Critical Muslim 21

Relations

Editor: Ziauddin Sardar
Deputy Editors: Hassan Mahamdallie, Samia Rahman, Shanon Shah
Senior Editors: Syed Nomanul Haq, Aamer Hussein, Ehsan Masood, Ebrahim Moosa
Publisher: Michael Dwyer
Managing Editor (Hurst Publishers): Daisy Leitch
Cover Design: Fatima Jamadar
Associate Editors: Tahir Abbas, Alev Adil, Nazry Bahrawi, Merryl Wyn Davies, Abdelwahab El-Affendi, Marilyn Hacker, Nader Hashemi, Jeremy Henzell-Thomas, Dilwar Hussain, Vinay Lal, Iftikhar Malik, Boyd Tonkin
International Advisory Board: Karen Armstrong, William Dalrymple, Anwar Ibrahim, Robert Irwin, Bruce Lawrence, Ashis Nandy, Ruth Padel, Bhikhu Parekh, Barnaby Rogerson, Malise Ruthven

Critical Muslim is published quarterly by C. Hurst & Co. (Publishers) Ltd. on behalf of and in conjunction with Critical Muslim Ltd. and the Muslim Institute, London. *Critical Muslim* acknowledges the support of the Aziz Foundation, London.

All correspondence to Muslim Institute, CAN Mezzanine, 49-51 East Road, London N1 6AH, United Kingdom

e-mail for editorial: editorial@criticalmuslim.com

The editors do not necessarily agree with the opinions expressed by the contributors. We reserve the right to make such editorial changes as may be necessary to make submissions to *Critical Muslim* suitable for publication.

© Copyright 2017 *Critical Muslim* and the individual contributors.

All rights reserved.

C. Hurst & Co (Publishers) Ltd., 41 Great Russell Street, London WC1B 3PL

ISBN: 978-1-84904-823-1 ISSN: 2048-8475

To subscribe or place an order by credit/debit card or cheque (pounds sterling only) please contact Kathleen May at the Hurst address above or e-mail kathleen@hurstpub.co.uk

Tel: 020 7255 2201

A one year subscription, inclusive of postage (four issues), costs £50 (UK), £65 (Europe) and £75 (rest of the world).

The right of Ziauddin Sardar and the Contributors to be identified as the authors of this publication is asserted by them in accordance with the Copyright, Designs and Patents Act, 1988.

A Cataloguing-in-Publication data record for this book is available from the British Library

IIIT Publications

APOSTASY IN ISLAM
A Historical & Scriptural Analysis

Taha Jabir Alalwani

What is the legally prescribed penalty, if any, for apostasy (*al-riddah*)? The work contends that both the Qur'an and the Sunnah grant freedom of belief including the act of exiting the Faith and do not support capital punishment for apostasy.

ISBN 978-1-56564-364-2 *hb*
ISBN 978-1-56564-363-5 *pb*

APOSTATES, ISLAM & FREEDOM OF FAITH
Change of Conviction vs Change of Allegiance

AbdulHamid AbuSulayman

The Qur'an mentions no earthly punishment for apostasy and also stresses no compulsion in matters of faith (Q 2:256). This *Occasional Paper* uncovers the origins of the debate to present the correct Islamic position and refute wide misconception. In reality many continue to leave the Faith freely.

ISBN 978-1-56564-554-7 *pb*

Marketing Manager IIIT (USA) 500 Grove Street, Herndon, VA 20170-4735, USA
Tel: 703 471 1133 ext. 108 Fax: 703 471 3922 • E-mail: sales@iiit.org Website: www.iiit.org

Kube Publishing Ltd MMC, Ratby Lane, Markfield, Leicester, LE67 9SY, UK
Tel: 01530 249 230 Fax: 01530 249 656 • E-mail: info@kubepublishing.com
Website: www.kubepublishing.com

Critical Muslim

Subscribe to Critical Muslim

Now in its sixth year in print, Hurst is pleased to announce that *Critical Muslim* is also available online. Users can access the site for just £3.30 per month – or for those with a print subscription it is included as part of the package. In return, you'll get access to everything in the series (including our entire archive), and a clean, accessible reading experience for desktop computers and handheld devices — entirely free of advertising.

Full subscription

The print edition of *Critical Muslim* is published quarterly in January, April, July and October. As a subscriber to the print edition, you'll receive new issues directly to your door, as well as full access to our digital archive.

United Kingdom £50/year
Europe £65/year
Rest of the World £75/year

Digital Only

Immediate online access to *Critical Muslim*

Browse the full *Critical Muslim* archive

Cancel any time

£3.30 per month

www.criticalmuslim.io

CM21

January–March 2017

CONTENTS

RELATIONS

SAMIA RAHMAN	INTRODUCTION: THE RELATIONS MATRIX	3
AAMER HUSSEIN	ANNIE	19
SYED NOMANUL HAQ	BEST OF ALL PATRONS?	34
PIRO REXHEPI	BORDERS	45
ANNALISA MORMILE	EU'S OTHERS	57
BENEDIKT KOEHLER	CAETANI AND EAST/WEST RELATIONS	66
JULIAN BOND AND FATIMAH ASHRIF	DISSOLVING DIFFERENCE: A DIALOGUE	73
MOHAMMED MOUSSA	KITH AND KIN IN JAPANESE POLITICS	87
ELMA BERISHA	HOMOGENEITY	99
MICHAEL VICENTE PEREZ	FEMINISM IS FOR EVERYBODY	109
SAULAT PERVEZ	READING ALOUD	123
AYISHA MALIK	HIJABI DATING	132
ZIAUDDIN SARDAR	TWO BOOKS AND AN AUNTIE	141

ARTS AND LETTERS

MUDDASIR RAMZAN	SHORT STORY: DRIFTING BARBS	157
MOHJA KAHF	SIX POEMS	163
PERZADA SALMAN	TURKEY AND KASHMIR	170
SAFEENA RAZZAQ	PROBLEMS OF A BROWN GIRL	173

REVIEWS

Nadiah Ghani	HIJABISTAS	183
Aysha Garaeva	SOVIET TERROR	191
Hannah Kershaw	SELF-REFLECTIONS	196
Hassan Mahamdallie	HOLY IGNORANCE!	202

ET CETERA

Henry Brefo	LAST WORD: ON AFRICAN CHIEFTAINCY	211
The List	TOP TEN RELATIONSHIP BREAK-UPS	217
Citations		226
Contributors		235

Learning how to make a chapatti by the age of 5.

Illustration by Safeena Razzaq

RELATIONS

INTRODUCTION: THE RELATIONS MATRIX
by Samia Rahman
ANNIE *by Aamer Hussein*
BEST OF ALL PATRONS? *by Syed Nomanul Haq*
BORDERS *by Piro Rexhepi*
CAETANI AND EAST/WEST RELATIONS
by Benedikt Koehler
EU'S OTHERS *by Annalisa Mormile*
DISSOLVING DIFFERENCE: A DIALOGUE *by Julian Bond and Fatimah Ashrif*
KITH AND KIN IN JAPANESE POLITICS *by Mohammed Moussa*
HOMOGENEITY *by Elma Berisha*
FEMINISM IS FOR EVERYBODY *by Michael Vicente Perez*
READING ALOUD *by Saulat Pervez*
HIJABI DATING *by Ayisha Malik*
TWO BOOKS AND AN AUNTIE *by Ziauddin Sardar*

INTRODUCTION
THE RELATIONS MATRIX

Samia Rahman

Spring 1999. With all the precocious privilege of a gap-year student, I walked into the police headquarters in Allahabad, India and strode up to the information desk. Looking every inch the backpacker in my creased linen trousers and retro shirt, I explained in carefully practised Urdu: 'I'm the grand-daughter of Dr Sabir Hussain. I wonder if I could speak to anyone who knew him?' It was my first time in Allahabad, the birthplace of my father and both sets of grandparents, and my first trip to India. I had visited Karachi on many occasions as it was where my mother was born and where most of my relations had moved after Partition, but now I was travelling around South and Southeast Asia with friends. An entirely different experience. They had stayed behind in nearby Varanasi while I took an early morning bus and set off on the two-and-a-half-hour ride to seek out relatives. My grandfather, the former Police Commissioner of Allahabad, had died a few years earlier and my parents had since lost touch with the few, rather more distant, relatives still residing in India. I had met him only once as a child when he briefly visited us in London. He would love watching *Sesame Street* on television and my mum had to make extra-soft chapattis for him because he wore dentures. He seemed so gentle and a million miles away from the austere and stern man I had grown up hearing about. His wife had died in 1943 when my dad was just three years old and by the late 1950s he had sent his sons to England, via Pakistan. My uncle, Dad's older brother, excelled in his studies to become a professor of entomology and a writer of Islamic books, while Dad dropped out of his maths degree to work as a DJ at BBC Radio Nottingham, grew a long (non-Taliban) beard and soon resembled a latter-day hipster. He was eventually persuaded to finish his university studies on the promise that if he got a proper job he would finally be allowed to marry my mum, which he did on a trip back to Karachi in 1972.

There was a flurry of activity at the police station and before long I was introduced to some of my grandfather's former colleagues who regaled me with tales of his much-feared discipline, authoritarian manner and great religious piety. The respect they obviously afforded him was extended to me and I felt a little embarrassed by their deference. I also felt keenly that I was absolutely not how they imagined the grand-daughter of Dr Sabir Hussain to be. Every time someone would enter the room I was certain I could detect a look of incredulity before murmurings of 'she is from England' would be offered as way of explanation, as if that made perfect sense. I began to hope I hadn't done my grandfather's reputation a disservice. Phone calls were made, relatives were tracked down and I was whisked away to stay with them. Their first gift to me as I entered their home: a freshly washed and ironed *shalwar kameez* and a copy of the Qur'an.

In that moment, as my new-found relatives pampered me with their hospitality, all the while seeking to re-mould me in the imagined expectation of my grandfather's gaze, I understood the complex interplay of power that determines our relations with others. With a well-thumbed copy of Edward Said's *Orientalism* and William Dalrymple's *City of Djinns* among my meagre possessions, I had not travelled to India to 'find myself' but had been ready to expand the boundaries of my own understanding of identity, through the human interaction that finding 'others' would invite. India was to be experienced on my own terms, without the social conformity that my perfectly enjoyable visits to my mother's family home in Karachi inevitably entailed. Yet, in the vein of social exchange theory, the argument that the equity of any relationship is measured not by an individual's possession of power but instead by society's constructed assessment of the benefits of each interaction rang true. It occurred to me that I had trampled all over the carefully assembled relationship parameters my grandfather had constructed over a lifetime.

It wasn't, and still isn't, clear how that should make me feel. What was apparent, though, was that however far apart the spaces we occupy, whether in time or distance, in life and even in death, relations cannot exist in a vacuum; they are entrenched in a complex matrix, have a context. It was the French philosopher Michel Foucault who asserted that, once born into a society we are introduced to the concept of power through our formative relationships. Our parents and guardians resolve how they will bring us up and our families particularise the manners and social etiquette that become our norms. Upon entering education it is ultimately the teacher who filters our knowledge streams and decides what we should learn and how. Our relationships deny the possibility that we can live as oases of autonomy minding our own business. The part reflects the whole and at the very minimum we must abide by the law of the land because the manner in which we relate to society will determine whether or not we will be allowed to exercise that same society's version of free will.

Free will in a free society is a contested concept. Not least because the notion of society and nations and states making decisions autonomously, without consideration for the nexus of global power within which they compete for a place, is impossible. So how do we reconcile that in Islamic texts free will is seemingly enshrined? There is no compulsion in Islam states the Qur'an (2:256). Our actions are our personal responsibility and we alone must account for them. How does this compute with entrenched societal roles and international geopolitics that determine the path an individual or community or nation takes in its journey of existence? Relationships can be manipulated to curb individualism and free will as Syed Nomanul Haq's fascinating discussion of patronage practices in Islamic history reveals. These acts of supposed benevolence that cultivated the wealth of scholarship and intellectual growth, so characteristic of the history of Muslim societies, are perhaps not quite what they seem. He writes in reference to the Ghaznavid Sultans, opulent Turkic rulers who reigned across central Asia, Iran and the Indian sub-continent from 977 to 1186: 'patronage was not simply a symbolic expression or a mere metaphor of glory and dominion; rather, it was irreversibly integrated into the actual running machinery of the empire… courts and rulers and individual patrons often treated scholars literally as commodity, something that came as part of the booty or loot of conquests, or acquired as gifts from friendly neighbouring dynasties, or as material tokens of surrender from weak ones.' Could it really be that the wealth of intellectual riches that provided the hallmark of Islam's golden era, were in fact the result of symbiotic relationships and the commodification of talent? Were the Muslim world's great advances in the arts, science, music and scholarship the upshot of kidnap and exploitation by a power-hungry and wealthy elite? The romantic notion of the benevolent patron who takes under his wing those among his people who are gifted and skilled, out of a quiet passion to foster the growth of thought and knowledge, is laid bare. Patronage was rather more likely a trophy in the power play of competing civilisations, a display of superiority and dominance in accordance with the value signifiers of the day. Yet, Noman reminds us, the balance of power remains complex and non-binary. He relates that ibn Sina, the Persian polymath born in the tenth century and regarded as one of the most significant thinkers and writers of the period in the history of Islam regarded as the Golden Age, was involved in his own machinations to secure patronage when and where it was available. He would adjust his loyalties as befitted his ambition, abandoning posts with the shrewdness of a political player and aligning himself with those in the ascendant. To assume that relationships between benefactors and their charges entailed a one-way conveyor belt of leverage, would be simplistic. Nomanul Haq explains: 'scholars here were not only passively subjects to or acted upon by these elements, they were themselves actors.'

Nomanul Haq's exposition illustrates that to varying degrees we are all actors in the story of our lives, yet our personal relations equally have the potential to define the fate that stretches before us, sometimes even proving instrumental in our deaths. Families are notorious bubbles of dysfunctional harmony that nurture, frustrate, gladden and also break our hearts. Warring couples, sibling rivalry, in-law disputes, overbearing mothers, authoritarian fathers, inheritance tussles, infidelity, delinquent or neglectful children: the capacity for inflicting pain and suffering on our nearest and dearest is immeasurable. History is built on the trajectories of imploding relations, with wars of succession shaping the fate of communities since time immemorial. The Mughals had no structure in place that automatically qualified an eldest son to assume his father's empire upon his demise. Instead, vying heirs were expected to use political and military intrigue and even assassination to seize power. The Mughal Emperor Aurungzeb, whose father Shah Jahan built the Taj Mahal in memory of his beloved deceased wife Mumtaz, famously had his brothers killed and his father deposed in his seventeenth century campaign to become the sixth Mughal Emperor. His father had favoured his eldest child Dara Shikoh, a sophisticated intellectual who championed plurality of thought, the arts and cultural syncreticity. Aurungzeb, on the other hand, was deeply conservative and found this religious liberalism distasteful. He railed against what he considered Dara's deplorable and lascivious lifestyle, illustrating the fissures in the brothers' relationship to be more than a power struggle or a Lacanian desire for Daddy's approval. Their feud was ideological. Ultimately it was Aurungzeb's qualities as a military leader that guaranteed his success, with any threat to his position irrevocably quashed when he ordered Dara's execution on grounds of apostasy. Similar stories can be found about the Ummayads and the Abbasids.

Such audacious dynastic familicide is thankfully rare these days. Yet, navigating the tightrope of relations is a precarious fate for no other reason than that relationships themselves, the exchanges, interactions and memories that form our identities are complex, fractured and fraught. What is it about our role in a family that anchors us and sets us adrift at the same time? I had never understood why my father, upon leaving India at the age of sixteen, never once returned. But, fleetingly, in the excitement of meeting long lost relatives in the midst of surroundings that my grandfather would have found so familiar, I felt the ache of a past that was long gone, unimagined in the condition of exile and un-belonging. As Aamer Hussein movingly writes in his journey of diaspora, 'Annie', the dislocation so intrinsic to the individualistic migrant experience is ongoing, existential and uniquely dispossessing: 'I was drawn to displaced people. Miruhi's family had left Ethiopia via Sudan and Egypt during a time of tumult; she'd married an Englishman, but was always nostalgic for the Nile. Fari was from Tehran; halfway through his PhD in Chemical Engineering, from Imperial College, Khomeini took over Iran and Fari didn't want to return there. Roman had defected on a holiday from Poland, and was also at Imperial. He was stateless and didn't know where he would go when he graduated.' For a generation that had no recourse to the luxury of global technological communication to keep relationships with 'back home' alive and dynamic, to be dispersed into the Western imagination was perhaps preferable to a return to an unrecognisable homeland.

Yet we continue on with our lives in the knowledge that there is no consistency or equity in relationships, imagined or otherwise. My grandfather and I never had the opportunity to cultivate a relationship in the way that he did with the police officers he commanded or those who knew him well. Yet, I entered his world of accepted behaviours and usurped his control. Authority in relationships can be subverted but we can never assume its limits are ours to define. An African-American male must now fear for his life if pulled over by the US police for a trivial traffic violation, unlike his white counterpart. As the 'Black Lives Matter' movement illustrates, there is no righteousness in the power relations we navigate. But neither can these regimes of truth, as Foucault describes them, be reduced to hierarchical structures. To view relations in terms of one entity interacting with just one other equally separate entity, blinds us to the unwieldiness of interaction.

Instead, what we experience is an interconnected relationship web across which power is disseminated at a dizzying spectrum of levels and intensities. In the course of their heartfelt and tender interfaith conversation, Fatimah Ashrif and Julian Bond exemplify such amplified reciprocity. Their exchange is premised on the notion that they represent two disparate theological positions. However, as they come together to read religious scripture drawn from the Islamic and Christian traditions, their shared experience transcends any dichotomy of faith. In spaces that are neither mosque nor church, or are sometimes mosque or sometimes church, their compassionate study and contemplation of the same sacred texts that divide them, draw them together and into a relationship of collective worship and intimacy with God and each other. By exploring their own interpretation of religion and taking responsibility for their relationship with the divine, the permeation of each other's belief shines a light on all that they already share. As Ashrif explains, 'Julian and I are not interested in dissolving Christian-Muslim difference. There is a clear spiritual creativity, which is inspired by doctrinal difference. What we are interested in is dissolving with kindness and compassion where possible, the dogmatic attitudes, and the fear which prevents us having open-hearted communication about each other's journeys.' Their relationship is not contained within two vessels but is all-encompassing, informing future conversations and interactions they may have with countless others who exist across their networks and with whom they may have even the most fleeting passing personal exchange.

In their lived experience of the democratisation of power through relations, Ashrif and Bond illustrate the mastery of the concept. Their impact upon each other is not total but is beyond the spheres of influence that unite and divide them, perpetually creating knowledge and deepening bonds of understanding. The process of self-disclosure that drives relationships is, in their case, organic, unhurried and substantive. In an increasingly individualistic world, transformative relations celebrate collective experience to strengthen the web of connectivity that is our reality. Society benefits and we are all empowered.

Collective experience is regarded as the converse of individualism, which is the inescapably prevailing condition of contemporary first world society and shapes our view of governance and our ability to cope with globalisation. So-called spoiled, self-absorbed millennials who can't see past the smartphone screens glued permanently to their faces plunge into precarious social relationships that are as superficial and transient as Julian and Fatimah's relationship is rich in depth. According to sociologist and philosopher Zygmunt Bauman, this generation, coming of age in the 2000s, is slave to 'liquid modernity'. He describes their relations as a continuum of weak and ephemeral liaisons that require minimal commitment. Social attachments remain brief and are characterised by self-interest and narcissism. The consequential heightened emotional anxiety and insecurity felt by your average millennial leads to a cycle of fragile entanglements that lack stability and trigger chronic retreat into isolation. Such detachment from society stifles the development of personal responsibility or collective interest, undermining social cohesion and any sense of community. The microcosm is instructive of the macrocosm, providing fuel to the catastrophic fire of hyper-reality and post-truth politics that renders facts obsolete when they dare to not reflect the designated acceptable reality. His outlook is bleak but perhaps rather more pessimistic than it needs to be, especially when we think back to the opaque power dynamic Noman outlined in his analysis of patronage practices. Bauman laments the resultant decline in the importance of duty and obligation in family relations but does not acknowledge that such ties can sometimes restrict and impede. As Mohammed Moussa's essay on 'Kith and Kin in Japanese Politics' shows, there are societies still in a default of rigid pathways linked to lineage: 'Party politics in Japan is an elite endeavour that has in some instances become the preserve of established families.' Just as the Mughal dynasty dominated Indian governance from the early sixteenth to the early eighteenth centuries, Japanese politics is mired in genealogical accumulation of power. Something Bauman would surely find problematic.

Reframing family relations can liberate many from restrictive concepts of honour and shame and challenge structures that oppress and stifle or monopolise access to power. Innovative solutions for the care of the elderly, for example, are very gradually being embraced by Muslim communities who had once viewed with horror and disdain the idea of residential care homes. Traditional communities are balancing the benefits of such options against the sometimes inadequate provision that loving or even resentful and duty-bound children are providing for their elders, which simply do not meet their needs. A stroke nurse working in London's Tower Hamlets once remarked to me that close-knit and devoted extended families with roots in the Indian subcontinent were killing stroke survivors with kindness by wrapping them in cotton wool and waiting on them hand and foot. Such over-protective and indulgent attention was motivated by duty as well as love, but impaired the recovery of patients and any prospect that they may regain their strength and confidence to once more lead an independent life. Expectation coupled with desire to take care of our relations may not always be in the best interests of those we hold dear. Frequently we are told that Islam commands us to be kind to our parents and that paradise lies under the feet of our mother, a thoroughly noble concept. Yet to be so beholden to relatives is to misunderstand the vibrant and versatile concept of relations in Islamic thought, putting those who are vulnerable to the abuse of power at risk. The classic drama of a mother feigning illness and taking to her sick bed in an effort to emotionally blackmail her son into marrying the girl of her choosing is a devastating manifestation of archaic and disempowering family obligations. Honour crimes reveal the most extreme pathology of a minority and are by no means exclusive to Muslim communities, but let us be clear: a mindset that thinks it is shameful for one to fall in love because you are betraying the expectations of your family or community and not shameful to murder an innocent person out of a perverse sense of 'honour' has lost all its ethical bearings and must be disassembled.

While addressing a variation of this mindset, Edinburgh-based Safeena Razzaq's wry series of illustrations 'Brown Girl Problems' provide light relief to such poignant issues and have a universal resonance with which many will identify. She sketches awkward, uncomfortable scenarios with wit and sensitivity, drawing on her own experience of cultural confusion, and attempts to locate her identity in the vortex of patriarchal and hyper-real 'liquidity' that is our global construct. Her illustrations may be specific to her personal history as a second-generation Muslim girl from the Indian sub-continent growing up in the UK, but her crises are universal, resonating with all those who seek to subvert the generational norms in which they feel constrained. Nadiah Ghani similarly writes about her struggle to maintain her identity as a 'freehair', or unveiled, girl in Malaysia. Family and societal pressure to conform to the increasingly narrow definition of religiosity in the country, is projected onto the female form. Control of women becomes the contested battle ground for the formation of Muslim identity in the experience of both Ghani and Razzaq. Each chooses to walk away from the definition that has been chosen for them as Muslim women and in Ghani's words: 'women like me will simply carry on leading our dual existences because it is our right to uphold the identity we choose for ourselves'.

Does the vision of the self to which we aspire lead to a cohering of what we term identity? If identity is fixed and complete then where do we weave in Aamer Hussein's journey of diaspora or Ghani's, Razzaq's, and my own experience of cultural shift? What are the implications for an individual whose identity sits at a crossroads of multiple pressure points? Once again, relationships refuse to be quantified as hermetically sealed entities colliding and parting in repetitive isolation. We can begin to consider the way in which identity is not inscribed on the self but is part of a matrix of relationships that mesh together from all angles to constitute our being. If identity is considered less in terms of being about singular perception or exclusive experience, we are able to appreciate the impact of the structural apparatus that regulates society and administers free will only as they deem fit. Expanding on Foucault's position, bell hooks argues that it is here that we must carve out the space in which multiple relationships are configured but not cohered. It is by embracing intersectionality that we may tackle the exclusivity of social justice movements and categories of differentiation such as feminism. As far as she can see, we can only do this by identifying the overlapping and multitudinous traits that interact to make up what we refer to as our social identities. It is when we direct our chimera of ourselves through this prism of intersectionality that we will realise that *Feminism is for Everybody*, including Muslims, insists Michael Perez. He cites hooks' work to problematise the essentialism of feminism, wherein patriarchy and injustice are charted according to the lived reality of the white, middle-class, educated female, as informing his thesis. The relationship between structures of power and a white, university-educated professional will not be the same as that between a woman of colour who is of a different class or a Muslim woman or a woman with disabilities. Once we tear down universalist and simplistic versions of truth, we can speak to the struggles of the marginalised, the voiceless, the individual.

The attempt to re-define feminism and acknowledge the heterogeneity of female experience is to once again comprehend the non-linearity of relationships in our culturally diverse societies. How we administer and translate relationships is unequivocally defined according to hetero-normative, patriarchal structures, which Piro Rexhepi recognises and deciphers in his essay 'Borders'. Just as Michael Perez subverts the assumed relationship between Islam and misogyny by asserting a space for feminist Muslims, Rexhepi turns his attention to the interplay between Islamophobia and homophobia. Employing a mesmerising mix of reportage and lived experience, he documents the exploitation of queer politics in Muslim-majority Balkan countries as European Union expansion becomes premised on the LGBT-friendly credentials of the applying nation. There is much to be said about the current state of the European Union, to which we will come shortly. Suffice to say the aim to choreograph acceptable queer subjects along Western normative lines to serve as tools to identify 'good' secular, traditional Muslims as opposed to those Muslims who adhere to foreign and un-European interpretive practices is a consummate example of the hegemonic power relationships of globalisation and its destructive effluence, that has compounded the insecurity and uncertainty we face today.

INTRODUCTION: THE RELATIONS MATRIX

Whatever one's view on the rise of individualism and its impact on relations, it is apparent that in our increasingly interconnected, interdependent and globalised world, relationships are splintering and no longer conforming to type. Bauman looks to social media in particular as wreaking havoc on human interaction by encouraging anti-social and solitary behaviour. With so many mediums enabling us to connect, there are an equal number of ways to feel ignored and disconnected. Social networks encourage us to disclose more and more of ourselves both emotionally and visually to a ravenously consuming public with a short yet unforgiving attention span, in a dynamic of questionable trust. The potential for emotional and sexual abuse in these domains is exponential and devoid of sanctuary because, digitally, we are permanently plugged in. In an age of hyper-real expressions of intimacy and the constant desire for validation, romance and desire become a minefield of arbitrary relations. Ayisha Malik, author of the feisty and highly relatable romantic comedy *Sofia Khan is Not Obliged*, introduces us to the trials and tribulations of a Single Muslim Female looking for love. Her essay is a foreword that ties together the episodic strands that led to the novel. She adores *Bridget Jones' Diary*, she tells us, but found she could not entirely identify with her icon's escapades: 'here's the thing: she drank alcohol. A lot of it. And she had sex. She complained that she never had enough because she was always single, but Bridge, trust me, you were way ahead of the Muslim game… no sex before marriage. Not even a little sex. Like, phone sex… I've never had an occasion for *genuinely tiny knickers*. Because as a practising Muslim the only person seeing my genuinely tiny knickers would be me, and perhaps my mum when she accidentally walks into my room.' If Bauman worries that millennials are on the precipice of perpetual anxiety in an age of unpredictable social mores, perhaps he should spare a thought for young Muslims. Caught in the glaring headlights of relentless and meticulous scrutiny, they have had the misfortune of waking up to an age in which all the assumed conventions they were led to believe should form a yardstick for that random chore, otherwise known as getting through life, are hideously outdated. Malik sums it up perfectly when asked for the umpteenth time why she is not married: 'Well, Auntie number three-hundred-and-twenty-six, I'm trying, but it's not like it was in your day.'

Therein is the crux of the matter: it's just not like it was in our parents' day, or our grandparents' day or anyone's day for that matter. Contemporary postnormal times appear to have flung us into an entirely unknowable set of circumstances and there is no guide-book in sight. Long-gone are the extended family networks that would intrigue and conspire to marry this person with that person and neatly package everyone up, complete with a tight ribbon guaranteed to bind them together. While growing up, it seemed to me that it was the entire raison d'être of my mother's generation to live their lives through their children and to successfully and auspiciously marry them off. What we see now is a disintegration of the world wide web of extended relations meddling in your love life, along with which, the surety of acquiring a half-decent spouse becomes a little more illusory. This is not to say that a half-decent spouse is better than no spouse at all, after all who actually wants to end up with 'mister or miss let's-make-do'? The breakdown of kinship bonds has doubtless created more opportunities for individuals to follow their own path in their expression of desire. It is also worth mentioning that internet dating and matrimonial events are potentially democratising ways to secure everlasting love. But, there's no getting away from the fact that these days it all seems a bit harder.

Anxiety-ridden love, sex and emotional intimacy are the emblem of postnormal times. The insecurity we play out in our intimate relationships reflects the tumult that is projected in the arena of global relations. Faltering personal and social relationships are a small-scale snapshot of a wider phenomenon. In today's post-truth society, fallacy has brought about its unravelling and the repercussions are infiltrating every aspect of our reality as we know it. The most troubling manifestation has been the rise in extreme and populist far right narratives in the media and in the political domain. The stuff of nightmares, the worst-case scenarios, our deep-seated fears that we dismissed as just too far-fetched to possibly be taken seriously are morphing into reality. Writers of satirical political programmes such as *The Thick of It* and *Black Mirror* are seeing their wildly imaginative tales of allegory metamorphose into true life. After the savage austerity of the UK coalition government led by David Cameron and Nick Clegg, it did not for one second enter my realms of possibility that sit comfortably in my London-based liberal bubble, that the General Election of May 2015 would sweep in a Conservative government. All the polls were wrong. Every single person I know in real life and across social media was distraught. Who were these shy Tory voters and why would they confound my logic so resolutely? Confirmation bias is tangible in its power to redraw reality to reflect the narratives that social media reflects and reaffirms. Did I even realise how definitively social networks clump together to ping right back our values and friendship preferences? Who knew that there were so many people in the UK with such radically diverging values to my own? Worse was to come. On 23 June 2016, the day of the EU referendum, I sat in my favourite cafe with friends and reassured them that there was simply no way the British people would vote to leave the EU. At the very worst, I meandered, the result may be closer than we would like, which would indicate a worrying ugliness within British society, but they would still be overwhelmingly in the minority. I had planned to go to bed by midnight but as the first votes came in, revealing the Leave campaign to have garnered a far greater number than the polls had predicted, I had that same sinking feeling I had when the exit polls were announced for the General Election. I stayed up all night watching the unwelcome drama unfold in disbelief, just as I had done then. I was blindsided. So was everyone I knew. Everyone. A handful of friends had voted to leave due to perfectly reasonable left-wing concerns surrounding free trade legislation and the shoring up of fortress Europe, but certainly not to protest at immigration. I was shaken. The sheer fact that everything I feared most was coming true was horrifying and there was worse to come. You would have thought I would have learned my lesson and not dared to entertain complacency but on 8 November 2016 I was admittedly nervous, yet could not in any realms of fantasy comprehend the possibility that the next US President would be a misogynistic, xenophobic, reality TV celebrity and tax-avoiding billionaire who utters untruths with absolute abandon. It confirmed that nothing was knowable. The surreal was becoming the actual.

I wasn't the only one. In her excellent analysis of disunity in the EU family, Annalisa Mormile echoes the sentiments of Bauman: that the valuing of difference in this great human adventure called the European Union has not benefitted everyone. Those who feel their invitation to the EU party was lost in the post have lashed out in the most visceral way possible. The vote to leave, for many, was a rare opportunity to voice their desire for sovereignty, 'to get our country back' and to varying degrees an objection to migrants. In Mormile's words, immigration 'provoked among the majority the most common of human fears: the fear of losing one's job and personal security.' She goes on to examine the EU project in relation to the crisis of asylum seekers and refugees, highlighting the 1990 Dublin Convention, which was designed to establish the common framework for deciding where an asylum application should be processed and to ensure it remains that country's responsibility. The appalling handling of the refugee crisis has unfolded with all its stark human misery over the past couple of years, emphasising that the convention is 'built on an illusion of EU common standards, whereas both reception conditions and recognition rates vary considerably.' For Mormile, the tragic debacle demands a reassessment of the core notion of responsibility upon which the EU design, and the Dublin Treaty in particular, is based: 'the English word *responsible* stems from the Latin *spondeo*, which means "offer, promise". If we consider the term *spondeo* together with *re-spondeo*, we must assume that *re* points out that a counter-offer has been made in response to an initial one. So, in the very act of responsibility, two aspects are fundamental: a feeling of reciprocity and the response to the other. Whereas with the first offer the "other" demands of us responsibility, exchanging his or her offer with another one means we become responsible not only for ourselves, but also for the other.' It is this 'other' – the refugee who flees wars in which Europe is implicated and abandons a homeland that Europe once colonised – who represents our worst fears and insecurities in this liquid age of anxiety. Mormile's rallying cry that 'a Europe worth its name, will always respond to the call of the "other"' is sadly falling on deaf ears. The thousands of heart-wrenching deaths have no doubt elicited public sympathy. Yet the fact remains that those hundreds of thousands of refugees seeking nothing more than safety and a better life will step into a Europe that is barely papering over its cracks while public opinion continues to lurch to the right.

Mormile recalls waking up to the news of the Brexit result, shocked and disappointed. An Italian national living in the UK, her fears were heightened, but are soon offered some repose in the form of her students, who are as dismayed as she is. Will the next generation prove more outward looking and strident? All we can be sure of is that we are all exposed to the impossible irony of our perception of self, communities and nation-states, in the contemporary context of precarity. Power relationships are by nature unequal and indeterminate. The idea that being a member of the EU bloc means that a nation, and by sequence, an individual is therefore afforded incremental power is pure fantasy. Correspondingly, to regard exiting Europe as having taken power back is equally ludicrous. No government is able to make autonomous decisions and act only unto itself. We must reconcile to our status in the globalised world; we are but mere supplicants in a complex and haphazard web of interconnectivity, that we can try but will fail to press into service. If a rogue algorithm, triggered by a remark by French President François Hollande about the need for tougher Brexit negotiations, can cause a flash crash of the value of the British pound to historic lows in October 2016, the 'let's take our country back' game surely has to be up.

But the game is not up. Populations are rebelling against globalisation in their droves as the Leave vote, the rise of UKIP and the march of the far right across Europe, as well as the obsession with immigration shows. Governments are resorting to jingoistic rhetoric in an attempt to acquiesce the populist appetite. Prime Minister Theresa May defied all rationale in her statement 'if you believe you are a citizen of the world, you are a citizen of nowhere' but her naked pandering to nationalism was carefully crafted to reach out to a disaffected and seemingly impenetrable chunk of the electorate. Similarly, Trump's odious promise to build a wall to keep out Mexican 'rapists' and to ban Muslims from entering the country resonated with more than just someone out there. We live in an age of insecurity, and the foregrounding for this existential state of being is the unequal distribution of the benefits of interconnectivity. While the elites have become enriched, there are many, including those to whom the British PM and Trump were directing their sophistry, who, whether perceived or real, simply see no benefit in the current status quo.

The ties of family relationships, origin, culture and heritage bind us into power vortexes that equally dispossess in our age of anxiety. Everything that we took for granted has been turned on its head. But how did we get to this point? Cancun in Mexico was the location in 1981 for a summit called the International Meeting on Co-operation and Development, informally known as the North-South Conference. World leaders gathered to discuss how northern countries could aid southern countries in their efforts to develop and prosper. US President Ronald Reagan challenged the desirability of such co-operation. Self-reliance was far more worthy an aim, he argued, calling on poorer countries to show more initiative in the free market system in order to attain growth. Growth was all he was interested in, his own country's growth. This attitude of self-interest has, above all else, shaped the evolution of globalisation in our lives. Western hegemony has supplanted international relations by tipping the balance in favour of Western corporations in our nations, which go on to mutate into multinational corporations dominating global trade and disseminating their own form of cultural imperialism. President Reagan and Margaret Thatcher were the architects of the 'me' generation that has stamped its mark on our reality of today belching out the likes of Trump and his ilk. Of course there were winners, of which he, a billionaire who, born into extreme wealth is a poster boy of the power of multinational corporations and global elites. But there were so many more losers. The disparity in wealth distribution was not just between nations but also within nations. More than three decades of parochial government policy and under-investment in communities existing on the fringes has precipitated a rage that seeks easy scapegoats. The likes of UKIP and Donald Trump capture the imagination of those who feel that the political establishment does not speak for them or to them. The vote to leave the EU and Trump's win was a resounding message to say that the interconnectivity of global relations is not working for everyone. Relationships do not need to be consistent to be authentic. As the web of relations become ever more complex and interconnected, attempting to circumscribe every connection to its boundaries is both impossible and unwelcome. Much like an ecosystem, relations are a vibrant and pulsating maelstrom of entities that would not exist if placed in isolation. I think back to my disordered relationship with the memory of my grandfather and I realise we sometimes fall into the grooves a needle runs through on a record. Every now and then a jolt can bring us out of complacency and help us to discover that a singular path is not the only way to bring creativity to the world and our lives.

ANNIE

Aamer Hussein

1.

'I want you to meet Annie', my mother said that afternoon…

May, 1968. I hadn't seen Mother since I left Karachi in December, to attend a family wedding. My father and I had taken a two-day trip from Gwalior, via Bhopal, to receive her in Bombay. She whisked me off to Breach Candy, where Annie lived, with one woman who cooked and kept house, in an economically furnished ground floor flat.

Annie was small and spare in her smart sari, with a shock of cropped curls. She was forty-one and single; she'd lived for a decade or so after partition in Karachi, and then in London. In the early '60s, she decided to return to India when an enormous novel she'd written was controversially received by Ayub Khan's military government and she no longer felt happy in Pakistan. In Bombay she'd worked for a journal called *Imprint*, and had just moved to the *Illustrated Weekly of India*. Her conversation with Mother was probably about their mutual friends: it wasn't easy in those days to travel between India and Pakistan unless, like us, you had a British passport. She took an immediate interest in my precocious reading habits. I'd grown up with women journalists – Mother was still managing a women's magazine in Karachi, which was owned by my father's sister, a Member of the National Assembly who was usually busy with politics. I was used to chatting to adults with literary inclinations; I'd met many artists and writers as a child and I didn't consider them much larger than life.

A few days later, I set off on a three-day journey with my father by air and train to Ootacamund in the Blue Mountains, unprepared for the bleakest, rainiest and longest months I'd ever known in my thirteen years. I walked or rode three miles to school. On holidays I watched Hollywood and British films in the local cinema, or spent hours in the dusty old library. The main reading room had newer books that were specially transported from Madras every few weeks, novels by Kingsley Amis and his generation – I preferred historical fiction, and memoirs, and since I couldn't get enough of those I read my way around histories of the British theatre and biographies of Madame de Stael and Chopin I retrieved from rickety shelves upstairs, full of books that some colonial librarian had chosen for the English readers 'domiciled' in the Blue Mountains.

Every month, parcels arrived from Annie: back issues of *Imprint*, and current issues of the *Illustrated Weekly*. *Imprint* carried excerpts of foreign fiction. I sweated and shivered my way through *Rosemary's Baby* in Ooty's rainy cool climate. (I couldn't recall whether I had fever when I starting reading it or it came upon me as I read.) I also read *Conspiracy of Women*, by Aubrey Menen, a half-Indian writer who lived in England, about the women who surrounded Alexander of Macedon.

In the eclectic *Illustrated Weekly*, I read about the life and times of Mirza Ghalib, whose poems I'd heard recited and sung all my life, in a centenary issue, with translations by Annie. (I now knew from her byline that she was a public figure called Qurratulain Hyder whose writings straddled two languages and several cultures.) There was also a special number dedicated to a pioneering singer-actor called Balgandharva, who had played women's roles in the Marathi theatre, and an article about the Southern dancer Balasaraswati. I began to stock a mental library that included the entire subcontinent in addition to the exclusively western catalogue of my early years.

Bad times do eventually come to an end: after eighteen months, so did my Ooty days. I decided to study in London. After our long farewells to Mother's family in Indore and Gwalior we came to Bombay to catch our flight. A few days before we left, Annie took us all to tea: a grand send-off at a café on the seafront. Deftly switching languages in a voice that was gruff for someone so slight, she peppered sentences with quirky English acronyms – MCPs (male chauvinist pigs) and LMC (lower middle class was an aesthetic, rather than class-bound, judgement). She delivered a few blistering comments about Nirad C Chaudhuri's *Continent of Circe*, who may have been the MCP she referred to.

My sisters and I left for London at the very end of May. One of the few books I carried with me on the flight was a translation by Khushwant Singh, Annie's colleague at the *Weekly*, of the turn-of-the century novel *Umrao Jan Ada*, which I'd heard my parents discuss in muted tones when Mother was reading the Urdu original. I'd picked it up at a bookstall in Colaba. Re-titled *The Courtesan of Lucknow*, it had a lurid pink jacket portraying a bare-bellied dancing girl, accentuating its slightly scandalous elements. I was riveted by its confessional story of the eponymous courtesan-poet and her account of a period I'd read about only in passing – the so-called Mutiny of 1857, and the decline of Awadh in its aftermath. I left it behind in Beirut where we were changing planes.

2.

My first three years in London flashed past. Readjustment to living, once again, in a metropolis, which at first I found rather shabby. Freedom to wander around the streets until sunset. A profusion of books in the public libraries I found at every corner in the nerve centre of London where I lived during those years. Schools, friendships, and my first full-blown romance, with a Korean girl, which ended traditionally in heartbreak and drove me to write poetry.

At eighteen, I didn't know quite what to do with myself. I sang, and performed occasionally in folk clubs, but singing wasn't meant to be a profession. My father's wish that I study law wasn't effective either. I had no notion of a 'home' to go back to, as London was where I'd landed up: I'd be staying on at least until I graduated. I wanted to study something Eastern at SOAS, but when my application was rejected I lost all interest in scholarly pursuits.

We moved from Sussex Gardens in West London, to Wimbledon Park where I had my twentieth birthday. I felt cut off from everything familiar. Once again, my only refuge was the little public library down the lane, and the folk music I was drawn to. I learnt many traditional songs from Punjab: though I wasn't Punjabi they were songs from 'home'. I recorded an album that spring, but it was never released.

I had trouble with the Urdu script, so my mother found me a tutor. Gigantic Mr Shah was something of a London legend. He had been researching a thesis on Fort William for decades, but also gave evening classes in Urdu at the Polytechnic of Central London. When I'd attended two semesters, he decided I was ready to sit an A level in Urdu. He'd tutor me privately.

In London I'd come to identify with the poems of Faiz Ahmed Faiz, some of which I sang, though Shah Sahib made fun of them and called him a plagiarist of western poets. Meeting Faiz several times was an inspiration.

The set text for my exam was *Umrao Jan Ada*. I read it in Urdu, with some help from Mr Shah. Within a month or two I passed with an A. It was too late to apply for University. Instead, I got into technical college in the last-minute 'clearing' process, to study librarianship as a stop-gap. After a year's study, in 1977, I left the college and Wimbledon, and came back to West London. I worked in a bank before using my Urdu A level as my passport to SOAS, where I finally fulfilled my dream of studying Persian and Siraiki. On the way I acquired a sound knowledge of Urdu poetry from Ralph Russell, David Matthews and, later, Christopher Shackle.

My mother often visited her family in India. She frequently saw Annie, who was still in Bombay. In 1980, she came home with a book that Annie had worked on for at least a decade: *Akhir-e-shab ke hamsafar*, a chronicle of East Pakistan and the creation of Bangladesh. Annie hadn't dried up after her magnum opus; she was starting on a new phase. Mother was entranced by several chapters that evoked the seasons in a manner that reminded her of Kalidas and old Hindi poems, but my head was full of Persian grammar. I'd suffered through a couple of weeks the previous summer reading the Progressive Writers, Premchand, Krishen Chander, Manto, for one of my first Urdu exams. My interest in Urdu was limited to poetry.

I was drawn to displaced people. Miruhi's family had left Ethiopia via Sudan and Egypt during a time of tumult; she'd married an Englishman, but was always nostalgic for the Nile. Fari was from Tehran; halfway through his PhD in Chemical Engineering at Imperial College, he didn't want to return to Iran as Khomeini was now in power. Roman had defected on a holiday from Poland, and was also at Imperial. He was stateless and didn't know where he would go when he graduated.

My mother went back to India to visit her mother in 1981 as I sat my final exams. By the time she reached Indore, her birthplace, my grandmother had died. Annie had gone to Aligarh, or Delhi, where we heard she was now teaching; Mother didn't see her on that trip

I hadn't considered returning to Pakistan even for a holiday after Bhutto's hanging and Zia's military coup. So I decided to travel around in India after I took my degree. I'd been in the West eleven years: I wanted to see my mother's family. My father was going to Delhi, where he'd had spent some youthful years – he'd probably have stayed on if he hadn't been summoned by his family to Karachi just before partition and his house there declared evacuee property. I'd never seen Old Delhi, where the first of my father's ancestors to arrive in India were buried; its monuments and gardens were calling to me. I decided to spend a fortnight there, en route to Bombay.

I lost direction for a couple of years, after that trip. Then, after wandering around the Rajasthan desert with a film crew on another Indian journey, and a broken engagement, I started research on a dissertation on loss of motherlands and artistic practices. It was 1984. In the gaps between philosophy and psychology, I switched from writing poetry to experimenting with fiction. I knew, with the naive self-determination novices have, that literature was my direction. I was prepared for a long journey with some detours.

3.

'Come along to hear Annie read at SOAS,' Mother said.

October, 1986. The audience at SOAS was enormous. Qurratulain Hyder was flanked by Urdu poet Iftikhar Arif, Pakistani critic Fateh Malek, BBC broadcaster Raza Ali Abidi, and the grey eminence of Indo-Anglian letters, Mulk Raj Anand. She looked somewhat disdainful throughout the long speeches, which were all in Urdu and acknowledged her as the greatest living novelist in the language. The critic analysed a long prose poem she'd published recently, in which she berated the Iranians and the Arabs for the murders and wars that were taking place in Iraq and lamented the decline and fall of Muslim civilisation. When it was her turn to speak, she mentioned that one of the characters in her new, unpublished novel went around India delivering lectures on 'Me and My Art': that wasn't her style at all. And no, she wasn't berating only the Muslim world:

she'd switched on the television the night before and the fighting in Ireland had shocked her: violence was endemic everywhere. Wasn't there such a thing as humanism anymore? And why couldn't people, and nations, live and let others live?

'Do you write too?' Annie asked me when she visited my mother three days later. (Since my unaccustomed exposure to the public face of literary Urdu, I'd been filling up my diary with despairing pages about history, exile and the loss of language. Perhaps her words – 'write as if rain was falling on the page' – had affected me.) Though I hadn't published anything yet, I mumbled, truthfully, that I did write.

'Do you write in Urdu?' she asked.

'No', I said.

I glimpsed a flicker of regret in her eyes. (And, perhaps, an unspoken question: Why not?)

Annie was researching a book at The India Office. She looked the same as she had sixteen years ago, though her short hair was henna-red now, and she wore western clothes for her research stints. But there was an ease about her that I didn't remember from earlier days, when she'd acted like a busy jobbing journalist and seemed somewhat distracted.

In Delhi, where she'd settled, she'd finally seemed to have found a place that suited her. There had been a revival of her creative energies in the shadow of those monuments and relics of the city's past. Delhi wasn't her birthplace: she was born in Aligarh, where her father had a post at the University, and she'd studied in Lucknow, so UP was her homeland. And Delhi, until '47, the epicentre of Indo-Muslim history, was now the capital of an independent nation.

The following October, back in London, she stayed with my parents. She was in the third and grandest stage of her career. She'd published another masterwork, *Gardish e rang e chaman*, which covered some of the same ground as *Umrao Jan*, bringing the story of India's courtesans right up to the present day. She'd also translated one of her novels into English: *Fireflies in the Mist*. An eminent London publisher was considering it for publication.

I'd given up my postgraduate studies to write and teach, and had a couple of stories accepted for publication. I'd also begun to review fiction. Though it was my sister who interviewed her that year, it was to me that

Annie handed a manuscript she was working on, of her own short stories, freely translated into English. I found it absorbing but patchy, and wondered whether something was lost in translation. But I wasn't ready to read her in Urdu, not yet.

On a Roman holiday the following April, waiting on a rainy morning for friends to take me out to lunch, I began to write a story. I had just turned thirty-three and had avoided memories of my thirteen years in Karachi. But that day in that dark hotel room with the sound of falling rain as accompaniment I completed 'Little Tales', which, though it wasn't autobiographical, was set in the neighbourhood I'd lived in as a child, during the '65 war between Pakistan and India that had worsened relationships between our countries.

My mother gave my story to Annie, who folded the typescript and put it away in her handbag. 'I'm going to translate this', she said, her eyes twinkling. It was about a city we'd both known well and left behind, and I thought she recognised in my writing an affinity to her 'Memories of an Indian Childhood'.

'Your hand was on mine when I wrote it', I told her later.

She smiled and nodded.

4.

In London, during the first Gulf War, I sat with Annie as she mused: 'There were three great tragedies in our history, the fall of Baghdad, the fall of Grenada, and the fall of Delhi. Closer to our time, the fall of the Ottoman Empire. Now, again, bombs over Baghdad – is there a flaw in our basic structure that dooms us to civil wars and decline? When the rationalist tendencies of the Mutazilites were superseded by the foregrounding of predestination doctrines by the Asharites our religious philosophy, too, fell into a time-warp.' She traced every current event in the subcontinent, and in the Middle East, to the vicissitudes of Islamic history.

Annie was often in London in those years: launching her new novels, reading at the India Office Library, speaking at SOAS, and discussing a new project, her translation of *Nishtar*, an eighteenth-century memoir about the love affair of a courtesan and a clerk, both minions of the East India Company. That translation, which she re-titled *The Dancing Girl*, was the first of her works I reviewed, and the first of her works to be published in the West. (*Fireflies* had been rejected by Cape.) She'd won award after major award in India. Her reputation was soaring there. In Pakistan, though she'd left it suddenly and under a cloud, she still had the status of an icon.

She spoke about history and the past with a nonchalant authority that was sometimes taken for arrogance. By contrast, she was tender when she spoke of her parents, the Turcophile writer Sajjad Hyder Yildirim and the pioneering feminist novelist Nazar Sajjad Hyder, who had started to write at the height of the Freedom movement, in the first decades of the twentieth century. Annie thought the Raj was historically inevitable. 'Wouldn't Pakistan have been in the state that Afghanistan is in, if you hadn't inherited western systems of government?' She admired Sir Sayyed and his reforms, of which we were all, she held, a product. Yet she decried the excesses of empire, yesterday's and today's.

That year I decided it was time I read Urdu fiction from Pakistan. I taught Urdu to foreign students at SOAS and had easy access to the library. I read everything I could find. Annie would guide my reading, criticising one writer and praising another in a dialogue that continued from trip to trip. I asked her if there was anything she'd like me to translate for an anthology of Pakistani stories I'd been commissioned to edit. She suggested '*Ek Makalma*', from her collection *Patjhar ki Avaz*: a dramatic dialogue between two men in the garden of an exclusive Karachi club, it moved between gossip and local politics to international affairs with terrifying prescience.

Other stories from that collection moved me even more. The title story was a model of laconic narration: a woman recounts her experience of migration in a flat tone that belies the darkness of her tale of loss of home, emotional vagrancy and sexual migrancy. '*Jalavatan*', written the year I was born, was set in London, in the dark, dark dawn after Partition, when the intellectuals from India and Pakistan who gathered here were divided from each other by political allegiances and the borderlines which split and separated families. Its abrupt temporal transitions and stylistic fragmentation reflected the anomie and displacement of its subjects. Even after decades I could identify with its exiles: in spite of my British passport I found it increasingly difficult to get a visa to visit India, but I been back three times as my mother's family all lived there and I hadn't yet gained the courage to return to Pakistan. 'Housing Society', which reflected her disenchantment and her self-exile from her adopted country, was a novella about migration and the making of new fortunes and identities in Karachi in post-partition. At its climax was the murder in jail of a radical migrant intellectual imprisoned by the military regime. The milieu that had formed me, even to the eponymous neighbourhood, was depicted with a subtlety and brilliance I'd never before found in contemporary fictions about Pakistan.

I published my first collection of fiction in winter 1993. The next spring, a copy of *Fireflies in the Mist* arrived, that magisterial version of *Aakhir-e-shab* she'd rewritten in English some years before, a novel about East Bengal and the war for Bangladesh. Formally daring and hugely inventive, it was Annie at her mature best. Because I had been in Dhaka the winter before, the scenes and sounds of the book came vividly to life in my mental theatre. Her quote from the poet Lalon Shah: 'There is a house of glass in which my neighbour lives. I have never seen him. A deep river separates us. How can I cross it?', made me wonder if I'd ever cross the deep river to meet my unseen neighbours in Bangladesh.

Annie read my book on her flight back and wrote: 'You write very well. Hope to hear one day that you've won the Booker.' By then, we had another common bond – I was writing about her parents' generation, those forgotten pioneers of Urdu fiction, many of whom appeared in her two-volume family chronicle. She regaled me with anecdotes that reached beneath the mazes of her own recollections into the memories of her parents and their friends. 'We Urdu writers wallow in emotion,' she'd told me, 'while you have an English restraint.' 'But Annie Khala, you're subtle too,' I said. 'Oh, no,' she responded. 'There's a lot of *taam jhaam* (ornaments and frills) in my writing.'

5.

Back in Karachi after nearly twenty-eight years, I was happy to meet Urdu writers I'd read, but the city, once open and inclusive, was riven by ethnic tensions between Sindhis and Muhajirs. Annie had written about Sindh, with an understanding and love of the people and that land which had also seen an enforced migration and an influx of incomers. Like those characters of Annie's who return to their native cities and feel out of place, I was both insider and outsider there, caught between feelings of homecoming and of unbelonging. I wasn't part of the current conflict. Though my father was born in Karachi and his family had settled in Sindh several generations before his birth, he'd grown up in Delhi, Dehra Dun and Oxford; my 'Urdu-speaking' mother had come to Karachi six months after Partition, not as a migrant but as a bride, a few days after her wedding in Bombay. Neither wore badges of identity. I didn't feel like a bridge between communities. Nothing was as I remembered; the centres had shifted. I didn't get to see the sea which I'd seen from my classroom window in Clifton every day, or make a trip to the beach I'd often visited on Sundays. But one night I did walk down to the house where I'd grown up, in P.E.C.H.S (Annie's 'Housing Society').

I also visited Lahore and Islamabad for the first time, that summer of '96. I wanted to prove to myself that I felt at home in every part of the subcontinent where I had friends or relatives. But I was surrounded by strangers who saw me as a British writer interested in Urdu literature. I was amused and annoyed to be introduced inaccurately as someone who'd written about Annie and others for '*The Times of London*' (it was the *TLS* I wrote for regularly).

I spent a year in London writing about Karachi, but abandoned my stories when I lost my father in the year that we were celebrating fifty years of Independence. He was my closest link to Karachi; he'd travelled restlessly between three countries until the end, saying he felt at home in all of them; but he was probably entirely at ease in none (it was he, after all, who'd chosen to bring us all to London). I finished a new book as an act of remembrance, four months after he died. Writing was both torment and cure.

Annie's English version of *River of Fire* finally appeared in India and the US in 1998. In the final section of this early masterpiece she explored in depth the conflicts of her own generation, particularly in the region to which she'd chosen to return: the exiles and migrations, the comings and goings and divisions and rifts, the hardening of religious factions, of regional and cultural identities, the nationalisms that tried to confine the pluralism of nomadic minds like hers and my father's within their artificially created frontiers.

River of Fire was launched in London's Nehru Centre in the summer of '98, with the poet Katherine Raine among the other Indian and British luminaries on stage with the author. Annie was frail; she'd been unwell, lost the use of her right hand, and her eyesight was poor. She asked me to join the panel and read passages from the book: we chose the lyrical opening of the novel, and a segment set in '50s London.

We avoided the many pages that evoked partition.

6.

River of Fire's Kamal Raza evokes, in a letter, Karachi's post-partition euphoria, its affluence and progress, its poverty and its greed. On his return from a brief visit to India, Kamal feels that the guards at the border will eye him with suspicion and even the wheels of the train are calling him an Indian spy:

I have to search for a ship whose lights have gone out, a ship which will quietly enter the dark ocean, going towards a place where there is nobody to say, 'welcome home, Kamal Raza'. He stood up and started walking back towards the sea. Then he repeated, 'there is no one to say "welcome home"'.

Long-sighted words. Annie had chosen to return to a country and a city where no one was waiting.

In the millennium, *River of Fire*, which had started its life in Urdu as a Pakistani book, was acclaimed in its English version as one of the twentieth century's greatest works of Indian fiction.

I am the corpse and I am the gravedigger and am the singer of dirges, Kamal reflects on his flight back to Karachi in *Aag ka Darya*.

The author deleted the lines in *River of Fire*.

7.

'Come right on over!' Annie growled over the crackling line to Mother. 'I'm sending the car. And be sure to bring Aamer with you.'

We were in Delhi that winter, 2005–6. I'd worked all year in a new academic post at the University of London, was struggling to complete my fourth book of stories, and had decided to spend December with my sister who lived there. We all wanted to visit Ajmer, where Mother's mother was born. That summer, there had been a series of explosions in London that had killed many and turned 'Muslim' into a bad word, making even those of us who prized ourselves on pluralist ideals, secular politics and composite identities, defensive when we were asked to 'explain' the causes of our fellow-Muslims' disaffection. I'd been commissioned to write about that for a Delhi local weekly and had started work on it almost as soon as I arrived. When they saw it in print my friends there protested: 'Why did they label you a Muslim writer? Didn't you object?'

I visited monuments I'd seen on my last trip – Humayun's tomb, Lodhi Gardens, Juma Masjid – with my brother-in-law, who also took me places I hadn't seen. The Old Fort. Jamia Millia, the pioneering educational establishment where novelist Saliha Abid Husain and her husband had lived for many years, among many other young and progressive intellectuals. Annie had taught there when she moved to Delhi from Bombay. I came home with an armload of Urdu books that, in the winter afternoons, brought back a Delhi that was almost invisible now.

Annie had heard from her publisher Ritu Menon that we were in town and hadn't been able to reach her on the number she'd given us. She'd rung at once. The trip from South Delhi to Noida was at least an hour long. On the way, as we drove along the banks of the Jamuna, Annie's loyal driver remarked: 'The river has become a drain. Dhobis wash their laundry in its trickle and people grow watermelons and cucumbers on its bare bed.'

Annie was waiting in the veranda of her house, basking in the glow of the mild winter sun. Her welcome was loving, even expansive. A feast was laid out on her table. As we ate, I saw two generations of household retainers who had looked after her for years. In contrast to the Bombay flat I'd seen her in nearly forty years before, here she was surrounded by her drawings, her books and papers. A close relative lived nearby; the literary world that had given her increasing acclaim was a brief phone call away. I wondered whether, in her years in Bombay – hardly the heartland of the rich syncretic culture she celebrated – she'd missed Karachi's artistic circles. She spoke about her friends there indulgently now.

We shared a past in three countries and two languages. I'd read her obituary of Saliha Abida Husain, and reminded her she'd written that Saliha

ANNIE

and her husband had now become an object of research for social historians, perhaps because the ideals and dreams of the early years of Jamia Millia had been forgotten. Animated, Annie told me how, in her early years there, she'd often visited Saliha Abida Husain, and spent long evenings listening to her discussing literature, politics and religion with her neighbour, Anis Kidwai. In spite of their formidable erudition, Saliha and Anis had both been schooled at home and didn't have a university degree between them.

'Have you read Anis Kidwai's diary, *Azadi ki chhaon men?*' she asked. 'A penetrating account of the effects of partition in Delhi, when hundreds of Muslims were refugees in their own country. They were herded into the Old Fort awaiting resettlement, or transportation to Pakistan, where many of them didn't want to go. Anis Kidwai's husband was murdered during the riots, but she went on and worked with refugees....'

On the long drive away from that home she'd finally created for herself, I thought of Annie's words about that lost period of broken ideals. The previous year, she'd published her translation of her first novel, *My Temples Too*, originally published just after partition, when her memories of the events in Delhi, from where she'd left for Pakistan, were raw:

There were young Muslim volunteers of Jamiat ul Ulema in the camp, attending to casualties and carrying corpses. It was like living through a blood-curdling nightmare. Syed Iftikhar and his colleagues were either busy demoralising the Muslims or taking the first opportunity to run away to the new dominion. Most of them had already gone, leaving their followers to face death. Corpses lay about in the streets or rotted in the sun or became decomposed and swollen in the rain...the blood of the Muslim citizens of Delhi flowed in the streets, dripped into gutters and mixed with muddy rain-water.

What had made her rewrite this book after nearly three decades? Had she witnessed those scenes at the age of twenty? Did she leave for Pakistan in fear, or in desperation, or in hope of the promised new dawn? Had she spent much of her life answering those questions in the voices of her characters and remained silent about her own feelings?

I found a copy of Anis Kidwai's book in the SOAS library when I got back to London. I was haunted by its images of the Old Fort, where I'd walked a few days before, only half-conscious of its hidden history. When I finished reading it, I wanted to write a story about a woman of that generation, who lived through partition and stayed on in Delhi after the riots, as Saliha and Anis had done. A couple of months later, after another trip to Delhi, Agra and Fatehpur Sikri, I did – but in my story the narrator, like Annie, decided, or was forced to, flee to Pakistan. In the end, my heroine didn't return, as Annie had chosen to do.

8.

About eighteen months after that meeting, I came back from Andalusia to hear that Annie was dead. She was buried in the graveyard of Jamia Millia. I hadn't known as we drove away that day before the early winter sunset that it would be the last time I'd see her; that with her gone, I'd said goodbye to my India, the country I'd escaped from in my teens but continued to yearn for, return to and miss; that the next piece I would write about her would be an obituary; that when *Fireflies* and her short stories were reprinted she'd have been dead a year and would never know how her reputation would keep on growing, that she'd never read or comment on my lengthy introductions to those books in the way she'd relished commenting on my reviews. I didn't foresee that, when I went back to Karachi after a gap of sixteen years, I'd be launching my novella set there that had been nominated for a prize, and my story about the city by the sea that she'd liked so much all those years ago would be reprinted in an anthology about Karachi; that in a symposium about her, on a platform with the grey eminences of Urdu literature who would damn her with faint praise I, who was there to talk about her short stories and her English writings, would say I thought Qurratulain Hyder was the best of us in everything she ever wrote. I didn't know, when I was asked to write a fiction piece about Pakistan for an issue of the *New Statesman* about Pakistan when I came back, that my story would be, in structure and technique, a tribute to the story Annie had asked me translate all those years before, transposing her vision to the present, or that it would be published later that year in an Urdu translation. I didn't even begin to guess that after that trip to Karachi I'd be back in Pakistan ten or eleven times over the next five years, that people there would begin to ask me to stay on, and London friends wonder if I intended to move back to Karachi for good. Above all, I wouldn't have predicted that five years after her death I'd be writing and publishing stories in Urdu, along with an afterword I'd title with her words to me: *Do you write in Urdu?* I'd like her to know, I did keep the promise that I made to our shared mother tongue and, tacitly, to her, and tell her as I had at that last meeting: Annie *Khala*, your hand was always on mine.

BEST OF ALL PATRONS?

Syed Nomanul Haq

A slave boy of Byzantine origin, who had grown up to become a scientific scion of Archimedes in the annals of world intellectual history, was offered a hefty sum of 1,000 dinars as a gift from his royal Seljuq patron Sultan Sanjar ibn Malikshāh in Khurāsān (r. 1097–1157). This gift was sent in celebration of the young scientist's completion of the tedious astronomical tables that he had painstakingly composed in crowded pages for the grand patron. Owned by the treasurer of the court, this humble client of Sultan Sanjar – Abu'l Fath al-Khāzinī, whose *Kitāb Mīzān al-Hikma* (*Book of the Balance of Wisdom*) is both a theoretical and practical breakthrough in the science of hydrostatics, possessed the courage, confidence, and, above all, the grit to refuse this generous reward! 'I have ten dinars already,' he is reported by the twelfth century polymath Zahīr al-Dīn Bayhaqī to have said, 'and I live on three a year. Besides, in my household there is nobody except one cat'.

When we reconstruct in our historical consciousness the grandeur and the worldly might of the Seljuqs, this 'audacity' of a slave-servant (*khādim*) appears to be quite remarkable, manifesting the stature scholars enjoyed while in the service of a patron or patrons in royal courts. Note here that the generic appellation 'scholars' in this exposé denotes not only scientists but also philosophers, writers, historians, poets, artists, artisans – that is, all those preoccupied with matters relating to human thought and imagination, with historical enquiries, or with the creative arts. The boundaries between many of these disciplines being invisibly blurred anyway in the earlier periods of our human history.

But back to Khāzinī. Demonstrating the simplicity of his lifestyle despite royal patronage and high-level connections, he could turn down a massive material gesture from the powerful Sanjar – and get away with it, facing no ensuing adverse consequences. One also remembers that he had expressed such impudence twice: once before he had turned back the same financial reward of 1,000 dinars sent to him by the wife of a Seljuq emir. But then, neither the Sultan nor the majestic lady felt slighted by what seems to be an abrupt refusal on the part of a 'lowly' slave in their service. Khāzinī seems to have been valued as a favourite of the court whose idiosyncrasies were to be admitted.

Is this kind of security that Khāzinī felt typical for scholars attached to royal courts? Indeed, the patron-scholar/protector-protégé relationships seem so varied in Muslim societies that it is difficult to make risk-free generalisations about their precise nature: stable and secure in some cases, precarious and sinusoidal in others; long-lasting and mutually loyal here, short-lived and subject to changing political winds there; now happy, now strained; scholars being beneficiaries of rich favours at one time, suffering the wrath of the same benefactor at others. An expert of the phenomenon of patronage in the Islamic intellectual history, one of the very few let's note, Sonja Brentjes, had told us categorically that theoretically grounded investigations in this area are non-existent. All one can do at this juncture of contemporary scholarship is show to the reader a few glimpses of empirical history and tentatively identify some enduring patterns.

And yet, despite all the variations in the patronage practices, there seem to be two characteristics of this phenomenon that are to be found universally in the history of Muslim societies. One is that scholars brought with them to the royal courts, and to individual rulers and their empires, much glory and prestige – but this is a trivial observation. The important point here is that such glory and prestige performed not only a symbolic function but were also items of concrete acquisitions that demonstrated real majestic power and served as efficacious political instruments. This last characteristic, I tentatively claim, is unique to Muslim societies. Take the Ghaznavids for example, the opulent Turkic rulers during the period 977 to 1186, whose empire at their greatest extent exercised its imperial power over much of Transoxiana, Iran, and Hindustan. The Ghaznavid Sultans loved splendour and luxury and, not unlike all other highly developed Islamic cultures of the times, their courts too embodied an elite cultural ethos. This fundamental attribute was brought into focus with much perspicacity by the historian Clifford Bosworth in his learned study of these kings.

What is the implication of Bosworth's observation that might lead us to further historical enquiry? Patronage, he tells us, was the very foundation on which the Ghaznavid culture could rest, given the latter's elite nature. Again, patronage was not simply a symbolic expression or a mere metaphor of glory and dominion; rather, it was irreversibly integrated into the actual running machinery of the empire. Listen to Bosworth: 'the financial basis of patronage was exactly the same as that upon which the fortunes of the dynasty and state rested; one cannot condemn [or explain] the one without the other'. Small wonder, then, that courts and rulers and individual patrons often treated scholars literally as commodity, something that came as part of the booty or loot of conquests, or acquired as gifts from friendly neighbouring dynasties, or as material tokens of surrender from weak ones.

Talking about the practitioners of the mathematical sciences in Muslim societies, Brentjes starts off by noting that the languages in which they were writing, and this means largely Arabic, there existed no direct equivalent of the term 'patronage.' Thus there were many ways of denoting the patron's acquisition of a protégé, and among these was the tell-tale appellation *hamala* (to carry [away] something) – yes, in many cases this denotes the phenomenon with graphic accuracy and one can legitimately go as far as to translate *hamala* contextually as 'kidnapping,' 'snatching,' or 'looting.' So we see: while the adventurous Sultan Maḥmūd Ghaznavī, who ruled over a vast area during 998–1030, brought to his capital in Ghazna entire libraries over from Ray and Isfahan, he also acquired for his royal company and for the prestige of his empire numerous scholars, and he did this by force if he found it necessary. The canonical historian of the literary world of Central Asia and Iran, E. G. Browne, is quoted as saying that Sultan Mahmud 'has often been described as a great patron of letters, but he was in fact rather a great kidnapper of literary men ... whom he often treated in the end scurvily enough.'

The accounts of Bayhaqī whom we have met above, as well as those of his contemporary, the not-always-reliable chronicler Niẓāmī ʿArūżī, record many Ghaznavid anecdotes of 'kidnapping' – kidnapping physical embodiments of letters, such as books and manuscripts, together with men of letters – literally apprehending them, and carrying them away on horses. But here also exist in these sources reports of acquiring such cultural and human booty by means of vicious coercion wielded by the political and military might of the empire. Bayhaqī tells us categorically about Sultan Mahmūd that 'whenever he came across a man or woman who was an expert in any skill, he deported them tither (namely, to Ghazna)'. This is how the Tabānī family of Hanafī legists had ended up in the Ghaznavid capital from Nishapur. And when in the wake of his advance on the left bank of the Oxus and his sacking of the Ma'mūnid Khwārazmshāhs in Gurgānj, Mahmūd sent an ultimatum to the defeated ruler Abu'l-'Abbās Ma'mūn, the victor's demands were typical. This ultimatum is recorded by Nizāmī 'Arūżī in his *Chahār Maqāla*:

> I have heard that there are at the Khwārazmshāh's court several men
> of learning, each peerless in his science, such as so-and-so and so-and-so.
> You must send them to our court, so that they may have the honour of
> being presented there and that we may derive prestige from their knowledge
> and capabilities ...

One recalls that the redoubtable intellectual giant of the times who is elevated by contemporary historians to the station of the 'greatest scientist of Islam,' Abū Rayhān al-Bīrūnī (d. c. 1050), was a *nadīm* (boon companion) and adviser of the Khwarazmshāh Abu'l 'Abbās, lavishing upon his patron not only private sessions of learned and witty company but also helping him in sensitive diplomatic missions. We have reports in our received historical legacy that the Khwarazmshāh court had become known for its high cultural refinement and its intellectual assets and that Mahmūd Ghaznavī had grown quite jealous and, what is uniquely revealing, he was rather fearful of this reputation due to its implications in practical politics – hence his ultimatum it seems. Indeed, the royal entourage at the Gurgānj court could boast the glow of a brilliant stellar cluster: other than Bīrūnī, the short-lived Khwarazmshāh dynasty had among its protégés the philosopher 'Isā Masīhi, the mathematician Abū Nasr Jīlānī, and the physician Abu'l Khayr Khammār. But perhaps the brightest star in this cluster, a star that illuminated the chambers of world culture until almost the sixteenth century, was ibn Sīnā, Latinised Avicenna, the 'Grand Shaykh' (al-Shaykh al-Ra'īs) of the Arabo-Islamic tradition.

Now Bīrūnī had served many courts. At the Samanid capital of Bukhara, for instance, he had secured the patronage of another eastern ruler, the emir Mansūr II ibn Nūh II (r. 997–999). This royal embrace of the scholar yielded decisive results for intellectual history, for it was here that Bīrūnī corresponded with ibn Sīnā who too happened to be in the same city at the time, the latter serving the Samanid rulers both as administrator and physician. This elegant correspondence has been preserved for posterity and exists in a modern edition. So here we have one of numerous examples of the intellectual harvest of patronage relationships. And more, Bīrūnī moved in the year 998 to the service of the Ziyarid emir of Tabaristān and Gorgān, Shams al-Ma'ālī Qābūs ibn Voshmgīr. Then, under the protection of the Qābūs court, reinforced no doubt by the financial security generously provided personally by the emir, our scholar wrote his first major work on historical and scientific chronology with its internally rhyming title, *al-Āthār al-Bāqīya 'an al-Qur'ūn al-Khālīya*, usually translated as *Chronology of Ancient Nations*. Let's recognise at once that the Ziyarid patron of Bīrūnī has thereby served as a building block in the intellectual history of the world.

In the end, upon Sultan Mahmūd's terrifying ultimatum for the surrender of what was considered human intellectual commodities, Bīrūnī had to leave Gurgānj of his ancestral region and relocate to Ghazna to serve his new patrons. Did Bīrūnī choose his new patrons willingly or was he forced? We know that some scholars serving the Khwarazmshāhs had refused to serve Mahmūd's court, and stories have it that Bīrūnī was taken prisoner by the soldiers of Mahmūd – if so, one imagines him being delivered to the Ghanznavid sultan in chains. And yet, once in the Ghaznavid court, Bīrūnī began to practise the same art of flattery and boon companionship in which he indulged in the service of all other royal courts. In this court-scholar trade of patronage, did loyalties shift so smoothly, so painlessly, and instantly?

The answer to this question is neither straightforward nor easily found. Chroniclers tell us that in Mahmūd's court there were as many as four hundred poets, acolytes of the *amīr al-Shu'arā'* (poet-laureate) Abu'l-Qāsim 'Unsurī, singing songs of praise, uttering hyperbole, and composing panegyrics (*qasā'id*, sing. *qasīda*) in honour of the majestic Ghaznavid patron. Bīrūnī too sang in this chorus, accompanied Mahmūd in his expeditions and territorial exploits, and dedicated his monumental astronomical treatise, the *Qanūn al-Mas'ūdī (Mas'ūdī Canon)*, to Sultan Mas'ūd, Mahmūd's son; then, this was followed by yet another major dedication: he dedicates his comprehensive work on mineralogy, *al-Jamāhir fī Ma'rifat al-Jawāhir (On Gems)*, to Sultan Mawdūd Ghaznavī, Mahmūd's grandson. But perhaps the most outstanding, well-known and enduring work of Bīrūnī is his *Book of India* – the full title is *Tahqīq mā Li'l-Hind min Maqbūla Ma'qbūla fi'l-'Aql am Mardhūla* (literally, *Research on the Reasonableness or Unreasonableness of What is Said about India*). Given that it was indeed Sultan Mahmūd who brought, by force or by mutual consent, our Khwārazmi scholar to the gateway to India, we ought to give this patron credit for what may be considered Bīrūnī's supreme work, his historical magnum opus that he completed just after the Sultan's death in the year 1030.

But the question rebounds. Was it out of his free will and a display of his true loyalty that Bīrūnī acknowledged his patrons, dedicated his books to them, and stood beside them in their travels and even in their regional military adventures? Or were these acts of his carried out as a matter of disciplinary conventions of the court, mere tropes, a client's drill, being part of his 'job requirements' that he had to fulfil mechanically as it were? We might never know. And yet it remains plausible to assume that it was the financial comfort and leisure that the Ghaznavid provided him, together with his travels into the inner territories of Hindustan in the fully protected royal company of his thirteen-year long patron Mahmūd, that gave Bīrūnī the opportunity to learn Sanskrit and Hindu philosophy, and to experience Indian cultural practices first-hand; and it was precisely this specialised body of theoretical and empirical knowledge that made his India the rigorous and authentic study it is. But then, on the other hand, the famous translator of this work Edward Sachau tells us that Bīrūnī shows no enthusiasm for Mahmūd, that he speaks about this particular Sultan perfunctorily without elaboration in the book, and that we have no evidence to show that he enjoyed any kind of patronage. The matter must rest undetermined at this juncture.

But in the intellectual history of Islam we do meet people who, like the Byzantine slave Khāzinī, assert the independence of their will even in the face of ruthless royal authority. So we have the eminently dramatic and eventful case of the Grand Shaykh ibn Sīnā: he refused to make his will pliable to Sultan Mahmūd Ghaznavi's whims. We have noted that at the time of the Sultan's annexation of Gurgānj and his ultimatum to the fallen Abu'l 'Abbās Ma'mūn requiring the handing over of scholars to Ghazna, Ibn Sīnā too happened to be in that Khwārazmshāhi cultural metropolis serving under the patronage of the Ma'mūnid ruler. While Bīrūnī ended up in Ghazna in effective compliance with the Sultan's demand, ibn Sīnā moved out of Gurgānj and travelled South to Khurāsān and then West to Jurjān. Was the Grand Shaykh's refusal to deliver himself at the Ghaznavid court an act of defiance? Or was it simply avoidance? Again, there can be no simple answer to this query. In his autobiography, he is vague: 'necessity' called me to leave Gurgānj, he says. This 'necessity,' the American Arabist Dimitri Gutas figures out, means political reasons.

The biographical story of this monumental philosopher and physician is intriguing. At the age only of seventeen, he was summoned to treat the Samanid ruler Nūh ibn Mansūr in Bukhārā, the city in the vicinity of which the young physician was born around the year 980. The ruler recovers and the physician is admitted to the royal court. Upon the death of his father while this promising son had barely grown out of his teens, ibn Sīnā begins his career as a state functionary. Like his father, it is highly probable that the son too was now given the governorship of a Samanid district. Following this, after the Turkish Qarakhanid overthrow of the Samanid state, he moves from court to court, from one patron to another, from this city to that city. In many cases, these moves were made due to what is described in the autobiography as 'necessity', that is, political exigency. This is the time, we recall, when the authority was disintegrating and many Iranian and Turkic states were coming into being and passing away, sometimes in quick succession. Ibn Sīnā served many of them.

From Bukhārā, where he must have been identified closely with the defeated Samanids, ibn Sīnā moved in 999 to Gurgānj where we have already met him in the service of the Khwārazmshāhs. Here, not long after the defeat of the dynasty at the hands of Sultan Mahmūd, he moved to Jurjān, avoiding or defying the Sultan's ultimatum. Now he was looking for another patron, the Ziyarid emir Qābūs ibn Voshmgīr who had been protecting Bīrūnī. Ibn Sīnā arrived in Jurjān in 1012, only to find that his prospective patron had died. The ruler at the time was Manūchehr ibn

Qābūs who probably took ibn Sīnā under his patronage, but there exists an interesting twist in this story. Manūchehr had declared his allegiance to Sultan Mahmūd Ghaznavī and took the Sultan's daughter as his bride. Now one impression keeps nagging at us: for some reason ibn Sīnā was desperately determined to stay away from the Ghaznavid Sultan! It is perhaps for this reason that despite the patronage offer of Manūchehr, as it seems likely, our Shaykh did not live in the Ziyarid royal quarters; he found a private patron who offered him his residence in Jurjān. Then, very soon, he left that city too. We note that it is here that he had met his famous biographer and companion Abu 'Ubayd Jūzjānī.

And then on to his twin patrons in Ray. These were the ruler Majd al-Dawla Rustam of the Shī'ī Buyid dynasty and his mother Sayyida in whose hand lay the real power of the throne. Ibn Sīnā got himself recognised as a skilled physician, treating Majd to full recovery from a nasty illness, and thereby also gaining access to the political elite of the area. But things were unstable in these politically turbulent times, and we see Majd's own brother Shams al-Dawla, who controlled Hamadan, attacking Ray. Ibn Sīnā moved again, now via Qazwīn to Hamadan, the city of the attacker. The reasons, again, seem to be political.

Ibn Sīnā's biography is highly instructive. For example, from his vitae one can practically find leads for the reconstruction of the very dynastic history of his times. When the Abbasid Baghdad was steadily receding into political irrelevance, Transoxianan, Persian, and North African rulers were arising all over from Spain to India. But more to the point, ibn Sīnā's life story throws into sharp relief the second defining characteristic of patronage in Muslim societies. We have noted that one attribute of this phenomenon, tentatively claimed here to be unique to Muslims, is the political valence of scholars, hence their status as commodities to be acquired as booty in conquests or as surrender from a weak or a client state. Ibn Sīnā opens for us another vista: we now see the role of scholars as state functionaries, and this appears to be a pattern. Acquired or kidnapped scholars generally became part of the state machinery; they served as diplomats, viziers, governors, administrators, negotiators, and government advisors. And again: with some trepidation, we can declare this second characteristic of patronage to be unique to the world of Islam.

Let's pick up the thread of ibn Sīnā's story where we left it. Ibn Sīnā began his career in Bukhārā where he served as a high administrator, perhaps as a district governor; now in the year 1015 he is in Hamadan under the patronage of Shams al-Dawla. Here he becomes the ruler's vizier. This grand philosopher and physician serves as a Buyid vizier for nearly six years. Upon the death of Shams in 1021, and the accession of the new emir Samā' al-Dawla, ibn Sīnā abandons the high post. This was the decision, it seems, of a shrewd politician, so we gather from his eminent biographer Jūzjānī: 'ibn Sīnā saw fit not to remain in the same state nor to resume the same duties and trusted that the prudent thing to do ... would be to hide in anticipation of an opportunity to leave the region.'

Foreseeing and dreading the end of the Buyids, ibn Sīnā withdraws from the public eye. Now his story becomes more and more intriguing and complex, and this brings before us in full focus the messy drama of state machinations in the Muslim patron-scholar dynamics. Indeed, particularly from hereon, the Shaykh's biography reads more like accounts of petty kings and scheming court climbers than those of a stereotypical sage, and this is hardly surprising because, after all, he was typically a state functionary scholar. Already during his ministerial service, some bad blood had developed between him and Shams's Daylami and Turkish soldiers; there was even an army rebellion against him according to some reports.

So, ibn Sīnā went into hiding for several years under the protection of a private patron to whom we ought to be grateful since it was in this secret haven, when the former minister was unencumbered by the chaotic pressures of the Buyid state, that he completed a large part of his encyclopaedic work, the *Kitāb al-Shifā' (Book of Healing)*. But during this time, from 1021–1024, ibn Sīnā was also involved in some clandestine activities: historians tell us that he corresponded secretly with the Kakuyid 'Alā al-Dawla, a cousin of Sayyida whom she had placed on the throne in Isfahan. He was caught, and thrown into prison. The intelligence network of the Hamadan Buyid court, led by the Kurdish vizier Tāj al-Mulk, had charged him with the crime of treachery.

There are many versions of ibn Sīnā's life story, some authentic, some spurious, and one is often tempted to opt for the most sensational. But this temptation ought to be resisted. The safest thing to do is follow Dimitri Gutas who tells us that ibn Sīnā was incarcerated by the Buyids in a castle outside Hamadan called Fardajān. He remained in prison for four months and was freed when in 1023 his prospective Kakuyid patron 'Alā' al-Dawla advanced towards Hamadan and sacked Samā' al-Dawla. The political winds changed again and ibn Sīnā was offered an administrative position here; he declined. One day, perhaps after one year, ibn Sīnā escaped to Isfahan. He escaped with two slaves, his brother, and his biographer Jūzjānī – all disguised as Sufis.

Incarcerations, court intrigues, military adventures, high offices, administrative manipulations – all these are, quite typically, historical elements in the life of patronised scholars in Islamic intellectual history. What is uniquely important, scholars here were not only passively subject to or acted upon by these elements, they were themselves actors. Thus we see ibn Sīnā, in the wake of his royal reception in Isfahan with much fanfare, dedicating a Persian book, *Danishnāma-i 'Alā'i* (*'Alā'i Encyclopaedia*), to his yet another patron 'Alā' al-Dawla, and accompanying him on most of his military campaigns and trips. In fact, it was during such a trip to Hamadan that our Grand Shaykh died. He is buried in Hamadan, the very place from where some thirteen years earlier he had escaped in disguise. Now he was back with a vengeance in the company of the victor.

So scholars should indeed figure in the political history of Islam, a body of history that cuts across ethnic and sectarian boundaries. Bīrūnī served both Shi'ite and Sunni and ethnically diverse dynasties, and so did ibn Sīnā. The case of the twelfth-century Andalusi ibn Tufayl, the author of the world classic *Hayy ibn Yaqzān* (*Living, Son of Awake*), shows a slight variation, but again this variation is of an ideological not sectarian or ethnic kind; an ideology packaged in theological terms but in fact riding upon political doctrines. The court career of ibn Tufayl embodies an eminent case of the public role of patronage relations, based on state function. He was a close confidant and trustee of the Almohad (al-Muwahhid) Caliph Abū Ya'qūb, who ruled Spain and North Africa from his seat in Marrakesh, so close that one word of favour from the scholar was enough for one to gain access to his royal master. What is more, the philosopher ibn Rushd is a gift of ibn Tufayl for it was he who had introduced ibn Rushd to Abū Ya'qūb, and it was this very ibn Tufayl who had encouraged ibn Rushd, considered to be the greatest Aristotelian in the history of philosophy, to work on Aristotle.

One must recognise the importance of ibn Tufayl's *Hayy*, a work that celebrates the power of human reason. Since its seventeenth-century Latin translation by Edward Pococke, its influence and its long shadows are found all over. Indeed, as I have said elsewhere:

> *Hayy ibn Yaqzān*'s historical impact in world intellectual culture was massive; in fact, mind-boggling. We hear its chimes all over Europe – in pure philosophy, in science proper, and in educational doctrines, not to speak of literature and that liberating genre of fiction that is part of the world literary canon. The founder of empiricism in modern-day philosophy, John Locke, happened to be a student of Pococke and knew his teacher's translation since he refers to it. But what is more, historians say that the English philosopher's classic *tabula rasa* (blank slate) theory – the theory that the human mind at birth is a blank slate – is inspired by the *Hayy*; this observation is highly plausible. Historians have also traced the Arabic tale's diffusion in, and in many cases direct impact on, the thought of Robert Boyle, Voltaire, and even Karl Marx. This includes *Emile: Or, On Education* by Rousseau.

It has been observed that, apart from the Qur'ān and *Thousand and One Nights*, there is in all likelihood no work in the entire corpus of classical Arabic that has been translated into so many other languages and published so many times.

Yet, this ibn Tufayl was a state functionary of the Almohads. One of his duties was that of a propagandist: promoting the ideas of the dynasty's founder ibn Tumart. Here again one begins to be fascinated by the yields of patronage in the field of intellectual culture. And like ibn Tufayl we have another compelling case of ibn Khaldun, the fourteenth/fifteenth-century North African 'father of sociology.' His meeting with Tamerlane is familiar to us, and so is his successful role as an official negotiator between tribes, and as a royal emissary to Peter the Cruel in Seville. He refused to be recruited by the world conqueror; and he also turned down flatly the historic offer of the post-Reconquista Spanish ruler: that if he returns to his ancestral Seville, all the Khaldun family property will be restored to him. Ibn Khaldun seems to have possessed the same confidence and grit that we saw in Khāzinī with whom we began.

BORDERS

Piro Rexhepi

It is a fine summer evening and I am with my parents in Lake Prespa, Macedonia while Muslimgauze's Ali Zarin is playing in the background. The tranquillity of the season belies the tension in our midst. News of refugees being rounded up in Greece, hunted on the Bulgarian borders or stuck at the Macedonian ones crowds our thoughts. We watch intently as Deutsche Welle maps the movement of people in transit to Europe via a new route at the Greek-Albanian border. A few days later we watch the Turkish coup unfold on television as mass protests continue in Skopje against the government and more images of Syrian children captivated in terror appear on TV. My parents switch through channels nervously and settle for their new favourite Indian soap opera: *Diya Aur Baati Hum*. They can't watch or talk about the refugees, too close to home, too many memories, too much pain. Later, I drive to Salonika to meet my friend Saffo who I met at a failed queer collective, ambitiously and somewhat appropriately named the Balkan Queer Initiative – for it remained just that, an initiative. Disappointed with the anti-racist festival we had attended earlier in the month, we hoped to go to the No Borders Camp together; an initiative to summon the precarious commons into togetherness and think of ways to confront EU borders in the face of refugee pleas on all sides. Greece, or as Saffo likes to call it, the former Ottoman Province known as Yunanistan FOPOY (a pun on Greece's persistence that Macedonia be called the Former Yugoslav Republic of Macedonia FYROM), seems to be boiling too. We join a group of demonstrators on Via Egnatia attempting to re-take Salonika's Theatre Academy. Local activists, Syrian refugees, European anarcho-tourists, all surround the building and then wait, using the moment to meet, reflect, watch, exchange.

We talk about homonationalism, transphobia in the queer community and what is to be done about the incorporation of queer political formations into the EU enlargement project in the Balkans. Saffo insists that the discourse needs to be decentred from Europe. That it is imperative to talk to ourselves instead of wasting energy persuading the European ga[y]ze that all people in the Balkans, including the refugees, Roma and Muslims, are human too. Our friend Velina joins us from Bulgaria. More conversations about the Bulgarian law criminalising radical Islam proposed by the far right Patriotic Front and adopted in parliament the previous month; of European vigilantes arriving at the Bulgarian borders to defend 'Europe' from refugees. We talk about the possibilities and limitations of Novi Levi Perspektivi in Sofia to 'do something.' We conclude that they are too small and fragmented, like all leftist movements in the Balkans. Being in Greece reminds us of Syriza, the once promising leftist alternative, now in power and for the previous two weeks gathering up refugees around Greece, evicting them from migrant squats set up with the help of local Greeks and ultimately deporting them to Turkey. Saffo tells us about a protest she attended, against the evictions and deportations of refugees, that took place in front of the Syriza offices which saw members of the Syriza Political Party show up to protest against Syriza the government. All the while Syriza the government has been facing EU pressure to start expelling refugees after the EU reached a deal with Turkey for their containment there. Paradoxically, the coup in Turkey, with its entire terrifying unfurling and the consequences, gives us a glimpse of hope that the EU-Turkey trading deal with refugee bodies may now have to wait.

We move through Ano Poli, the old Turkish quarter in the upper town of Salonika, commenting on the old Ottoman mosques, türbes and hamams – and the mayor's recent decision to preserve and transform them into tourist sites for the new Turkish travelling middle classes with a taste for Ottoman nostalgia. After we pay our respects to the Musa Baba Türbe in Terpsithea square, we end up at Egli Yeni Hamam turned into a hipster café and order our overpriced Turkish coffees. We agree that we too suffer a little from Ottoman melancholy but pretend to be less sentimental about it. Svetlana Boym has warned us of the dangerous seductions of nostalgia. After a long discussion on turbofolk, Turkish pop and failed attempts to sing rembetiko, we all agree that Aziz is the shining star of the queer Balkan

Turbofolk scene. Velina tells us about a recent interview where Aziz is being questioned for calling his latest song Habibi, for it sounding too Arabic and not Bulgarian enough and for promoting Arabisation in Bulgarian culture. Eventually we find ourselves at a queer squat in Ano Poli with Nasta and Sofia who have been providing assistance to refugees.

Wanting to get away from the heat in Salonika, we drive to Western Thrace, Drama, Xanthi and Kavala, the birthplace of Mohamed Ali of Egypt and the only part of Greece with a Muslim minority that survived the population exchange of 1924. Saffo tells me that a Kosovar queer is joining us. It happens to be Astrit Ismaili whose work I have written about but never met in person. As we walk through the streets of Kavala, Astrit dances through a quiet restaurant with live music. Everyone joins in, we get free raki from the owner and go our way. In a silent moment after the dance and the raki, Astrit reminds us 'we are all the same people'. Driving through Muslim villages of Western Thrace, we witness the continued coercion of the Greek state that can be felt in a way that cannot be articulated. We decide to leave Greece and head to Kosovo with Astrit for Dokufest, a film festival in Prizren that has become a favourite with the Balkan hipster crowd and their admirers. Anxieties rise as we cross the borders. Driving from Greece into Macedonia, we follow the same Balkan route refugees travelled through, but are no longer able to, as the Greek state has rounded up most of them and Macedonia has closed its borders. We fight over music in the car. I want Akhlaq Ahmed and Bülent Ersoy. He wants Dua Lipa, Era Istrefi and Beyoncé. When we reach the Macedonia/Kosovo border crossing at Blace, Astrit remembers being stuck here with his parents as a refugee during the Kosovo war in the summer of 1999. We travel in silence after crossing the border.

Astrit has been away for year in Amsterdam. Driving through Kosovo, he points out the obscure and bizarre postwar architecture or the freedom of architectural expression in post-war Kosovo as he calls it. We talk about our mutual friend Lorik Berisha, a queer urban legend in Prishtina who loved brooches and died too young. I press Astrit about his piece Trashformations. He resists the discussion, knowing my critique of his work doesn't bode well with some aspects of his performance, such as his wearing of a pink hijab in it, that I find problematic. In Trashformations, he questions the limits of defined and codified subjects and rights. He opens the possibility of trashforming those rights in the context and circumstances in which subjectivity is embodied and where bodies can take different shapes and forms. To illustrate the limits of confined rights, he wraps himself in adhesive tape symbolising the restricting nature of codified rights, their impossibility and the borders they create between bodies, communities, genders, classes and temporalities. The taping of his body to the walls of the studio suggests the binding nature of these rights to certain material and discursive realities that limit our ability to physically move and see and be beyond them. He points out during his performance that one needs a visa to pass through these borders and 'if you don't have one, you go to jail,' further illustrating how these borders sustain the biopolitics of who lives and dies, who passes and who does not. As we drive across three nations, we discuss the moment he throws money at the audience, to bring attention to the various economies that sustain and profit from drawing and maintaining borders. Reminding the audience that he does not want to be a victim and that he is not one, he questions the 'war is over' discourse in Kosovo as fictitious as his war is still ongoing. Finally, pulling out an EU flag as a symbol of the ultimate blinding and binding ideology that the EU has come to represent in post-war Kosovo, Astrit remarks that when he looks at the EU flag he does not see the stars and the sky. Nonetheless, he argues, 'we still have to use the things we don't like.' Questioning the promise and premise of what is the EU, he shoves the EU flag in his mouth and throws it up into a garbage bag, symbolically trashing it in a hope of trashforming EU sanctified borders and the violence that sustains them.

We discuss his work in the context of the humanitarian missions in Kosovo after the war, particularly the EULEX (European Rule of Law) Mission and how they have frequently exploited the issues of gender and sexual rights in the legitimisation of their continued presence even after the declaration of independence in 2007. How the funding for civil society projects that relate to gender and queer rights become the social ordering tools on questions that cannot be addressed by legal ramifications alone. I ask him what he means by his statement that he doesn't want to be a victim – he says he no longer wants to feel under threat, fear or in need of saving. As we discuss the victimisation of queer subjects in Kosovo, our conversation moves to a common acquaintance from queer circles in

Kosovo, Semi who features in a recent short video reportage called 'Living openly gay in Kosovo's homophobic society'.

The story and accompanying pictures and videos were published by a German initiative 'Facing the Balkans' in which young journalists from six different countries travel in the Balkans to chronicle minority stories. Semi, the Kosovar Muslim homosexual, is one of the minorities. The video piece and its various semiotic modalities conjure Kosovo as an oppressive space for Semi, pointing out that 'Semi is an exception' and that there 'are not many gay men who display their sexual orientation like him' because they 'are afraid'. The cause of Semi's fear is attributed to strong 'traditional and religious values [that] provoke prejudice and judgment in the Kosovar society where 90 per cent of the population is Muslim.' In one take, Semi is projected alone, behind bars, seemingly wanting to break free. The background of grey socialist architecture presents Semi as victim of both post-socialist and post-conflict conditions but also Islam. When Semi talks about his religious father the camera focuses on posters of mosques hanging in his parents' home. The piece is designed to illustrate the converging itineraries that the authors believe constitute the roots of homophobia in Kosovo. While we both agreed that this work is important, we find the trajectories in which this, and many similar narratives are situated, problematic. The individualised victim narrative not only renders the existence and work of a queer community in Kosovo invisible but it also bifurcates Semi from both the queer and Kosovar community, projecting him as an exception and a victim, whose liberation cannot be located in his immediate geographies but must come from elsewhere.

I left Astrit in Kosovo, with his friends and family, and travelled south to Albania. With my friend Duri in Tirana, we watched the documentary *Stigma* I was told about while in Kosovo. Funded by an EU project called 'Challenging Homophobia in Kosovo', the documentary is meant to illustrate the struggles of LGBT Kosovars. In it, the European Parliament rapporteur for Kosovo, Ulrike Lunacek appears during a press conference, explaining to the Kosovar viewers that homosexuality is not a disease. We don't know if we should laugh or cry. In another segment, she goes on to suggest that she is 'sure that there are artists in this country who are quite popular who are also lesbian and gay, but are afraid to say so' stressing the importance that some of these people should 'show their faces' and closing her remarks with 'I have said here in Kosovo myself that I am a lesbian myself, it is part of my life, so what?'. Similar to Semi's story, the rest of the documentary represents the queer community in Kosovo as almost entirely invisible and frightened. Kosovar society is pathologised as pervasively patriarchal and ignorant with an almost irreconcilable difference between queers and the rest of their communities. Duri and I worry about the consequences of this kind of framing of homophobia and transphobia and their promotion of normative EU LGBT rights that rely on homo-emancipation concepts of coming-out, visibility and institutional top-down and problem-solution imperatives.

We discuss a recent EU project, ironically (or not) titled 'normally different', where two organisations, one from Finland and the other one from Austria, market their project as necessary for Kosovo's EU integration. The Finnish National Institute for Health and Welfare points out that, 'Kosovo needs to embrace the European values of tolerance, diversity and understanding to make progress in the EU integration' and that the 'international project team will work in close cooperation with relevant stakeholders and with the newly established national Advisory and Coordination Group for the Rights of the LGBT community.' Whereas the Austrian contractor, the Ludwig Boltzmann Institute of Human Rights, identifies the project as 'a wide spectrum of awareness-raising and training activities across the public sector in order to enhance effective protection against discrimination,' pointing out that under the motto 'normally different' the project 'entails an analysis of the existing anti-discrimination legislation and the institutional structures in relation to sexual orientation and identity as well as measures for improving access for the LGBT community to legal and psychological counselling'.

We discuss the power dynamics of these projects and how they are characterised by the donor-contractor agenda of what they believe should constitute the parameters of homo-emancipation in Kosovo, which then comes to dominate public debates with recognisable EU models of sexuality. In the process marginalising queer voices who are critical of further EU interventions and incorporation of queer Kosovar politics into larger EU emancipatory politics. We wonder how an international staff, with no background, training or familiarity with the queer community in Kosovo, will relate and respond to the needs of the community or why EU funding meant for the queer community in Kosovo is not administered by local community organisations but through organisations that have little or no experience of working in Kosovo? Assuming that the EU wants to promote visibility, as Lunacek suggests, then why not allow grassroots bodies to define their own terms on visibility? In this context, we feel that coming out and the disciplinary call to visibility would mean locating oneself and identifying with the dominant recognisable LGBT identity promoted by EU projects.

Duri wants to return to the question of visibility and Lunacek's assumption that there are no queer artists in Kosovo who 'show their faces' in the face of the many common friends we share. He believes that this is an important discourse that needs to be exposed for it not only hides the important work that queer artists and activists in Kosovo and the rest of the Balkans have engaged in over the last decade but it also legitimises as permissible the EU discourse on LGBT rights denying local queers to tell their stories by controlling their narratives. We agree that EU pressure for visible queer subjects points to a more concerning direction: that of the incorporation of queer bodies into the EU politics of 'more' or less European subjects, of developed and underdeveloped or proper and improper Europeans, but also of good and bad Muslims in the Balkans such as the framing of the homophobic attacks in Prishtina in 2012 or the reoccurring homophobic attacks of the Merlika Queer Film festival in Sarajevo.

On 1st February 2014, a group of 14 masked men entered Merlinka Queer Film Festival at Cinema Kriterion in Sarajevo shouting, 'Where are you faggots?' and 'There will be no Pride Parade in Sarajevo, there will be no faggots in Sarajevo.' Agence France-Presse reported that because 'Bosnia is a largely conservative Muslim country ... the capital Sarajevo has usually been hostile towards hosting events linked to homosexuality.' This was the second time that the queer community had come under attack. In 2008, and more recently in March 2016, similar attacks took place during the Queer Sarajevo Festival. Some LGBTI voices that have dominated the discourse have generated a debate that naturalised the assumption that most, if not all, of the attackers were Muslim fundamentalists influenced by radical strains of Islamist thought and practice coming from the Middle East, troubling the supposed local, moderate, secular and European type of

Islam practiced in the Balkans. In a declaration after the 2008 attacks, the Bosnian civil rights organisation Front issued a statement asking if 'the tolerance of violence by a religious movement, which has nothing to do with the (traditional) Islam in Bosnia and Herzegovina, raises the question of whether Bosnia and Herzegovina is an Islamic or a secular country'.

The self-fashioning of Muslims in the Balkans as more secular, more tolerant and more moderate than the other Islams out there, but particularly in the Middle East, has been something I have struggled to understand in the last four years despite having been exposed to it all my life. I want to emphasise that the articulation of local, Balkan, European, secular and moderate Islam vs. Middle Eastern, radical, religious and backwards Islam is not exclusive to the queer communities. It has, however, become one of the dominant explanations for the multiple converging crises and pain that Muslims in the Balkans have undergone in the last three decades. It emerges everywhere, as an Islamist Middle Eastern threat lurking in the background with the possibility of being activated at any time to defy the secularism and Europeaness of Muslims in the Balkans and our possibilities of joining the EU as the EU may find us too Muslim to let us in. It is racist, with disturbing undertones of self-hate and is complicit in the larger racialisation and vilification of Muslims in Europe. It strikes a chord with all of us for it was these and similar allegations that justified collective violence on our communities during the wars in Bosnia, Kosovo and Macedonia. Long before the emergence of the war on terror that has now become a standard excuse to persecute and coerce Muslim communities from Burma to Britain, Yugoslavia had developed its own Islamist threat in the 1980s, a discourse that would became lethal in the conflicts that accompanied its disintegration. That this discourse converged with the larger post-cold war and post/911 debates on clashes of civilisation and the threat of radical Islam, only intensified the articulation of Balkan Islam as an exceptional type of Islam, one that should not and could not be identified with other Islams.

This is a discourse that can now be observed in much of the Muslim world. Think of the projection of Southeast Asian Islam as a lighter, folksy, syncretic and more peaceful Islam that has supposedly come under threat by Arab, Middle Eastern fanatical Islam. Mahmood Mamdani has written brilliantly about the divisions of good and bad Muslims in the larger narratives of the war on terror. What is specific about how this discourse operates in the Balkans is how it produces and draws ideological divisions among Muslims while materialising physical borders and the geopolitical division of Europe from the Middle East. As the borders of Muslim majority countries in the Balkans merge with those of the EU, the markers of extremist, suspect and fundamentalist move from us to our fellow Muslims in the Middle East, drawing clearly defined boundaries of acceptable Islam that can be integrated into the EU and 'extremist' Islam that must remain outside. It has been painful to see this debate play out in queer communities, for it, intentionally or unintentionally, ignores the continued marginalisation of our communities by singling one over the other – making intersectional and cross-sectional belonging seem like a natural impossibility.

At the end tail of the summer, I returned to these thoughts and put pen to paper once again. It has been difficult to include everything or even most events, meetings, conversations and digressions that took place over this summer that got me thinking and writing about Muslims and Islam in the Balkans. How to convey in a story all the little details that shape us and we shape in return; our subjectivities, gender queer, trans*, Greek, Muslim, Albanian, Bulgarian, Balkans, Middle Eastern, Eastern European… all coming together and traversing (and hopefully trashforming) borders and boundaries? How to also write in English conversations, their impact and all that is not said but understood and communicated in Albanian, Turkish, Greek, Bulgarian, Bosnian-Serbian-Coratian and English with Ottoman expressions in between that we could all identify? To write about our frames of references, our shared histories, our common struggles and desires, but to also write about Islam while not all of us are Muslim.

To write about Islam in the Balkans is to write about the painful experience of being allowed to live. To be always reminded of how trauma shapes and structures our desires and struggles so as to make sure that we never bear witness again to the bodies of our loved ones being piled at border crossings, refugee and concentration camps, the cemeteries and mass graves of Srebrenica and Reçak. It means to be inscribed with the possibility of expulsion before you are born, until, and after you die. For your memory to be laced forever with the images of your grandparents hanging over graves, pictures, always waiting for news of some missing person in the family, always fearing that one could go missing while bearing the childhood guilt of our harsh angry gaze at them for believing still, for hoping, for going over the ceremonies, for reminding us that this too shall come to pass – for they have seen it all before. It means to be reminded that the assimilation and expulsion of Bulgarian Muslims in 1989, the mass and organised expulsion and violence faced by Yugoslav Muslims in the 1990s, the continued destruction and erasure of Islamic sites in Macedonia and Bulgaria form part of a long persisting project to erase not just Muslim communities in the Balkans but all that they leave behind.

Engendered by these memories and embedded in the violence that produced them, we want to avoid watching the Syrian crisis unfold as it triggers our own hidden wounds. The common circumstances that have produced us, should also remind us that we need to love each other. Need to be there for one another. When you emerge from violence though, and begin to breathe, you are reluctant to look back, to be reminded, to revisit the conditions that made that violence possible. Guilt. We want to hide this pain, put it away, make it bearable by seeking out and imagining painless possibilities while performing resilience, reconciliation and reconstruction in the now familiar post-conflict humanitarian governance langue of multi-ethnic coexistence circulating in Bosnia, Kosovo and Macedonia. We know not to ask the uncomfortable questions of what happened. Our pain must be sublimated and sacrificed for the foundations of a new Balkan future and fraternity. Just as in socialist Yugoslavia, we are now recruited by the EU to be the good exemplary Muslims, the tokens of multiculturalism, our only capital to be allowed to stay and live in the politics called 'Europe' that has constituted us as the weak link in fulfilling its imagined geographical wholeness. EU saviours come to remind us that we need to Europeanise quickly because we have no other futures but that of Europe, that Europe is the destination we had imagined and hoped for all along. How can we question this seemingly great proposal to enter Europe and Europeanise at a time when people leave their lives at its borders in a hope to gain access to it?

Beholden and relieved by this possibility, we have shut our mouths in the face of the violence we witness at these borders and only speak to voice reassurances to the European missionaries who come to measure our progress of Europeaness that we are the Muslims they are looking for, the good, peaceful, tolerant ones, the white European Muslims. The ones who when allegations are made against us that we may harbour undercurrents of Islamist fundamentalism, recalling how these allegations played out during the wars in Bosnia, Kosovo and Macedonia to justify our collective death, destruction and displacement, we raise our voices to refute those claims. No we say, we are not observant Muslims, we are secular, civilised and European, the radical Muslims among us, we say, are those gone astray and brainwashed by Arab radical missionaries from the Middle East. This reassurance, the border that designates us as different from those Muslims further east, prevents us from identifying with the pleas of the Syrians, the Palestinians, the people of colour, the migrant and Muslim inside the EU or Trump's US. It asks us to fragment and sanitise our memories of colonial histories and decolonial belonging. We leave our pain unclaimed, tone everything down and let others write and sing about the 'Siege of Sarajevo' and the 'children of Kosovo'. We whisper only timid, acceptable, protests. Afraid to develop our own language that reflects and reckons our pain we become overjoyed every time someone else writes a couple of words about us. How can you blame us? We want to escape and avoid the recent past.

No one seems more committed to this future than queer communities in the Balkans. Sometimes marked for violence because of our sexuality; other times for our religion or ethnicity; we have aligned ourselves with the EU project uncompromisingly. When EU Missionaries single us out for protection, we keenly regurgitate their language, we appreciate and appropriate it, we self-fashion ourselves in the hope that if we reproduce the same LGBT rights narrative, our communities will think twice before harming us. We keenly read the EU reports that assess our countries' progress towards EU integration, pressuring the governments to pay close attention to the references they make for our rights if they want to join the EU. We are tokens within tokens. We expose homophobes, radical Muslims, nationalists, EU haters…anyone who is against us, is against Europe. That hate crimes against Muslims within the EU have intensified, that the EU has closed its borders in the face of refugee pleas and sends them back to the violence they try to escape, doesn't seem to concern us. Our self-fashioning as different type of Muslims, autochthonous, white, European requires that we distance ourselves from the refugees, from the second and third generation Muslims gone crazy abusing European hospitality, from all those unloved bodies that must be produced as different and dangerous to service our validation as Europeans. And so, like good Europeans, we have learned to think of second and third generation Muslims within Europe at their point of arrival as foreign and threatening. We are Balkan Muslims: the poster child of EU resilience, diversity, intersectionality. Estağfurullah.

EU'S OTHERS

Annalisa Mormile

The morning after the EU referendum vote, I woke up earlier than usual and immediately turned on my TV. I couldn't believe my eyes. The British people had voted to leave the European Union – a result that I had feared, but never actually expected. My first reaction was disappointment. Huge disappointment. Why on earth would they vote this way? I could barely take it in. I got ready for work and, when I arrived at school, found my students in a chaotic state. 'We are worried for this country. We are scared for our future', they told me. It was impossible to discuss any other topic. Instead, we embarked upon a long discussion about the possible effects of Brexit. I was surprised, and at the same time greatly encouraged, by how much passion there was in their arguments, and how indignant these young people were at being part of a country that, essentially, had 'given up'; unable to foresee a relationship within the European Union (EU) – a relationship that compels all member states to find effective communitarian solutions to the issues they face.

During the pro-remain campaign, dire financial consequences were predicted by respected economic institutions such as the IMF and the Bank of England. But a crucial deciding factor was one long-standing national concern: migration. This provoked among the majority the most common of human fears: the fear of losing one's job and personal security. Yet, among those who voted to leave, there were some who were not even clear what the EU was and what it had contributed to their disillusionment. Even though the UK has never been traditionally 'Euro-phile', it became apparent that there was a groundswell of opinion that much of the nation's ills stemmed from the unsolved dysfunctions of EU politics and the 'threat' represented by migration and its poor management.

From this perspective, we may interpret Brexit as the last, evident symptom of an EU crisis – a state of affairs which had already been defined since the internal divisions provoked by the arrival of thousands of refugees undertaking perilous journeys from the global South. Even more than Brexit it was the recent impact of migration, often demonised by the negative rhetoric of the media, which significantly put into question the political legitimacy of the EU – not only in terms of democracy and human rights, but also in relation to its spiritual tradition and historical identity.

Since the beginning of the migration crisis in 2010, the lack of an EU approach, both political and collective, has shed further light on the inherent paradox of a Europe which is not united in political terms, only through a shared economic background. This is why it is a timely and urgent task to re-examine the notion of 'Europe' along with its relationship with the 'other'. In particular, what do we speak about when we refer to the EU family's approach towards the 'other', namely a foreigner, a migrant, an asylum-seeker?

Since the end of World War II, most European countries experienced increasing flows of asylum-seekers, but concern over the rising number of applications only began to be raised in the late 1970s. As signatories to the 1951 Convention relating to the Status of Refugees, they had little choice but to consider asylum claims. Since 1990, EU member states have then sought to exercise this choice collectively through the Dublin Convention (1990) and its legislative successors, which established a series of criteria for determining the EU member state responsible for the application of the asylum law and maintenance of asylum-seekers. However, although the Dublin Convention takes into account family and health issues, allowing a refugee to be transferred to another member state, the responsibility is generally allocated to the first country of entry. Crucially, its purpose failed to standardise national approaches to the reception of asylum-seekers. Instead, it aimed to quickly decide which country is responsible in order to prevent asylum-seekers from making multiple applications. Between 2003 and 2014, after the beginning of the migration crisis, the Dublin Convention was not replaced, but developed further, introducing new criteria for assessing responsibility and the 'Eurodac' system for the comparison of fingerprints.

Over recent years, as all evidence pointed at its poor performance – bureaucratic difficulties, lack of adequate resources and failure to protect the best interests of asylum-seekers as well as the host country – the

Dublin Convention became a matter of judicial attention at the Court of Justice of the European Union (CJEU) and the European Court of Human Rights (ECHR). Significantly, it has been accused of fostering mistrust and suspicion among EU member states and asylum-seekers. On the one hand, the process of assessing responsibility had not led to any tangible results, given the low transfer rate of asylum applicants among member states; on the other, the number of refugees unwilling to be fingerprinted by Italian or Greek authorities has progressively increased, as it reduces their chance of continuing to other preferred destination countries. According to EU Northern countries' authorities, this attitude is often matched by Italian and Greek officials, who are not eager to register asylum-seekers who then become their responsibility. Given these circumstances, what does the Dublin Convention tell us about the EU's responsibility?

First of all, that there is a climate of mistrust among member states, which are more likely to call for a comprehensive approach when the situation involves them in the first place. Secondly, that the criterion of 'illegal border crossing' does not guarantee an equal sharing of responsibility, often assigned to member states at the Southern and Eastern EU periphery, which are facing greater financial pressure and expenses. This unbalanced situation proves that the Dublin Convention is built on an illusion of EU common standards, whereas both reception conditions and recognition rates vary considerably.

In 2015, after the dramatic number of tragic deaths of people attempting to cross the Mediterranean Sea, Germany effectively suspended the Dublin Convention and offered to accept Syrian refugees' requests, even though they had entered the EU through another member state. Simultaneously, the EU negotiated a new agreement with Turkey, which has received significant financial concessions in exchange for reducing the number of refugees crossing European borders. Due to its geographical position, Turkey plays a crucial role in an EU strategy that is not devoid of contradictions: a strategy that should help *to prevent* asylum seekers from entering Europe. In this light, how can the EU and its member states be said to be fulfilling their responsibility towards refugee protection? This is where the question of Europe – what 'Europe' is and if it represents a 'good' political example – becomes relevant.

According to Aristotle, the name 'Europe' was first used by the Phoenicians, and later by the Greeks, to point out the direction towards the indefinite lands where the sun sets. The myth of Europa, the Asian princess abducted to Crete by Zeus (disguised as a bull of 'incredible whiteness') further confirms the non-European origin of this name. Amazed by his 'uncommon kindness' and 'incredible whiteness', from a state of initial fear, Europa becomes increasingly confident and eventually decides to climb on the bull's back. In that moment, the bull runs away. Significantly, in the ancient myth Europa does not offer any resistance to Zeus, but rather seems to accept her destiny and the *necessity* of her departure. Once she arrives in Crete, she carries in herself the 'other' whose gaze has been first set upon Europe – a gaze from 'outside', from Asia, which has been interiorised to such an extent so as to be *forgotten*. But who is this 'other' that Europa has interiorised? It is the figure of the migrant or the asylum-seeker, the transcendent being who, upon arriving in Europe, demands hospitality. Yet, how do we understand this relationship between hospitality and responsibility?

The English word *responsible* stems from the Latin *spondeo*, which means 'offer, promise'. If we consider the term *spondeo* together with *re-spondeo*, we must assume that *re* points out that a counter-offer has been made in response to an initial one. So, in the very act of responsibility, two aspects are fundamental: a feeling of reciprocity and the response to the other. Whereas with the first offer the 'other' demands of us responsibility, exchanging his or her offer with another one means we become *responsible* not only for ourselves, but also for the other.

Let us return to the myth of Europa. Once she arrives in Crete, Zeus finally reveals his identity and, after making her the first queen of Crete, he gives her three gifts: Talos, a giant man of bronze to protect her; Laelaps, a hunting dog who can provide her with food; and a javelin, so she may protect and fend for herself. In other words, Zeus *honours* Europa, greeting her in a land where she is only a foreigner, a land where she is going to stay and give birth to the 'Europa' that we currently inhabit; and Europa accepts the 'offer' made by Zeus, who has become *responsible* for her the moment she accepted her destiny, giving herself in the form of an 'offer'. This demonstrates that an 'ethics of responsibility' is already inscribed in the mythological history of Europe, founded on the *offer* of the 'other' and the *response* that brings Europe to life. However, if we consider where we are today, can we say that Europe follows the same spirit of its tradition, from whence its name and identity were born?

Evidence shows that the current EU asylum system mostly coincides with anti-immigration feelings, detainment camps and the violation of the principle of *non-refoulement* (forced return to certain persecution). Possibly, the only time the term 'responsibility' comes to the legal surface is through the Dublin Convention, where it is not conceived as a collective political issue and is incapable to 'respond' to the call of the 'other'.

In *The Gift of Death* (1992), the French philosopher Jacques Derrida explored the meaning of 'responsibility' in relation to his main question about religion. He argued that Europe ignores its history of responsibility, and this is why it fails to assume it. To understand the reasons that Derrida used to reach this conclusion, we must look to the work of the Czech philosopher Jan Patočka, who re-examined Greek classical thought with the aim of reconstructing the origin of Western rationality. In his essay *Is Technological Civilization Decadent, and Why?* (1966), Patočka identified this origin in the figure of the ancient Greek philosopher Socrates and his injunction of 'care for the soul', which, according to his opinion, is inseparable from the idea of 'responsibility'. His main point is that the Socratic appeal starts with the premise that 'being themselves' does not come naturally to human beings, as the process of 'becoming responsible' implies an act of inward looking, rather than an external outlook over which we have no control or authority. However, from Derrida's point of view, whereas Socrates extorted his disciples to 'know thyself', understanding the external as well as the internal as an experience of the 'I', both Platonism and Christianity, which represent the next two main contributions to the formation of a European spirit, developed the Socratic motif in relation to an external object: a supreme Idea or being, who sees into the soul without being accessible. In this sense, Christianity took a step further than Platonism, as the subject lives in relation to a superior being who is the 'other', namely an Almighty God who judges the morality of his actions, making him feel guilty if he is not capable to respond to his infinite *gift* of love. As a result, Derrida writes, the figure of a superior being provided Christianity with an escape from 'responsibility', as the self is still caught in a relationship of dependence. The subject becomes a singular individual who acts and prays in a constant state of anxiety, in knowledge of his sins and in the hope of eternal life. He trembles, fears and dreads the divine presence, caring no longer for his soul, but for the *salvation* of his soul. Through the *mysterium tremendum* – the Christian experience of being paralysed by the gaze of God – and the logic of messianic eschatology, Christianity, thus, succeeded in placing a stronger emphasis on the soul and the notion of individual responsibility, but it failed in the attempt 'to universalise', being unable to develop the Socratic motif to its full extent, without the intervention of a metaphysical God. However, as Derrida recognised, its existence through Western history is fundamental as it created a bridge between how 'responsibility' was so far understood and how it should be considered. As a matter of fact, the idea of 'responsibility' that Derrida advocated is born out of a 'demythologised Christianity', as Patočka called it, or a 'religion without religion': an 'ethics of responsibility' that preserves the morality of religion, but abandons its dogma. It is a personal accomplishment that originates within oneself, without the intervention or *gift* from a transcendent being, which does not involve any religious-messianic guidelines. After the emancipation from the dogma of Christianity, what would remain is an ethics grounded on the absolute singularity of the subject and the inner structure of his conscience, influencing the moment of decision-making.

It is exactly at this point, however, that we also face the *aporia* of responsibility. As Abraham's emblematic gesture in the Judeo-Christian tradition, Derrida argued that responsible men must be able to *sacrifice* themselves – their own affections, interests, desires – and be alone in front of their duty, which for Abraham was to obey the divine law without knowing the reasons for it. For Derrida, it seems that we can respond to the call of the 'other' only by sacrificing ethics, which means that we cannot respond in the same way and at the same time to 'all the others'. In the case of the Dublin Convention, for example, this *aporia* could be translated in a set of criteria that would give priority to those asylum-seekers in urgent need of international protection, regulating their fair redistribution within each EU country.

But before this, there is another question to consider. Although the era of globalisation has led to a new process of regulation that ended up denationalising many of the state functions, EU countries can still exercise their national sovereignty advancing the right to determine who is a 'refugee' and whether he or she could be a potential 'security risk', or an 'economic burden'. As state functions become progressively decentralised, this newly perceived weakness results in an excessive performance of sovereignty, especially at the borders. Such a pattern of behaviour is not new. The political distinction between friend and enemy underlying the actions of a state perfectly coexists with the theological division inherent to religion between civilians and barbarians, dating back to ancient Greece. It follows that in times where religion is 'by no means disappearing in the modern world', sovereignty has become more openly and aggressively theological.

At one point in *The Gift of Death*, Derrida makes it clear that the theological paradigm of Western politics is deeply related to the history of European responsibility. Again, he draws upon his critical reading of Patočka, who was the first to warn against one of the most common experiences of the 'sacred': the 'orgiastic', which the Czech philosopher understood as an irrational 'enthusiasm' or 'fervour' for fusion. According to Derrida, for Patočka the existence of the 'orgiastic' would automatically bring the loss of individual responsibility, endorsing the sense of belonging to a specific community based on a theological paradigm of inclusion/exclusion. This sense of belonging becomes stronger than any other principle or ethics. This is why Patočka opposed the 'orgiastic' to his understanding of 'responsibility', which instead originates within the single individual, rather than a multitude. Once the 'sacred' has been integrated into religion as the relationship between a single subject and the divinity, it leads the community to the passage from multitude to singularity. However, although disciplined and subjugated through religion, a return of the 'sacred' in the form of the 'orgiastic' could happen any time in the future, resulting in an *abdication* of individual responsibility. According to Patočka, then, everyone should learn how to surpass the 'orgiastic' separating themselves from the community of fusion.

To be responsible, in the end, means to avoid the risk of falling into particularistic assumptions of belonging. The rising waves of nationalism that we are experiencing today instead suggest that the modern state is far from reaching a secular model, whereas the theological paradigm of inclusion/exclusion is still alive. National fears towards the non-Western 'other' indeed symbolise the current challenge to the conventional meaning of state sovereignty, as he or she comes to be perceived as a 'security threat'. However, we must bear in mind that an objectified subject can never be a 'threat' in itself, but must be understood as such by a third party security actor. As both Patočka and Derrida would recognise, it is the theological 'fervour' inherent within the current configuration of state sovereignty that forces people to consider the high numbers of asylum-seekers in terms of an 'alarming' or 'destabilising phenomenon'. It follows that, although migration has always been an intrinsic human phenomenon, today it can be perceived as a hostile or peaceful 'invasion' by the local community, depending on the circumstances. All the particularities of the migration process – with its different reasons, conditions and desires – become completely erased.

This is particularly true if we think that, after the 1930s, the figure of the 'migrant-as-nomad' turned into the figure of the 'border-crossing migrant labourer'. With the rise of what scholars have defined as *homo economicus*, the migrant labourer, displaced from his or her own country in search of a better life, was racialised and equally perceived as an 'external' subjectivity, as opposed to the citizens who belonged to the national community. In many ways, this scenario is reminiscent of the history of European colonialism, a topic of discourse that so far has been slyly avoided through two different means: a negative rhetoricisation of migration, and the prevalent attitude to 'forget' European identity alongside the colonial origin of its wealth. Nowadays, it seems that the 'dark side' of this history is coming back in the shape of a 'request' from the same people who had previously been exploited.

Within this picture, Europe is no longer the place for democracy, the adventurous place 'heading to the other', as Derrida once defined it. It becomes insecure and forgetful of its own identity, tied in a historical relationship with the 'other', as 'others' are the Europeans themselves. The discourse of securitisation – often protracted through the complicity of the media – seems to position the EU as the 'innocent victim of an unprovoked transgression', whereas the main tasks of Europe, as Derrida remarked, should be inscribed in the duty 'to respond to the call of the European memory, to recall what has been promised under the name of Europe, *to re-identify Europe*'. What Derrida tried to suggest is that the essence of

Europe has always come along with the right of hospitality, the capacity of addressing the 'other' without turning it into a restrictive condition. This does not mean, however, that vigilance or any other kind of regulation must be abolished. As hospitality by its ideal nature can be perverting and pervertible – inhospitality and xenophobia always representing a possibility – vigilance and rules are also necessary. Derrida himself remarked that if *unconditional* hospitality could be perverted by the realistic shape of the law, it needs to become *conditional* with its rules and restrictions in order to be truly effective.

'Pure hospitality' cannot exist in the reality. Whenever it becomes law, it consists in two contradictory imperatives: welcoming the other *unconditionally* and welcoming the other *'with a particular name, identity and origin.'* It requires reciprocity, some kinds of obligation, a duty from guest and host alike. It needs to take shape from the question of the name – the identification at the threshold-border – from which we can start to formulate a different path also for the Dublin Convention: welcoming the other *unconditionally*, without regard of its origin, and welcoming the other *with a particular duty*, which requires from all member states collective procedures to determine how asylum-seekers can be integrated into EU society. The introduction of a 'quota system', for example, which would allow a fair redistribution of the number of refugees among member states, could represent a better path to follow compared to the current process of allocating responsibility. At the same time, decisions on transfers should take into account the refugees' will and personal circumstances, whereas those who are granted the right of asylum should be able to move freely around the EU in respect of norms unanimously approved in order to make the system work at its best. An implementation of this kind – in which all member states equally participate – would promote an idea of responsibility that is *conditional*, but still based on the ideal of 'pure hospitality'.

A responsible Europe, a Europe worth its name, will always respond to the call of the 'other'; it will recognise the European history of colonial dominations and risky undertakings, accepting to become that adventurous continent that we have been bequeathed. Whether we call it Europe or the European Union, this territory has often been home to universal questions, and as such, it will always go back to its mythological point of origin, where the 'other' is allowed to reside at the roots of European identity.

CAETANI AND EAST/WEST RELATIONS

Benedikt Koehler

The invasion of Libya was going well, much better than anyone had expected. With ground forces outgunning resistance and attacks from the air showcasing military technology to best effect, proponents of the campaign were riding high and detractors looked woolly and pusillanimous. The prime minister of Italy, who had coaxed his country into sending troops to Libya, ridiculed one oppositional Italian parliamentarian in particular, Leone Caetani, calling him *principe turco*, 'Turkish prince,' a taunt that picked on his target's social background. Caetani, everyone knew, was descended from the upper reaches of Italy's aristocracy and had a reputation as a scholar of Islam. It was not hard to see what the prime minister was getting at: by attacking government policy, Caetani, whether he meant to or not, had been playing into the enemy's hands. But when news trickled in of a successful counterattack on the expeditionary corps, early euphoria waned. Worse was to come. Worry yielded to shock on news that Italian soldiers taken captive in a small town near Tripoli, Sciara-Sciatt, had been massacred. Italy mourned over 250 casualties (the true number may have been much higher).

This was a national calamity that Leone Caetani might have exploited to settle scores. Caetani's voice, after all, commanded attention in the political fray of the day; he was a member of parliament and son of a father who had served as Italy's foreign secretary. But Caetani had more important things on his mind than striking back at political adversaries; writing as a scholar of Islam, Caetani came forward with an essay, every line reflecting a lifetime's study of Islamic history and the author's personal exposure to Islamic societies of his time, wherein he placed current events on a trajectory that began in ancient history and extends into the future. This essay was first published in Italy and reached a readership across

Europe within months when it appeared in France as a book with the title *La fonction de l'Islam dans l'évolution de la civilisation*.

Caetani's essay was published in 1912. It invites re-reading. Often, responses to atrocities tend to become obsolete once the circumstances that triggered them slip from sight. But with the benefit of hindsight of a full century, we can check whether Caetani's insights have stood the test of time by placing his essay alongside Samuel Huntington's 1992 lecture *Clash of Civilisations?*, which was later expanded and published as a book in 1996. In the eighty years that separate Caetani and Huntington, what has been the progress in the West's understanding of the East? But first we need to recap the back story of Italy's invasion of Libya in 1911. Italy's economy in the nineteenth century did not provide enough jobs for its growing population and Italians were emigrating in numbers, mainly to the United States and Argentina. To stem the drain, policymakers in Rome latched on to what looked like a viable panacea: Italy ought to emulate Britain and France, colonial powers that had carved Cyprus and Tunisia out of the Ottoman Empire. Were Italy to conquer her neighbour across the Mediterranean, Libya, two benefits would ensue: first, Italian emigrants would be offered a destination much closer to home than the Americas, second, Italy would rank as a colonial power. In September 1911, Italy went to war, and by October 1912, Ottomans were forced to cede what became known as *Italian Libya*. The invasion looked like a risk that had paid off.

The Libyan campaign set several notable precedents for military incursions into an Arab country. One was to use aeroplanes to drop bombs: mechanised aeroplanes were a recent invention and the Libyan campaign was the first where grenades were hurled from the sky. Another, even more ominous precedent was the underestimating of how much manpower would be needed to subdue the enemy and what the bill for the campaign would come to. In many parts of Libya, Italian troops rarely dared venture outside their garrisons and within a year Italians had to ratchet up troop numbers from 20,000 to 100,000. Consequently, forecasts of campaign costs were out by a factor of more than ten. Hopes that Libya would attract Italian settlers with spin-off effects on Italy's domestic economy were dashed and so the investment of manpower and material did not pay off. Worse, the human cost was immense: Italian reprisals for the massacre of Sciara-Sciatt took the lives of thousands and guerilla campaigns that dragged on into the 1930s killed numerous more. Only by 1950 did Libya's population recover the level where it had been in 1911.

Leone Caetani was a scholar with an unusual background. He was an aristocrat whose lineage even by Italian standards was ancient. His family tree included a pope in the eleventh century, another pope in the thirteenth, and in the sixteenth the Vatican favoured the family through the award of a duchy that eventually became a princeship. His privileged background would be an easy target for political opponents. Caetani, born in 1869, grew up in the family palace in Rome; he began his study of Arabic in his teens, left home before he was twenty to find out what it would be like to take part in an Arab caravan, and in later life became a leading practitioner of the study of original sources of early Islam. The first volume of his monumental work, *Annali d'Islam*, chronicles of events as they unfolded year-by-year during the beginning of Islam, was published in 1905. The *Annali d'Islam* shed light on the progress of events, sometimes from one month to the next, by juxtaposing *hadiths* that to European readers had never before been accessible. There were to be ten volumes in all, the last one appearing in 1926. Caetani's scholarship went beyond minute historical research, he ranged from the history of the ancient Babylonian empire to the relations of early Islam to Christianity, ever reflecting his passion for excavating history's deepest layers. Caetani drew on his vast erudition to map a bird's-eye view of the history of East-West relations, and more importantly, to point out where they might lead in future.

If one wanted to understand why events in Libya had taken a turn for the worse, wrote Caetani, one needed to look back beyond the immediate past and to start by asking how, from the point of view of Orientals, the West's engagement in the East came across. The question to consider was, '*in what measure is it for them something bad and a threat?*' In the West there were those who claimed engaging meaningfully with the East was impossible because, at the bottom of the Eastern temperament, there lurked inscrutability, if not irrationality. But Caetani argued, one only needed to take a considered look to see East/West interactions had been dynamic for a very long time. In fact, the course of European history going back several thousand years had been determined by its engagement with the East.

Confrontation, it is true, often shaped these relations, a constant that reached back beyond the memory of historical records. Indeed, from the story of one such confrontation, the siege of Troy, the image of a distinct European identity was first fashioned. More campaigns were to follow once Europeans stepped into the light of history; those of Alexander the Great the most eye-catching, those of the Romans the most methodical. However, the East in turn made an impact on the West. The *pax romana* buttressed by Rome's arms and Rome's laws contained a fatal flaw, a defect that felled what had seemed an impregnable hegemony: at Rome's spiritual core, there was a void, because Rome's civilisation, for all the magnificence of her physical manifestations, offered little meaningful religious or spiritual substance. By the first century, by which time the empire encompassed most of the countries and cultures bounding the Mediterranean, Rome, host to a multitude of sects, had become a veritable *'Babel religieuse.'* The Roman Empire imposed law and order but failed to win over hearts and minds. The Orient's countervail to the West, when finally it succeeded, was not through the military, through the likes of commanders such as Hannibal or Mithridates, but through a challenge that emerged from a quarter where Roman might proved powerless: namely religious sentiment. What placed East/West relations in the first century on a new footing was Christianity. Spreading from a small base in Palestine to take root in Rome and gathering adherents of numberless sects and denominations, this process reached its apogee when Constantine the Great endorsed Christianity as a state-sponsored creed and moved the empire's new capital to the border of Europe and Asia. The vision of Byzantium was to blend the capacity for organisation of the West enriched with the spiritual roots of the East.

But that empire too had a flaw: the Christianity that returned to the East was no longer the spiritual force that once had originated there. Byzantine Christianity had evolved from a creed into an institution, acted and functioned like an institution, it had become, as Caetani for want of a better designation termed it, a bureaucracy. And as such, to civilisations that longed for spiritual depth, it was profoundly unappealing, even hostile. The history of the Christian church, from the founding of Constantinople in the fourth century to the emergence of Islam in the seventh, is replete with accounts of Christian dissidents – from Armenia to Syria to Egypt to North Africa – all, without exception, seeking to shake off the yoke of religious orthodoxy decreed and enforced by Rome.

And with every contest where Rome's authority grew stronger, its spiritual hold on its adherents in the East weakened. More and more, Christianity became a symbol of domination by the West. Enter Islam.

Caetani makes a point of reminding readers that misconceptions about Muhammad's intentions mar readings of the creed he preached. Muhammad did not project Islam as a novel religion, but as one that renewed the faith as conceived by Abraham, one which had pre-existed Judaism and Christianity. It was a mistake, therefore, to aver that when Islam swept up Rome's Middle Eastern and Egyptian provinces it arrived like a flash storm, unexpected and abrupt. Anyone tracing the trajectory of a long historical arc could have seen the course of centuries had prepared the ground for the invasion of Islam; peoples of the East rallied under the banner of Islam in a fight-back against 'dogmas that no one could understand and the tyranny of an ecclesiastic hierarchy'. Peoples in Syria, Egypt and elsewhere, who all shared an aversion to rule and to constraints imposed from abroad, recognised in Arabs a certain kinship. Much as Christianity in her early centuries in Rome had done with pagan denominations, Islam had the capacity of absorbing a broad gamut of religious affiliations – and it might have remained an exclusively spiritual creed had it not met with circumstances that favoured political emancipation from Rome. In this way, Islam, which started as a religion, became a 'social revolution on a global scale'.

When the East that so long had awaited a champion at last found one, in Islam, it became 'an intangible expression, a very powerful tool of a grand Asian revolution or reaction against Europe.' Islam was woven into the core of Eastern culture and became inextricable from the identity of peoples in the Middle East, in Africa, in Asia, indeed everywhere a counterweight was sought to Western intrusiveness.

In early Islam, attitudes were set. Later, these hardened due to an event such as the crusades, but then again from the nineteenth century onward due to the West's encroachment of the East by other means. Modern intruders, unlike crusaders of old who came armed with weapons, are equipped with the tools of business: 'Railroads, hotels, shipping routes, telephone and telegraph lines, schools, roads, agricultural technology' – with each technical and organisational improvement, however useful in and of itself, more and more the East was being transformed into a copy of the West, in the process unravelling the very fabric that made the East what it is. The West's material blessings brought with them a frame of mind that to the culture of the Orient was alien. 'Every day,' wrote Caetani of the West, 'it offends the feelings of people who see their most cherished characteristics immersed in the dissolving acid of our culture and they resent, through instinctive intuition, the threat of being reduced to a uniform, human mass, adapted to produce wealth for the more powerful nations beyond the sea.' Even Western fashion is irksome and repulsive, 'that horrible anti-aesthetic European dress sense'.

If Islam, then, houses the core of cultural identity of the East, what did Caetani think his analysis might bode for the future? The deepest layer of the fault line dividing East and West, Caetani wrote, is the same one that brought down the Roman Empire, it is the West's atrophy of moral and religious sentiment: 'In the West, one can scarcely appreciate how much ancient traditional religions have lost their hold over souls; in the East, however, Islam has not only maintained, but extended its sway and gathers secret awesome reserves of anti-European passion that one day, once the time is right, will emerge, take shape, and perhaps come forward as collective action of resistance and preservation.' Hence, Western innovations are seen as intrusions or worse, as threats issuing from a society where scientific advance is yoked together with a moral void, and they rouse resentment because 'the East without religion would be like the West without laws: it would be dead.'

Given the roots of Eastern culture are older than those of the West and that the East will never concede defeat, what is the West to do? Following Caetani, it behooves the West not to tamper with the East's organic evolution. The West should desist from spreading 'moral anarchy' (*anarchie morale*) in the East, stop fighting Islam and let the East develop 'their culture, stimulate and strengthen their traditions, their leanings and their indigenous educational resources, and favour in all spheres their religious evolution'.

The Italian government ignored Caetani and the Libyan campaign continued. By the time World War I broke out two years later leading to even greater confrontations, Leone Caetani was no longer a member of parliament. He volunteered for military service on Italy's northern front. After the war, he emigrated to Canada (for family reasons) where he died in 1935. In Italy, he was unpopular with authorities; Benito Mussolini's government forced his expulsion from the Accademia Nazionale dei Lincei, Italy's oldest scientific academy, which today, however, is home to the Fondazione Caetani, a thriving centre of Islamic studies.

If Caetani's essay did not influence policymakers, what impact has it had on academic discourse? Edward Said's *Orientalism* overlooked it. So let us turn to Samuel Huntington's 1992 lecture *Clash of Civilisations?* to see how far approaches to Islam have moved on. To be fair, the comparison between Caetani and Huntington ought not be stretched too far since an historian and a political scientist work in different disciplines. But, even a cursory glance can tell us something.

Huntington noted virulent strains of anti-Western sentiment in Islamic countries. He recommended that the West should 'require a much more profound understanding of the basic religious and philosophical assumptions underlying other civilisations and the ways people in those civilisations see their interests.' The fact that he dropped the question mark from the title of his 1996 book, *Clash of Civilisations* suggests that, for him, the clash was imminent. In the book, he described what he called an Islamic Resurgence, compared its importance to the Protestant Reformation, and pointed out it is locked with the West in a 'quasi-war.' He went on to explain: 'the problem for Islam is not the CIA or the US Department of Defense. It is the West, a different civilisation whose people are convinced of the universality of their culture and believe that their superior, if declining, power imposes on them the obligation to extend their culture throughout the world.'

Two differences with Caetani's approach stand out. Huntington identified 'Islamic Resurgence' as a recent phenomenon, not as one with roots going back to Europe's earliest history, and he described flash points of conflict but did not explain their deeper source. But to describe a phenomenon is not the same as to explain the reason for it; without an understanding of a cause, it is not possible to prescribe a remedy. How much richer on both counts was Caetani's offering. One wonders how events might have turned out had the *principe turco* been heeded – if the West had taken steps to demonstrate the East may flourish alongside the West, 'free, safe, and benefitting on our behalf from sincere goodwill'.

DISSOLVING DIFFERENCE: A DIALOGUE

Julian Bond and Fatimah Ashrif

Julian: It has been over a year that Fatimah, a Muslim, and I, a Christian, have been meeting to read scripture with friends from different faith backgrounds. The venues for our gatherings have been as eclectic as our discussions: churches in central London, Friends Meeting House in Euston, London, parks and green spaces and the London Central Mosque have all provided space for us to reflect for a few hours. During my time as director of the Christian Muslim Forum, I organised hundreds of Christian-Muslim events and initiatives but this dynamic idea of reading scripture and sharing heart-reflections in the hope of creating deep friendship was entirely Fatimah's.

I happened to be in the middle of writing Bible study notes for the Methodist Church's website, our most popular page, on the occasion of our first meeting. Fatimah has a great fondness for the Psalms and asked me to pick one. As I read the one I had chosen for her, many Qur'anic themes jumped out at me (as a Christian relating to Muslims and Islam I had read the Qur'an many times, and had just resumed for Ramadan). I had only recently left the Christian Muslim Forum and was still feeling its absence, as many of my regular opportunities for ongoing dialogue were now gone. I found that this could fill that gap but also transcend all formal interfaith activities. It allows us to appreciate each other's differences, and recognise ourselves in one another. We call our meetings 'scripture-sohbets' (*sohbet* is a Turkish term used to describe heart-to-heart conversations between teacher and students, and between students).

Fatimah: In present times (as ever), it seems important to challenge constructs and notions which aim to engender division. The Qur'an tells me: 'And God's is the east and the west: and wherever you turn, there is

God's countenance.' (2:115) If God's face or 'being' (as the word is sometimes translated) is everywhere, and the two directions belong to him, then where and how does the 'otherness' arise, save within the mind of the human being? Opportunities for dialogue become a possible way of dissolving this fear, and relating to each other as humans first.

Just as in relationships we are often attracted to opposites, I have always been drawn by difference, finding it beautiful and fascinating, though always returning to the realisation that under these layers of difference, we are essentially the same. I met Julian last year at a workshop he was facilitating with St Ethelburga's, a fifteenth-century church in central London. I remember his warmth. Despite our obvious differences such as race and religion, an immediate kinship was ignited.

Julian: Division is sown when we fail to see the truth of other ways of being and believing. In Malachi 1.10-11, God says: 'I wish that someone among you would shut the Temple doors so that these worthless sacrifices could not be offered! I am not at all pleased with you… and I will not accept your offerings. But my name is honoured by people of other nations from morning till night. All around the world they offer sweet incense and pure offerings in honour of my name. For my name is great among the nations.' This resonates for me with another verse from the Qur'an: 'For, if God had not enabled people to defend themselves against one another, all monasteries and churches and synagogues and mosques – in [all of] which God's name is abundantly extolled – would surely have been destroyed [ere now].' (22.40). Reading these passages convinces me that God does not discriminate between religions. Religious people may think they are on the sole right path but that is a simplistic view of God's thinking. I know of many Christians who like to critique Islam, publishing books and resources which take Islam to task for lacking Christian distinctiveness or supposedly proving that it is deficient in certain ways. I have never seen how this is helpful to anyone. It is fine to point out that which we believe or don't believe with relevant reasons, as well as to make the case for an article of belief, but to argue that the other religion is not as good or does not bring its followers as close to God is against the spirit of faith.

I was once asked to review a range of popular material produced by a Christian organisation which was aimed at encouraging Christians to get to know Muslims: a very worthy aim and initially I was impressed by this commitment. However, when I shared it with a Muslim colleague her reaction was quite different, she didn't recognise various aspects of the portrayal of Islam and was very concerned that it gave entirely the wrong impression. In my view such material could only properly be produced with full Muslim involvement, and this may well lead to some constraint of Christian evangelistic impulses. This goes to the heart of our joint outlook and the purpose of our dialogue. If we have the temerity to write about the 'other' we should only do so if we are able to write about it from the other's perspective, if we are unable to do that we need to think again.

Fatimah: In my youth I would hear Muslim preachers pour scorn over the beliefs of Christians. Picking apart their scriptures, and taking great pride in pointing out inconsistencies between the Old and New Testament while simultaneously using both Testaments to prove the legitimacy of the Prophet Muhammad's mission! Historically, many pamphlets have been written in such a vein. I recall a particular well-known Muslim speaker at a lecture I attended on a university campus many years ago arguing with a student who was part of an evangelical Christian group over who had been guided to the 'right way'. The Muslim speaker was marginally more articulate and well-versed in his arguments, and so the student had no hope of point scoring. But what it made me realise was that point scoring did not win hearts, and did not foster understanding. The young Christian man was made to feel humiliated, which saddened me even though I knew that he had hoped to inflict the same fate on the Muslim speaker. The exchange illustrated that this was not the type of conversation that interested me.

Though it is often borne out of good will, interfaith dialogue between Christians and Muslims can easily be reduced to superficial confirmation bias or, worse: reinforcing feelings of superiority of one faith over another. When learning about different beliefs and practices, one can easily fall into the trap of believing that somehow what is ours is better. We avail ourselves as having better proofs, greater coherence, more logic and so on.

I studied a module at university called 'Religious Truth and Dialogue' with a professor who described himself as a Christian-Hindu. I had never before met anyone who held two such apparently different religious identities with such apparent ease. I regarded myself as having a healthy respect for other faith traditions due to the time I spent studying Christian Theology. However, I was still conscious of feeling that my religion was that little bit better! In the course of my learning, I read about the religious experiences of people from various faith backgrounds. The one which remains an over-riding memory is the one which would be seen as the most divergent from Islam: the experiences of a Hindu devotee. I don't recall the name of the study text, what I recall is a chapter in which the devotee described his pilgrimage up a mountain, crawling his way to the top on his bloodied knees. I was blown away by that devotion. I couldn't claim any superiority over that. Years later, I visited Lhasa, Tibet where I saw pilgrims circumambulating the main Temple one complete prostration at a time involving their entire bodies, taking hours in all weather conditions to complete each circle. Chinese snipers sometimes watched over them from rooftops but the devotees were unperturbed, singular in their dedication to the act. What I realised then was that faith has less to do with intellect and more to do with heart, and individual life experience.

As I went through life, I realised the beauty of the diversity of faiths, and also grew to appreciate the spectrum within each faith tradition. My experience showed me that diversity is a gift from God. I found this confirmed for me in scripture: 'Unto every one of you have We appointed a [different] law and way of life. And if God had so willed, He could surely have made you all one single community: but [He willed it otherwise] in order to test you by means of what He has vouchsafed unto you. Vie, then, with one another in doing good works! Unto God you all must return; and then He will make you truly understand all that on which you were wont to differ.' (5.48)

This promise that Allah will enable me to truly understand all that on which we are wont to differ, is a reminder of how limited my vision of God and Ultimate Reality is, and yet I could strut around thinking I have the truth, the final word.

Such realisations must be at the heart of dialogue if it is to be truly honest, truly open, as must the starting premise that there is no 'other', only my sister, and brother (in 'faith', in 'humanity'). Dialogue is vital because it has the potential to remind us that despite our apparent and often beautiful differences, we, our struggles, and our concerns are the same. Relating to one another helps us appreciate our inter-connectedness, which is more and more evident in the physical sphere, and accept that we are made in the image of God. To take this further, we are all made of 'God-Stuff'! Such thinking can take us beyond the difference when it is meaningful to do so.

Julian: There is diversity in Christian outlooks and in the Bible too, although I only really first encountered religious diversity when I entered the world of interfaith, especially relating to Islam. I was fascinated by pluralistic verses in the Qur'an, prompting me to seek the same in my own tradition. Perhaps the most famous statement on diversity in the Bible is this one from Acts 10.34-35: 'I now realise how true it is that God does not show favouritism but accepts men (and women!) from every nation who fear him and do what is right.' Of course there are those for whom inclusive pluralism is a theologically threatening concept and the encouraging verses that I appeal to do not convince everyone, their interpretation often being contested.

Some years ago I organised a Christian Muslim Forum dialogue on Jesus and Muhammad. An imam, Dr Musharraf Hussain, gave a warm presentation on the Prophet. It surprised me then that it was almost 'Christological' in the way it offered 'high' appreciation of Muhammad as a unique human being and special creation of God. The imam talked about Muhammad as the superlative example of the light of God and shared this phrase *Allama Mahmud Alloosi*: 'He is the root and the world is the branch'. That Muhammad is referred to in the Qur'an as 'a mercy to all creation' was central to his presentation. One of our Christian colleagues, the Very Reverend Frances Ward who is now Dean of St Edmundsbury Cathedral, responded with an excellent overview of Christian beliefs about Jesus and the Gospel. He touched on thorny topics such as Incarnation, Crucifixion, Atonement and Resurrection. It seemed a surprisingly evangelistic presentation within a dialogue context but was a mark of our confidence and openness with each other.

After the opening presentations we opened up the conversation to the audience. I expected that there would be some Christian responses to the 'high' view of Muhammad but instead, the first comment was that Islam was all about rules and regulations, not grace as is the characteristic of Christianity. It was disappointing that this was the perception amongst those who had a track record of engaging with Islam, however it is the reality of those who have not seen the inner spiritual life of Muslims and their dependence on God's bounty. It also indicates that we can be so wrapped up in our own tradition and theology that we do not hear or appreciate that our dialogue partners are using the same words and frequently talking the same language. Once we allow ourselves to hear and appreciate, the experience can be transformative. I remember reading Dilwar Hussain's article 'The Hidden Heart of Islam' in *Emel* magazine, in which he describes the love of God. He quotes the famous Bible verse 'God is love' (1 John 4) as if it was part of his own tradition and theology and not from a different religion. It struck me that, for him and many other Muslims, Christianity is not a foreign concept but is indeed part of Islam. The question for Christians is – how far do we have to go to find or discover this common connection of love between our two religions and beyond? Until we can begin to recognise this we have not really connected.

Returning to our dialogue conversation, a Muslim colleague responded very well, challenging the suggestion that Islam was all about law and lacking in grace. Had there been no Muslims present I hope that I could have challenged the assumptions that lay behind the question just as successfully. In a subsequent conversation with an Anglican priest I picked up on this exchange with the possibly provocative comment that everything in Christianity, apart from dogma, exists in Islam too: love, grace, compassion. This seemed to be too much for my friend who responded in the initial stages of outrage, perhaps wondering what kind of syncretist, overly liberal Christian I was. Then, as now, I am convinced that it is doctrine and dogma, which both differentiate and divide us, but only at the creedal level. Though since this particular intra-Christian dialogue experience my engagement and exposure to Islam has only continued to deepen.

My experience tells me that there is much we could gain from sharing spiritual practice. At a Christian-Muslim retreat I once organised, a powerful experience of shared worship offers me solace and comfort to this day. It was a mesmerising exult of Sufi dhikr and Taizé chanting that none of us had ever encountered before. We took care to ensure that each word that we chanted was suitable for everyone and immersed ourselves in the pure energy and love. It was a tremendous experience of bonding and intimacy. I have participated in this only once since then, at the Sufi Centre in Feltham, though it was only the Sufi chants on that occasion, with women and men, young people and children. Any opportunity to pray, sing or chant together is a beautiful gift, which sadly is all too rare.

Scripture sohbet is one of the high points of my week, although at times I am restless if the text unsettles me. Any talk of wrath and judgement in either of our scriptures troubles me and I would prefer not to engage with it yet I cannot escape the fact that it is there on the page, though perhaps not in reality. When our sohbets began I had been reading the book of Revelation so was very sensitised to this theme. The Psalm that I hoped we might read at our first gathering, because it was the Psalm for the day, was soon passed over in favour of another as it spoke too much of the fate of the 'unrighteous'.

Fatimah: There is definitely something momentous about sharing spaces, and worship. I have a real love of churches and for many years have been venturing into these quiet spaces in a lunch time on a working day in the heart of a bustling city, to pray, meditate or seek solace during times of difficulty and challenge. Julian and I held our first scripture sohbet at St Paul's Church in Covent Garden. It was a sunny afternoon and we were both on our lunch break. We entered the church via a sensuous garden that was in full bloom. The church has high ceilings, and is simple but ornate with lit candles, and not at all vast yet still offering the feeling of spaciousness. When we first entered it was almost empty, and we seated ourselves in the pews at the back. We began as we now always do by praying for guidance. Sometimes this is led by Julian and sometimes by me. Often there is silence and meditation, but not always. It depends on where we are. We then reflected on the reading, which was Psalm 86. I was reminded of the opening verses of the Qur'an, and the Muslim mystics' loving beseeching prayers to God, 'Teach me your way, Lord, that I may rely on your faithfulness; give me an undivided heart, that I may fear your name. I will praise you, Lord my God, with all my heart; I will glorify your name forever.' It spoke to my heart of the untold mysteries of the greatness of our shared Creator. A Eucharist Service was set to begin, and we intuitively decided to participate. It seemed almost a seal of approval from the Divine to be offered this opportunity to share. The priest spoke of the passage in Matthew, chapter 5 which explains that one can know a good Prophet from a false one by the fruits they each bear. I couldn't shake the similarity with the passage in the Qur'an that speaks about the parable of the good word being like a good tree (14:24). It also felt like a tremendously apt teaching in the context of the barrage of news reports on the brutality of Daesh who continue to claim Islamic legitimacy. I pondered on how one might know the worth of a particular approach to dialogue: by the fruits it might bear! I was fasting that day and so could not receive the transformed wine and bread but I did receive the blessing from the Priest. Small groups took it in turns to kneel at the altar, to receive the sacrament. I felt incredibly moved. As the Priest placed his hands on my head, his touch connected me with something within him, and beyond both him and I. It was the shortest of moments but utterly timeless.

A couple of Christmases ago, I attended the Christmas Eve service at our local Unitarian Chapel. It is a tiny and adorable little chapel with a well-kept burial ground abundant with beautiful plants and flowers in the warmer months. On the night of the service it was packed full of delighted and luminous faces, young and old. We sang our little hearts out. For me, the experience felt no different from attending a *dhikr* gathering in which songs of praise and the names of God are repeated out loud or silently in the heart. The energetic resonance built by the congregation through the singing felt so similar to that created by my Islamic practice of remembering God.

Julian: In our sohbets Fatimah and I often recognise parallels in each other's texts and commonalities with the teachings of our own tradition. For example the Gospel parable which challenges the 'believers' for not visiting God, with its strident message about faith occupies a crucial place within Islam also. Abu Huraira reported the Messenger of Allah, peace and blessings be upon him, said: 'Allah the Exalted will say on the Day of Resurrection: O son of Adam, I was sick but you did not visit me. He will say: O my Lord, how can I visit you when you are the Lord of the worlds? Allah will say: Did you not know that my servant was sick and you did not visit him, and had you visited him you would have found me with him? O son of Adam, I asked you for food but you did not feed me. He will say: My Lord, how can I feed you when you are the Lord of the worlds? Allah will say: Did you not know that my servant asked you for food but you did not feed him, and had you fed him you would have found me with him? O son of Adam, I asked you for drink but you did not provide for me. He will say: My Lord, how can I give you drink when you are the Lord of the worlds? Allah will say: My servant asked you for a drink but you did not provide for him, and had you given it to him you would have found me with him.'

In an extract from the parable of the Sheep and the Goats in Matthew 25 it is quoted: 'Then he will say to those at his left hand, 'You that are accursed, depart from me into the eternal fire prepared for the devil and his angels; for I was hungry and you gave me no food, I was thirsty and you gave me nothing to drink, I was a stranger and you did not welcome me, naked and you did not give me clothing, sick and in prison and you did not visit me.' Then they also will answer, 'Lord, when was it that we saw you hungry or thirsty or a stranger or naked or sick or in prison, and did not take care of you?' Then he will answer them, 'Truly I tell you, just as you did not do it to one of the least of these, you did not do it to me."

The identification (or incarnation) of God, or Jesus, in both of these stories is staggering. It is poignant enough in the Gospel account, more so in the hadith where God uses language which is essentially the same. Both stories show true religion functioning at the level of the heart, and given their congruence, we cannot say that either is false. It is the same message, a Gospel message or one of human-divine contract. Both are inclusive of those who live with Divine Spirit, rather than, or even in spite of, their religion or creed.

Fatimah: It feels as though there is always something beautiful we can take from each other's tradition. I belong to a Facebook group called Returning to the Source: Repentance, Tawba and Metanoia. The main facilitator of this group is a Muslim who spends weeks sharing readings from the Holy Fathers such as St John Chrysostom, and St Mark the Ascetic. Why? Because they too are essentially concerned with the journey of the soul. There has been so much intermingling of cultures, symbols, ideas and practices throughout the ages. What Julian and I are engaged in, is not anything new. Even something as simple as the rosary and its use, cuts across religious traditions, as does of course, numinous spiritual experience.

Recently, I was involved in organising through Rumi's group, a small organisation which is concerned with sharing the wisdom of the thirteenth-century Turkish Muslim mystic and jurist, Jalaludin Rumi, two evenings of poetry, music and whirling with artists influenced by the Sufi tradition and Coptic Christian traditions. Both evenings were held in Churches. The artists hailed from Egypt, Iran and Manchester. The poetry shared was mainly that of Rumi on the theme of Mary and Muhammad. Mary and Muhammad share many commonalities, the main one being that they were both chosen by God to bear the Word. The gathering attracted an audience of all backgrounds. It was beautifully heartening to hear old and new Christian friends tell us how much the music, poetry and whirling had impacted them. How reminiscent lyrics and music felt of childhood or other religious experiences. Such moments bring me back to our unity as human beings. The same things move and touch us.

Julian: I am fascinated by Muhammad. He has such a key role in Islam, not just as its 'founder' but, as Fatimah mentioned above, as 'bearer of the Word' or *theotokos* in the Christian tradition. Additionally, through the Sunnah he is a role model for nearly two billion Muslims. I am intrigued by his goodness. There are many excellent facets in Islam and for that we must acknowledge and thank him, while bemoaning that, as in the case of Jesus, his followers do not always live up to the best of his message.

Having a positive perspective on Muhammad should, I would argue, be at the forefront of Christian interaction with Muslims, after all Christians hope, or even assume, that others will have an appreciation of Jesus, even those who have issues with 'Christianity'. So how is Muhammad any different? We are well aware of the ways in which people relate to or have preconceptions about Islam, for many people meeting real-life Muslims almost instantly shatters negative misconceptions. It is the same with Muhammad when we hear what Muslims, rather than what their detractors, say about him.

Some years ago, just before Eid, I spent almost two days on *i'tikaf* at my friend Musharraf Hussain's masjid in Nottingham. After lengthy prayers and recitations, which continued well into the night, there was a period of singing in praise of Muhammad. It was an honour to be in the middle of a tight circle of men pronouncing so devoutly their love for Muhammad and praise to God for sending him. This is what I think of when anyone asks me about Muhammad. This is how the spiritual descendants of Muhammad feel about him, they are not his followers because he is not Messiah or Lord but he inspires deep love and devotion. As a friend of Muslims I am also a friend of Muhammad.

Fatimah: One of my greatest challenges in this work is dealing with Muslims and Christians who are dogmatic. The struggle is to maintain openness of heart in the face of absolutism. I try to steer a path between being accepting of the dogmatism of Muslim and Christian friends but being honest and clear wherever possible of my own position. It is not easy when a 'live and let live' attitude comes up against a 'there's only one way' one! In such moments, the unity in the diversity feels momentarily obscured. But only momentarily. I recently attended the masjid of a minority Muslim group. It was an interfaith event with Christian and Jewish attendees. I was pleased to see Muslims from other backgrounds showing a willingness to embrace sectarian difference. This was a group which has a highly inclusive and tolerant image despite being emphatically excluded by other Muslim groups. Toward the end of the evening, when most attendees had left, I found myself in a conversation with a middle aged man of Iraqi descent who had come to the group only a couple of years earlier from a Sunni background, the same background as me. He became somewhat vocal and unashamedly so in challenging my faith and explaining how his was superior to mine. He said this without really grasping what mine was. I was surprised by this as I didn't expect such an overt attempt at conversion. I hope I showed as much grace as I know that Julian does, when Muslim friends tease him seriously about conversion. I tried in various ways to smoothly wrap up the conversation but it became increasingly difficult until a third party stepped in. He wasn't aggressive but just very persistent. There will always be those in any faith group with black and white thinking in which their way is the only way. The point was not that he had tried to convert me, what was depressing was that he was so adamant that he, and his group alone, in his view, possessed the truth.

I believe that all faith traditions carry the Divine spark, articulated in different ways for different peoples in different contexts, and different times. I appeal to the great Muslim mystics for much of my inspiration in relating to divergences in doctrine. Though the Christian narrative of Jesus' crucifixion might be difficult for some Muslims, I relate to it and his subsequent resurrection as a metaphor for the spiritual journey. For me, as for most Sufis, the journey of the human being is one of 'dying before death', which is a Sufi saying. That is dying to our prejudices, conditionings, attachments and fears, to lead a life which is more attuned with the All-embracing Divine Reality. Or, as Rumi put it:

> By nature, every spirit has the life-giving breath of Jesus,
> but one breath wounds, while another heals.
> If spirits were freed from the body's veils,
> everyone's words could be like the Messiah's.
> If you wish to speak words sweet as sugar,
> control your body's desires;
> don't run after this world.
> Children beg for candy;
> the intelligent desire self-control.

To die in this way involves coming to truly know yourself. To know what makes you function and tick as you do, and to come to know the part of you that is timeless. My concerns are rarely about dogma but are focussed on behaviours and those attitudes which prevent me nourishing my being with remembrance of the Divine. Difference exists but even these differences may mean something to us in our journey of return or resurrection. Even our response to dogma, and the dogmatic, can teach us about ourselves, bring us to higher consciousness, and help us on our journey home.

Julian: With the relentless horror on the news in relation to the Muslim world and the rise in negativity towards Islam and Muslims, I have become even more certain of the importance of my relationship with the faith and its followers. I have also become concerned that as I endeavour to become closer to and more supportive of Islam that it might alienate some more conservative or evangelical supporters of me and my work and I have considered how I might address this, though I am yet to embark on a proper conversation about it. Nevertheless, I have not received any negative comments about getting together with Muslim friends to read the Qur'an, though I usually emphasise that we also read the Bible and the Qur'an in church. I have ventured far outside the boundaries of my own faith, if we agree that such boundaries exist. I would argue that they do not, or not in my experience and outlook. My trajectory remains outward, though it also propels me inwards.

The depth and extent of hatred for Muslims or Islam troubles me, especially when expressed by Christians, or those of a Christian heritage. Somehow a few who follow Jesus, or are influenced by him, have put to one side his key command to love one's neighbour which he described as central to the life of one who is in tune with God. Sadly, I believe, some of Jesus' followers have put Jesus himself to one side, as well as stumbling over his command because it does not neatly fit into Christian doctrine. Some people seek to escape the command to love Muslims because, in their eyes, Muslims are the ultimate enemy – see how Muslims are described as terrorists, extremists, the enemy in our midst, not to be trusted, violent, liars, misogynists. I could go on repeating the hate speech that is so familiar from the media and my own virtual encounters on Facebook and Twitter. It breaks my heart. I want to respond with – these are my people, my friends, even my 'family', those with whom I pray and read scripture, exchange hugs, I'd even be prepared to say 'I am Muslim' if it made any difference and inspired people to think again . These many encounters have melted my heart.

I recall also the power of sharing prayer together in overcoming difficulty and conflict. I organised a prayer gathering in 2014 at the height of the Israel-Gaza conflict. I can hardly describe how wonderful it was for Christians, Muslims and Jews to gather to share their pain and then pray from the heart. We were united in our hearts even if we were divided by religion, politics and conflict.

Fatimah: The way I respond to hatred, ignorance, and misunderstanding is by working on grounding myself in love of the Divine. When my inner remembrance is strongest is when I feel able to act from a place of love and compassion. I have made a conscious decision to work with one of the many attributes of God referred to in the Qur'an, traditionally held to be 99: *Al Wadud* which means the Most Loving One. The belief is that recitation and meditation on the attributes of God, can help manifest those qualities in you in accordance with your capacity. I am keen to awaken the love within me further. The Sufi belief is that the Divine Qualities are latent within us waiting to be activated, as I recognise that there is a part of me that shies away from difficult conversations. I wish any that I have, to be grounded in love. Not only with those friends who hold similar views to me but also those who do not. Interestingly, my personal struggle is to also have these conversations with Muslim friends not only Christian ones.

Nourishing the love within, increases open-heartedness to the other, thereby creating the opportunity for deep friendships which enable all sorts of difficult questions and conflict to be held in a loving manner. I am part of a Sufi community, and have seen how sharing of the heart in safe spaces, can encourage endless trust, respect and love to develop.

Julian and I are not interested in dissolving Christian-Muslim difference. There is a clear spiritual creativity which is inspired by doctrinal difference. What we are interested in is dissolving with kindness and compassion where possible, the dogmatic attitudes, and the fear which prevents us having open-hearted communication about each other's journeys.

We both revel in sharing our different scriptures, practices and spaces of worship because often through them, we are reminded and rediscover our similarities, and are moved forward in our common goal and desire to connect to God in whichever way He invites us to.

KITH AND KIN IN JAPANESE POLITICS

Mohammed Moussa

> (Respect for) blood ties is something natural among men, with the rarest exceptions. It leads to affection for one's relations and blood relatives, (the feeling that) no harm ought to befall them nor any destruction come upon them. One feels shame when one's relatives are treated unjustly or attacked, one wishes to intervene between them and whatever peril or destruction threatens them. This is a natural urge in man, for as long as there have been human beings.
>
> Ibn Khaldun, *The Muqaddimah*

Blood may be said to be thicker than water in a world of power, status and hierarchy. Ibn Khaldun, the illustrious fourteenth century Arab historian on the rise and fall of royal dynasties, provides a pointed observation that echoes from the past into the present and is not restricted to any one place. My own observations in this essay are mere reflections of an erstwhile sojourner in Japan for whom society and politics are deliberate (as well at times unintended) consequences of collective actions of human beings in a series of interlocking relationships. Japanese politics projects an image that on the surface is a natural corollary of a unique 'national character'. However, families are a ubiquitous hallmark of politics throughout the world and one may add are the most basic unit for organising and transmitting political office. In the Middle East, the terms *gumlukiyya* (hereditary republic), a combination of *gumhuriyya* (republic in Egyptian Arabic) and *malakiyya* (monarchy), and 'dynastic republicanism' were coined in the pre-Arab Spring period to describe the then increasing importance of the president's family in politics and in the thorny matter of presidential succession. Where power, status and hierarchy slowly congeal, political dynasties are born.

Relations, particularly family, supply individuals with the opportunity, through close contact, to foster a unity of purpose, what Ibn Khaldun has described as *asabiya* (group solidarity), that is often required to maintain political power. The image of a mass society of countless atomised individuals in suits and ties tends to obscure the very personal and informal relationships of these same individuals bound to particular places. Parliamentary and other kinds of politics are not easily explained by the impersonal forces of the modern state. Personal links and affiliations of politicians and the electorate bestow upon observers a varied gamut of clues to draw an accurate picture of what is politics. A 'house', Ibn Khaldun tells us, comes into being when the ancestors of a man are considered to have great standing and nobility that are similarly held of him. Kinship among family members, nothing less than human nature according to Ibn Khaldun, can provide much of the human capital needed in politics such that popularly held esteem for the lineage of candidates is a vote clincher. The Khaldunian 'house' can be broadened to encompass not only vertical relations (one's ancestors) but also horizontal relations (one's spouse) with examples ranging from the Clintons (husband Bill and wife Hillary) in the USA to the Johnsons (father Stanley and sons Boris and Joseph) in the United Kingdom to the Gandhis (Jawaharlal Nehru father of Indira Gandhi and sons Sanjay and Rajiv and daughter-in-law Sonia) in India.

Names and all the electoral support they garner do matter in politics. A brand with a ready-made political machine, built up over decades or years, extends beyond the bloodlines of a politician's family to include other politicians and an electoral network in a 'tribal' fashion. However, the origins of dynasties in the form of royal authority, the inheritance of political power based on direct kinship, precedes that of the mass society and electoral politics characterising modernity. The role and status of family relations in Japanese politics emerges from the formation of the modern state in Meiji-era Japan during the nineteenth century, eventually illustrating the interdependence between the electoral system and Japanese political 'houses', a quasi-hereditary aristocracy.

Half a century before Japan would embark on a remarkable transformation of modernisation, dramatic changes following Napoleon Bonaparte's invasion set Egypt on a path towards the rise of the modern state. Muhammad Ali Pasha was a soldier who was determined to remake

Egypt according to his image (or more accurately that of the modern West) in a region which was experimenting with the possibility of institutional reform, inspired by the encounter with European powers, in the face of stubborn resistance from entrenched social and political interests. War-making provided much of the impetus and pretext for change in the Ottoman Empire and in Egypt, under the de facto control of Muhammad Ali Pasha, with unruly and conservative social forces alike being tamed and channelled into the political centre. Reform followed reform with varying successes in the Middle East, which also elevated the family of the ruling houses to a position of absolute authority. Modernisation often meant despotism in an era of rising nationalism, imperialism and colonialism. Similar motivations espoused by an equally zealous modernising monarchy pushed Japan on to a trajectory that has touched every facet of life.

Ottoman Turkey, Khedivial Egypt and Meiji Japan all began a process of abandoning certain established institutions that were deemed to be no longer functioning according to the greater interest of the emerging body-politic. Hereditary aristocratic organisations such as the Janissaries, Mamlukes and samurai were pushed aside in the rush towards the modern state. Most social intermediaries between the power of the state and the acquiescence of subjects were either co-opted or eliminated. Inheritance of political power was perceived to be legitimate and suitable only for the house of the ruler: the Sultan-Caliph, the Khedive or the Tenno or emperor. The houses of Osman, Muhammad Ali Pasha and Jimmu were the paragons of political virtue. Uninterrupted continuity of royal or imperial succession further strengthened the claim of authority enjoyed by a descendant in what can be described as the institutionalisation of charisma: bloodlines and virtue are entwined and inherited from generation to generation.

The personal aspects of politics shadow the impersonal dimensions of the modern state in ways that they do not contradict each other as one can see from the rapid modernisation of Ottoman Turkey, Khedivial Egypt and Meiji Japan. Although modernity is popularly believed to elevate the rationalisation of both society and the world for the benefit of the impersonal and the bureaucratic, the personal and the informal are not diminished in the newly created social spaces. Royal dynasties, backed by a ruling ethos or ideology and motivated by the idea of reform, supplied the initial start and continuity without which the overhauling of society could not be carried out based on direct and impersonal control of subjects previously buffered by a range of social intermediaries. A mass society was thus born defined more or less by a dynastic and bureaucratic political centre. These parallels can be made between Meiji Japan on the one hand and Ottoman Turkey and Khedivial Egypt on the other hand during the nineteenth century. Family relations acquired no less salience, quite the contrary, in shaping the ideology and mode of a fledging national politics.

Royal lineage was tantamount to divine lineage for the Japanese monarchy prior to 1946. The house of Jimmu is perceived to be the unbroken chain of succession of Japan's rulers for over two and a half thousand years in the land of the rising sun. Nearly 700 years of successive shogunates (military governments) had placed the exercise of political power in the hands of a feudal class of senior samurai at the expense of the emperors of Japan in a display of competing hereditary authority. The Meiji restoration was the culmination of a deliberate move to make the imperial dynasty the primary location for political legitimacy alongside various changes affecting Japanese society. And prior to the Meiji restoration, the cause of reform and the end of Tokugawa shogunate, the last dynasty of shoguns (military rulers) to reign, were vigorously agitated for by the nationalist *shishi* (men of high purpose or spirit) such as Sakamato Ryoma whose fidelity to the imperial state overrode one's family and former status as a samurai. Such kinship and solidarity to the ruling house subordinated any affiliations to one's immediate kith and kin in a time of rapid change, political disunity and a looming foreign presence.

Enlightened despotism of the type adopted during the Meiji era could not tolerate any potential interruption in the form of powerful and alternative family-based centres. This national project of modernising reform had to march forward with the efficiency of an army, revealingly a modern standing army was one such reform, to the drumbeats of a single drum. One question that can be posed about this reform is: what legitimacy or authority did these individuals possess to carry out reform? To answer this question, I will sketch out the mythology of the ancient origins of the Yamato dynasty currently occupying the Japanese throne. Founding stories dating back to antiquity often speak of divine-human relations with the offspring of the gods gracing the earth with their presence. Ancient Egypt was the land of divinely-descended pharaohs who were also regarded to be god-kings in their own right and Greek mythology documents with relish and amusement the relations between gods and humanity from amorous encounters to paternal protection. The Shinto mythic origins of the Japanese royal family similarly contain a semi-divine figure descended from the sun goddess, Amaterasu, born from the union of Izanagi and Izanami, deities who created the earth. Jimmu is a descendant of Amaterasu from whom all emperors of Japan are claimed to be descended.

Under the reforming monarchy of the Meiji era, Shinto became the religion of the state with the folk religious blend of Shinto and Buddhism consciously separated to allow the former to be the ruling ideology of the royal family, the state and society. Shinto beliefs and rituals were adapted in a newly crafted tradition which invoked the emperor as the descendant of the gods. Former rulers acquired the mantle of divinity through an intertwined process of the deification of past figures and the institutionalisation of hereditary charisma. Gods, spirits and deceased emperors received public and holy reverence in the creation of the Japanese nation-state. Bryan S. Turner, the neo-Weberian scholar of religion and sociology, illustrates the close affinity between the royal family and the nation-state in the following manner: 'in ideological terms Japan's march towards modernity involved a union between a divine emperor, the land of the gods and its people'.

Contemporary Japan is the culmination of a process combining expected continuity with sudden change. Nonetheless, a certain conservative inclination dominates the country's politics amid a tempestuous world. The current composition of the Japanese body-politic received its form in the aftermath of the Second World War where tragedy (atomic bombing of Hiroshima and Nagasaki), imperial hubris (occupation of Korea and China) and defeat (American post-war occupation) haunted the pressing question of how to turn a new page in the annals of Japanese history. Where the emperor was the sovereign in the pre-1947 constitution whose family lineage was both divine and continuous, the constitution, drafted under the direction of the United States, defrocked the living embodiment of the gods in Shinto mythology. According to Giorgio Shani, a British academic residing in Japan, the post-war emperor was 'secularised' and then contributed to the legitimacy of the American occupation of Japan and the dominance of the Liberal Democratic Party. A constitutional monarchy was established with the executive firmly located in the parliament with the emperor and his family perceived to be above politics and the incipient party politics, mainly the factionalism within the Liberal Democratic Party, which has since been a hallmark of the nation's parliamentary contests.

Symbolic, national and dynastic are three words which describe the postwar role of the Japanese emperor with the additional democratic safeguard of constitutional. A noteworthy feature is the dynastic nature of the symbol of the state and the unity of the people. Family relations still count in the body-politic. The remaking of the Japanese political tradition was necessarily anchored in the more conservative values, predispositions and practices of society. A constitutional monarchy now sat side-by-side with the National Diet shorn of the jealous and often violent conflicts in the past between different centres of political power such as the emperor, the shogun and a divided samurai class. Clear boundaries of political functions defined the rules of game among the various political 'entrepreneurs' through an electoral system that has also given rise to the phenomenon of dynastic inheritance and the *seshu giin* (hereditary parliamentarians).

Japanese parliamentary politics ostensibly differs from its counterparts in other parts of the world such as India, the United Kingdom and even the European Parliament. Family ties have contributed to the electoral competition (or lack of) in countries where entering into public life requires a great amount of money (donors), institutional resources (a political party) and name recognition (a relative formerly or still in politics). The name *seshu giin* has been given to this phenomenon to depict the growing trend of elected officials with a family member at one point present in Japan's National Diet. The inheritance of political power is neither an exceptional result borne out of a unique trait of a people nor an unchangeable essence of a society. Pretty mundane reasons can be found for the increasing rate of career politicians being followed by a son, daughter, grandson, granddaughter or a spouse. Political ambition is fostered by the impressive successes of a close relative. A wide and powerful network of donors and politicians can also light the fire of the enthusiasm for public life. In Japan, these and other compelling reasons have usually exerted more weight to the catalyst of a relative's death or political retirement.

Many lawmakers in Japan's National Diet, presently and in the past, hail from a political family in the strictest sense of the term. Yuko Obuchi, Shinzo Abe and Yasuo Fukuda have climbed up the parliamentary ladder thanks to their lineage: symbolic and material ingredients closely intertwined that make a rather potent brew for electoral success. Around two-fifths of the Liberal Democratic Party's parliamentarians are in seats previously represented by a relative. However, the highest number of *seshu giin* can be found in the ranks of the ruling party, the Liberal Democratic Party, which continued to form the government uninterruptedly for over half a century between 1955 until 2009: it has now picked up from where it left, under the current Prime Minister Abe. Political parties can be fairly conservative organisations which recruit members in a variety of ways. Nonetheless, one of the tried and tested methods for the survival of political parties and the transmission of their dream, electoral victory, to a capable and committed next generation is the next generation of family members. Japanese politicians, no doubt motivated by concerns similar to their peers in the world of politics, have found in their family relations reliable and trustworthy successors to continue their legacy.

An elite network of movers and shakers is united by a shared sense of unity, *asabiya*, which sustains the in-group often at the expense of electoral contenders or members of political parties without the requisite family connections. On one side of the social tie lies this influential network of entrepreneurs, for whom politics is a professional vocation, and on the other side the variously named electorate, clients, supporters and constituents. Numerically, the professional politicians are a minority to a majority of citizens. Party politics in Japan is an elite endeavour that has in some instances become the preserve of established families. What makes the quasi-polis of the hereditary parliamentarian in the specific context of electoral jockeying so efficacious rather than being widely dismissed to be simply the nepotism of the powerful? Convenience is one reply with the trinity of *ban* (bases), namely *jiban* (local constituency), *kaban* (literally purse, finance) and *kanban* (literally signboard, name recognition), providing a speedy arrival to the highest levels of politics.

Local politics can lead to a specific type of relations revolving around pork-barrelling, the allocation of official funds for projects in a constituency, to maintain the support of voters or win them over. An *oyabun-kobun* (patron-client) relationship, previously formed, often serves to benefit the son or daughter of a recently deceased politician in a quasi-extended family mobilising and bringing voters into the fold of kinship based on loyalty. Constituents are not simply citizens residing in an electoral district but bound to a lawmaker and his or her family in a paternal bond created over time. Political dynastic spin-offs emerge from a figure whose name and face have acquired popularity (or notoriety depending on the individual) for political know-how or competence. Reputations can smooth the path for a family relation to jump into the electoral fray. The two sides of the social tie in politics mentioned previously are centred upon a family's support groups or *koenkai* and ability to mobilise its *jiban*. Roger W. Bowen makes a general comparison of the *koenkai* 'to local machine politics in the United States, where a politician over time creates a very cohesive support base in his electoral district. The benefits are obvious – strong voter support at election time – even if the costs are not so obvious. To maintain loyalty of the local machine, members of the Diet are expected to give gifts to constituents upon the birth of a child, the loss of a parent, and at weddings and local celebrations'. Family politics often entails the politics of the family. Let me illustrate this with three portraits of Japan's *seshu giin*: the Obuchi, Koizumi and Abe houses.

Portrait One: Yuko Obuchi

Kinko (gender balance) was promoted by Abe's Liberal Democratic Party as part of the wider campaign of 'womenomics', a play on the prime minister's famous 'Abenomics' economic policy, for a greater role of women in politics and society. Currently, women only make up 9.5 per cent of the lower house in Japan's bicameral system and around 16 per cent in the upper house elected in 2013. These figures demonstrably show that Japan's gender balance in politics disproportionately weighs towards men at the expense of women. Public talk about change rests upon greatly entrenched private and informal relations that still largely perceive women to ideally dwell in the domestic sphere as mothers and wives. However, the rise of women in very prominent positions of power has indeed occurred within the very confines of the family as the example of Yuko Obuchi illustrates in bold terms. Family inheritance explains Obuchi's rapid climb to the pinnacle of politics when she became the youngest post-war minister in the cabinet. The 'princess' as Obuchi has been called, highlighting both her family's political pedigree and the paternalistic attention she has received as a woman, inherited the constituency of former prime minister Keizo Obuchi, her late father, who in turn inherited it from his own father. Yuko Obuchi was the same age as her father when elected to Japan's National Diet in 2000. A line of succession from father to son then followed by father to daughter signals the existence of a Khaldunian 'house' with ties to a local constituency beginning with Mitsuhei Obuchi. Initial and subsequent electoral successes for Yuko Obuchi would have been inconceivable without the carefully cultivated achievements of her father, for whom she served as an aide, in national politics and the establishment of her grandfather's position in the ruling party which had enjoyed virtually uncontested terms in government for over a half century.

Portrait Two: Junichiro and Shinjiro Koizumi

The case of Yuko Obuchi points to a wider trend more common among male parliamentarians in Japan's body-politic. A fairly long list of previous prime ministers come from families already part of the Japanese political establishment. One such individual is Junichiro Koizumi whose father and grandfather had served in the preceding governments dating back from the first decades and continuing into the middle of the twentieth century. Junichiro Koizumi's first overture into parliamentary politics arrived after the death of his father. Parachuting Junichiro into his father's electoral constituency did not succeed. Nonetheless, he was able to become a parliamentarian with the ruling party in the early 1970s. The culmination of Koizumi's electoral success can be seen in his occupation of the prime ministerial office between 2001 and 2006. During this time, his cabinet also resembled the prime minister himself with nine of his ministers at one time hailing from families with direct participation in the country's National Diet in the past. Political parties such as the Liberal Democratic

Party house prominent Japanese political families with competition between incumbents for its leadership exemplified by the victory of Keizo Obuchi over Junichiro Koizumi in 1998. A reversal of Koizumi's fortunes put him at the helm of government until he was succeeded by another product of dynastic inheritance in the person of Shinzo Abe in the leadership of the ruling party and by extension the post of prime minister in 2006. Abe himself resigned a year later making way for Yasuo Fukuda, a fellow hereditary politician, to assume the head of the executive. Shinjiro Koizumi has walked in his father's footsteps to represent his parliamentary constituency. A new face with an old name in Japan, Shinjiro is the fourth generation of his house to be a lawmaker. Political ties at the highest levels of society coupled with name recognition, over a century old, have enabled Shinjiro to be a rising star in the current Abe government. But not quite ready to be prime minister... for the moment.

Portrait Three: Shinzo Abe's War and Peace

Tumultuous times characterise Shinzo Abe's second try at the head of the executive, the first attempt was too brief a tenure in 2006 and 2007, specifically focused on the post-war constitution. Family history is often mentioned in analyses of Abe and his quest to change Article 9 which forbids military action, no 'right of belligerency of the state' is recognised, and the build-up of any capability to this end. The Liberal Democratic Party can be understood to be an organisation with a significant and influential cadre of hereditary politicians. Abe typifies both this trend and the acquisition of the most powerful post in the state: the prime ministership. Abe's political pedigree can be found on both sides of his paternal and maternal family. Most media attention on Abe's controversial pronouncements and actions regarding Article 9 talk about unfinished business for the grandson of Nobusuke Kishi who was a key figure in Japanese national politics as a post-war prime minister and as a member of the wartime government. Kishi opposed Article 9 and in his time as prime minister signed the treaty that put Japan under American protection in the case of an attack on the country and agreed to military bases in its territory. However, the latter led to the downfall of Kishi amid sweeping popular civil disobedience. Thus, commentators seem to suggest that Abe is determined to pick up where his grandfather left in adding military muscle to Japan in a flurry of nationalist and conservative fervour. The present prime minister has another family legacy that also goes back to the pre-war period in the figure of his paternal grandfather Kan Abe. He was a staunch pacifist who opposed the war effort by Japan in the 1940s and a lawmaker in Japan's parliament in the same period. While Kan Abe died in 1946, the house of Abe regained not a little political relevance under his son, Shintaro Abe, with Kishi, his father-in-law, in the Liberal Democratic Party first as an aide and then a parliamentarian in his own right. Against these somewhat contending family narratives, Shinzo Abe's political career has followed and identified with the track beaten not so much by his paternal grandfather, a pacifist whose death could be described as untimely, but the one by his maternal grandfather to 'normalise' Japan as a nation-state.

Conclusion

Political dynasties composed by the *seshu giin* have been hugely influential in modern Japanese politics through supplying stability and resources to the Liberal Democratic Party's continued existence. The Khaldunian 'house' has animated Japanese politics in accordance with the name recognition of a founding figure. A famous lineage of past politicians is not the only path for a political career but it certainly helps to enter public life and reach the most powerful offices of the state. Previous ages witnessed family relations at the centre of political alliances and conflicts. Pretenders to the throne vied with incumbent dynasties to place themselves and their descendants in positions of authority and wealth. The emergence of the shogunate had replaced the emperor's house as the principal hereditary aristocratic family until the cusp of the Meiji era in the 1860s. Dramatic changes to Japan brought the real exercise of power to the imperial Yamato dynasty and laid the foundations of the Japanese modern state. Parliamentary politics was also introduced in the creation of the Imperial Diet and later, during the beginning of the post-war American occupation, it was renamed the National Diet. One may, albeit tentatively, propose that the body-politic in the twentieth century mimicked the symbol of the Japanese nation, the emperor, and in the formation and survival of the *seshu giin* in parliament. Politics as a craft proceeds to induct the neophyte into its ranks through family relations in what can be seen to be an 'apprenticeship' in the art of winning elections and navigating parliamentary office politics.

Prime Minister Shinzo Abe is best understood to be a continuation of a family tradition of party politics in a body-politic chiefly defined by the historic dominance of the Liberal Democratic Party since the 1950s. A sizeable number of parliamentarians in the Liberal Democratic Party owe their success in no small way to their family relations which have equipped them with the very tools of electoral success: *jiban*, *kaban* and *kanban*. Local support, financial resources and name recognition have spurred on the creation and maintenance of a robust electoral machine or *koenkai* to the detriment of candidates of more humble means and without the familial popularity of incumbents. Institutionalised charisma, the very stuff of tradition, is associated with the transmission of a perceived extraordinary virtue to his children and grandchildren that was displayed by an individual. The reverence for bloodlines in politics can be traced to the belief in the inheritance of character in a family. Japan's *seshu giin* have responded to and benefitted from the mutually reinforcing relationship between the Khaldunian 'house' of hereditary parliamentarians and voters who have identified with a particular house in an interlocking relationship of patron-client.

HOMOGENEITY

Elma Berisha

When we were children we were explicitly told that we Albanians were unique people because we were the only nation in the world 'confessing three religions' – namely, Islam, Catholicism and Orthodox Christianity. That was taught to us with a great sense of pride, openly and emphatically even though Kosovo at that time was still part of Yugoslavia and in the official mainstream, communist ideology was as emphatically owned. As I grew up I wondered if the element of pride was indeed because we had historically managed to build a rich and unique culture of tolerance, or because we thought we were smart and downplayed religion and its effects in our civic lives. There were acquaintances who subscribed to either or both these explanations. Who was to be credited for our heavily cherished inter-religious tolerance? Anyway, the statement of pride remained for long and still remains. Once I grew up and travelled outside the region, I realised that after all, we are not unique in our religious diversity. However, it was not enough to meet the first Christian Arab, as shocking as it was, for the frozen mental notions to melt away.

There was another way the issue of homogeneity preoccupied me back then. Kosovo, comprising over ninety per cent ethnic Albanian population, was always an organic part of ethnic Albania. Their wholesome togetherness saw Roman, Byzantine and Ottoman empires passing by, not without an undeletable footprint. The partition of ethnic Albanian lands and the locking up of its severed population limbs in many of the neighbouring national states, the latter ones emerging after the disintegration of Ottoman Empire, began on the eve of the twentieth century. Thus, reoccurring Balkan wars ensued and the troubled times kept deteriorating further with our lands being at the cross-roads of wrestling powers during World Wars. Albanian lands were continuously overrun by neighbouring predatory armies that fought each other as much as the landowners. In those very few decades, Kosovo was to be occupied by Serbia, Montenegro, Austria-Hungary, Bulgaria, Germany, Italy and France. After a homogenised period of a thousand years of Byzantine Empire and five hundred years of Ottoman Empire, we had a diversified portfolio of occupiers within an unusually intensified period of time.

Diversity may as well beget homogeneity. Ultimately, local people of the diversified Balkan territories did orchestrate their national liberation movements and align their strategic efforts against the Nazi-fascists. In 1944, the Bujan Resolution was adopted, which defined Kosovo as a sovereign entity and a part of Albania. In it Kosovars expressed the aim to remain part of the Albanian state after the end of the Second World War. However, in 1945 once the war was over, Yugoslavia annexed Kosovo and its indigenous Albanian people by force. During most of my young age the border with Albania was hermetically closed. We did not know much of history at that age. We just underhandedly knew that a 'better version of ourselves', Albanians of Albania as opposed to Albanians of Kosovo, lived on the other side of the border. We sang their songs stealthily on given occasions with an utmost passion and longing. Yet, that border, cutting like a bloody knife across a fragile homogenous body, was haunted by horror stories of failed attempts to pass over to the motherland. Stories of those who never made it and of those who made it on the other side to be captured, tortured and never heard of again. One lyric line from our side goes 'leaving the mild winter only to find a storm', indicating the bitter version of communist totalitarianism prevailing in the motherland. Thus it turned out that we never were aghast enough at what was really going on in communist Albania. There was no way to know. Nevertheless, we knew that, these other versions of ourselves lived on the other side of the border with Montenegro, Macedonia, Serbia and Greece as well. Albanians were everywhere, locked up on both sides of all borders. We thought this was unusual, unseen and unheard of. This was an undesirable sort of map-making witchcraft and felt the pinch of painful destiny. Again, we thought we were unique and on this perhaps we still are, as this underlines an unresolved situation in which the majority of ethnic Albanians live outside the borders of Albania.

The irony was that, unlike Albania, we across-the-border Albanians within ex-Yugoslavia itself, could freely exchange visits and interact. We were

HOMOGENEITY

literally under the same roof as six 'socialist' republics, mostly of Slavic background. The 'Miracle of Yugoslavia' and its strikingly successful interethnic harmony was another uniqueness of diversity our young selves were not consciously aware of. Unlike history and its untamed interpretations, this diversity was incumbent as we were literally living it. Slovenians, Croatians, Bosnians, Serbians, Macedonians, Montenegrins, Kosovars and Vojvodinians, were all one. With a few glitches here and there, you could close your eyes and spell out the clockwork-like perfection of a socialist welfare system. Meritocracy in principle. Free quality education for all. Free healthcare for all. Freedom of religion in all its manifestations (loathsome as it was deemed by incumbent elites). Freedom of expression (of 'desirable' things) and self-determination (with supervision). Diversity in relations among people was the puzzle. Intermarriages, regardless of ethnicity or religion, were not taboo. Friendly neighbourly rapports, a blossoming interchange of intellectual, artistic, sportive creativity and an outpouring of a melting pot of addictive folk culture. Despite it all, voices murmured: this is an idyllic utopia, this is a time bomb. Nowhere in the world can you find anything like this. This diversity is improbable, it is an illusion. This diversity is unhealthy. 'We' are not like 'them'. This diversity is an aberration. Homogeneity is the normal way of life.

Living and working for years in the culturally melting pot of Asia Pacific did not greatly alter my cognitive frames of homogeneity as the standard expectation of normality. Over the years, I had consciously ignored the colourful heterogeneity of India and China, having cognitively processed it as a given exemption. These countries were huge, I fleetingly must have thought. They are vast in space and rich in history; their endless array of languages we constantly had to consider while dealing with multiple translations in survey projects, made sense. However, in hindsight it seems to me like every mini-melting-pot self-perceives itself as 'unique', as an 'exemption'. In the streets of Malaysia just about the same self-aggrandisement of diversity uniqueness randomly goes on. Malaysians think that they are an exceptional case, in their constituency of major diversity of Malays, Chinese and Indians, situated across the religious spectrum including Muslims, Buddhists, Christians, Hindus and traditional Chinese religions. And while with time I got used to the many churches in Malaysia, which were large in number and more modern in building architecture, I was completely thrown when I first came across the landmark Ban Ho mosque in Chiang Mai. Chiang Mai, with its majestic mountains and ancient temples, located north of Thailand, a country with a population topping more than ninety per cent of Theravada Buddhists, with a mosque ranked as one of its top landmark destination sites to visit. That was in total dissonance with my cognitive map of the Thai Muslims located in the southern region, on the Malaysian border. How can that be? My homogeneity lenses were beginning to crack.

It took time for me to connect the dots between the melting pots of Asia Pacific, North America or Africa; and unfortunately it was the post Arab spring events that opened the lid of the Middle East melting pot for many to view. Here, the negative spin of media kept highlighting the 'impossibility' of these diverse societies to get back on their feet, mostly due to intra-country irreconcilable diversity of local population. The common hints are that, for orderly societies to be viable, they have to arrange their diversity into orderly classification boxes, each with people of homogenous background. The multitude of diversity overlapping across the criteria makes this practically impossible. In the case of Syria, for instance, what was once a harmonious society under the Ottomans, consisting of peoples, cultures, intertwined histories, religions and denominations, now bursts into a life-or-death quest for homogeneity. Thus, all the horrors of the modern-bound, heavily equipped, tech-savvy murderers driven by global and regional power struggles are attributed to the problematic diversity of the population, a diversity that had been there since time immemorial. Or, it is attributed to the lack of what I would dub the *imagined homogeneity* of a population. This most likely was never there as a prerequisite for peace and prosperity prior to the modern concept of sanitised nationhood. We are talking about diversity of a population, as observed by N. N. Taleb, a renowned American author of Middle Eastern origin, in some of the iconic Syrian cities that can be traced back to ancient times. They retained their commercial autonomy and multicultural diversity through the ages and did not cease to be the most prosperous cities in the world until very recently. The words of an Egyptian friend uttered in a random gathering hosted in Kuala Lumpur still echo vividly: 'We Egyptians, 300 years under Greeks, 200 years under Persians, 800 years under Romans, then Arabs...then 1000+ under Ottomans...who are we, indeed!?'. Thus when the western pundits and so called experts come occasionally to KL conferences, fond of speaking of the deep-seated issues of Muslim societies that spring mostly from their incompatible heterogeneous consistency, rife with divisions particularly pinpointing the *shia-sunni* schism, I cannot help but smile. Based on what I had gathered, every single non-Muslim reader today has heard about the irreconcilable *shia* problem, even though worldwide the Shia communities comprise only about 14 per cent of Muslims. Upon closer inspection, the differences between these denominations are but superficial and historically speaking the inter-conflict is but irrelevant in scale. Today, homogenisation and pasteurisation of Islam is being forcefully prescribed in hindsight. While the rest of the world is being regionalised and globalised, some sort of pathological 'homogeneity' is being forced upon 'Islam' too. As if there ever was such a thing as monolithic Islam.

When I recently sat down to write a report about the launch of ASEAN Economic Community (AEC) at the end of 2015, I was already full of 'anti-homogeneity' munition. ASEAN, the Association of Southeast Asian Nations, an alliance promoting economic and political cooperation by fostering dialogue among its ten members, has been around since 1967. Not so far behind the establishment of the European Coal & Steel Community, I thought. It consists of Brunei, Cambodia, Indonesia, Laos, Malaysia, Myanmar, the Philippines, Singapore, Thailand, and Vietnam. The sheer diversity of ethnic backgrounds, languages, cultural and religious segments is striking. Indonesia alone is reported to have 1128 ethnic and 746 local languages and dialects. 170 languages and dialects are reported in the Philippines. The diversity is reflected in recent historic experiences of these former colonies too. The Dutch were in Indonesia; the French in Cambodia, Laos and Vietnam; the British in Brunei, Malaysia, Myanmar and Singapore; and the Spanish and the Americans in the Philippines. AEC launched in Kuala Lumpur and the headlines went haywire: 'We are now one big family'. After signing the declarations, the heads of government and state were ushered to the stage to make a single beat on the drum. The historic moment was marked by the beating of the ceremonial musical instruments of the ASEAN countries, symbolising unity in diversity. Among others, Malaysia's PM said that for the people of South-East Asia to understand the significance of the ASEAN Community, member countries must deliver 'tangible benefits that could evoke a real sense of belonging' towards the region. AEC goes beyond economy, said the PM, pointing out that it is also about 'making our citizens feel that ASEAN courses through their veins'. Can economic 'tangibility' bring about 'identity' and abstract emotional concepts such as 'belonging'? Such questions are raised in branding strategies whereby ways of transcending product functionality into emotional attachment are deliberated. That got me thinking about the process of regional identity-forging. With economic integration it is hoped cultural differences will wane. The 500 million people of ASEAN, more than those living in the United States or Europe, could thus be transformed into an homogeneous 'imagined community'. While working on the data I was reflecting on the different stages of regional integration AEC and EU currently experience. In AEC the citizens on the streets are hardly aware of what is going on despite high profile launches and signed treaties and are largely oblivious to the ceremonial drum beatings. The EU population, however, is struggling with the notion of a supranational identity; trading off national identity for Europeaness.

The European Union was set up with the aim of ending the incessant bloody wars between neighbours, which culminated in the Second World War. It was speculated that European economic integration would lead to political integration and a forged pan-European identity. So far this has not happened and as Brexit demonstrates so well a ferocious battle between national identities and European identity is taking place. Although, these two identity constructions can coexist with each other, the harmonious interplay has been disturbed by financial crisis and its implications, heightened xenophobia and vehement politicisation of the issue of immigrants. Immigrants are charged with threatening the cultural homogeneity of Europe. Why in the age of globalisation, do these issues still make headlines every day? In the age of rainbow multiculturalism in Canada, when the United States is losing its majority to its minority population, when Europe is coming together and ASEAN is drawing closer, why are immigrants perceived as a threat in Europe? Was this not supposed to be more about what makes economic sense and less about identity politics or culture? More about tangibility and less about intangibility? Moreover, historically speaking, homogeneity does not seem to make economic sense. Not long ago, immigrants contributed to the rebuilding of Europe from the ashes of World War Two. Looking further back the trail of diversity of the Roman Empire, Ottoman Empire or even British Empire, for example, illustrates that to make a civilisational quantum leap, homogeneity is not enough. And as we witness in many instances today, homogeneity has a poor prospect. Homogeneity is not productive enough so we need foreign workers; homogeneity is not creative enough so we need foreign talent; homogeneity is not competitive enough so we need regional economic alliances.

European countries within their own borders are ethnically homogenous. The notion of homogenous national identities tied to ethnicity originated in Europe, and spread across the globe. Contemporary Europe's borders with more-or-less ethnically homogenous populations developed over a vast period of conflict and inter-wars and hardly seems worth the trouble. But even as we look closer in scale and time, the texture of European homogeneity is not as smooth as we imagine. As late as 1863, around eighty per cent of the French population did not speak French but rather a range of other languages and dialects. Europe's homogeneity had its walls as recently as 1989. Is it about to rebuild its walls following the worst migrant crisis ever in 2015? While this is the case with national borders in Europe, the borders in Africa and Asia were carved up by colonial powers into territories and possessions with no regard for the background of the people living in the land. A cursory review of the data for diversity of the globe is telling. When five researchers set out to measure ethnic diversity for a 2002 paper for the Harvard Institute of Economic Research, those results measured 650 ethnic groups in 190 countries. Turning to regional variation, the highest ethnic division is spotted in sub-Saharan African countries. Africa accounts only for about quarter of all countries but has 43 per cent of the world's ethnic groups. African countries are the least ethnically homogenous. While the rest of the world's regions average between 3.2 and 4.7 diverse groups per country, the African countries' average is greater than eight diverse groups per country. Globally speaking, only 21 per cent of countries are 'homogenous' in the sense of having a group that claims nine out of ten residents in the country. Some 70 per cent of countries in the world have an ethnic group that forms an absolute majority of the population, although the average population share of such groups is only

65 per cent and below. That allows for huge diversity, making diversity the norm not an exception.

And this is diversity by the arbitrary ruler of borders. However, diversity is much more than ethnicity and far beyond any borders. In fact it is almost impossible to define diversity across all research parameters; language, ethnicity, religion, denomination and race. If you look at the Religious Diversity Index (RDI), the conclusion is similar. The Religious Diversity Index is a version of the Herfindahl-Hirschman Index, which is used in environmental and business studies to measure the degree of ecological diversity or market concentration. The 10-point RDI is divided into four ranges: Countries with scores of 7.0 and higher (the top 5 per cent) are categorised as having a 'very high' degree of religious diversity. Countries with scores from 5.3 to 6.9 (the next highest 15 per cent of scores) have a 'high' level of diversity. Countries with scores from 3.1 to 5.2 (the following 20 per cent of scores) are considered to have 'moderate' diversity, while the rest are categorised as having 'low' diversity. Looking at the percentage of each country's population that belongs to major religious categories included in the study, 12 countries have a very high degree of religious diversity. Six of the 12 are in the Asia-Pacific region (Singapore, Taiwan, Vietnam, South Korea, China and Hong Kong); 5 are in sub-Saharan Africa; and one is in Latin America and the Caribbean. By these criteria, no countries in Europe, North America or the Middle East-North Africa region have a very high degree of religious diversity. Singapore with scores of 9 out of 10 ranks the highest of all in the Religious Diversity Index. Kosovo ranks in the 'low diversity' group with only 2.6 out of 10. So much for our diversity uniqueness.

It is obvious that homogeneity as a norm was always miniscule in scale and if it was a norm beyond a provincial prospect, it was an aberration soaked in blood. Beyond a tribal or provincial prospect, it may have been due to social engineering, a 'pathological homogenisation'. We only need to look at the despicable situation in Myanmar. Driven by the myth of homogeneity, the Rohingya Muslims, who have lived there for centuries, are being eradicated by Buddhist fanatics. A relatively small minority has become a target of a hate campaign, that has led to barbarity and incomprehensible human suffering – all with the silent collusion of the Nobel Peace Prize Winner, and darling of the West, Aung San Suu Kyi. Or consider the violence in Rwanda's recent history. Global diversity data has shown that sub-Saharan Africa has only one 'highly homogenous' country and that is Rwanda with Hutus at 90 per cent. We know how and at what price this was achieved. I was witness and a victim of a very recent 'ethnic cleansing' enterprise in 1999 when almost the whole population of my home town was forced to flee their homes in a matter of days. Within weeks, it expanded to the whole country with thousands of hundreds of Kosovo Albanians driven out forcefully across the borders into neighbouring countries. Over-loaded lorries, buses and trains, including non-passenger modes of transport designed for livestock and material goods, filled up to an unbreathable level of all types of diverse human demographics and profiles; elderly, youth, scientists, children, celebrities, pregnant women, nuns, disabled individuals, university professors, to name but a few. I vividly recall the moment the paramilitaries, whose job was to drive citizens out of their homes, finally approached our neighbourhood. They had already cleansed the few upper neighbourhoods, as illustrated by increasingly closer shootings that could be heard and the sheer number of people who had taken refuge in our area in the previous 24 hours. We stood in the uppermost floor of our three-storey house and watched through the full-glass windows the apocalyptic Serb figures, only 25 metres across the street as they started breaking through the first gate. Mesmerised, we stood there as if watching another century unfolding in front of our eyes. It did not occur to us to escape until they finished all the upper row of houses one by one and turned their attention in our direction. Only then did we rush down the stairs and by the time we reached the back exit, the front gate was loudly knocked down. Why did we wait for the last moment to make our move? I later wondered. Was it that there was nowhere to go as they were all over the city? Was it some sort of negotiated permission to leave? Or an unconscious rationalisation or justification to our own deep consciousness that there was no choice but to leave?

Talal Asad suggests that the preoccupation with national unity or integration has been a hallmark of authoritarianism. The Nazi-inflicted holocaust of European Jews illustrates one such classic horrendous 'final solution' of diversity cleansing. One might be tempted to think that our human past has been horrendous anyway and that only today, in the age of economic regionalisation, multiculturalism and globalisation have we learned to co-exist. Living side-by-side in globalised offices, whereby every few weeks a cultural occasion is celebrated be it Christmas, Eid, Mid-Autumn Moon festival or Chinese New Year. Today's most prosperous global megacities, reminiscent of Syrian iconic cities of the past, are a fusion of everything. As Zygmunt Bauman puts it, 'today every society is just a collection of diasporas'. Strategies to manage and nurture 'diversity' are a major theme of cutting edge organisational policies and top notch change management programmes, addressing inclusivity of gender, culture, race, religion and so on. We think we finally are smart and have matured enough to look beyond our nose and recognise the need for 'others'. We always give credit to ourselves and our times. Just like we Albanians give full credit to religious tolerance to ourselves and none else. I remember being highly amused reading Slavoj Zizek who praised our Ottoman past for its tolerance which seems to have been part of Balkani culture prior to the nationalisation enterprise. But the Ottomans were demonised in our communist mainstream, as they were in the West, and their umbrella administration deemed outdated in comparison to our sparkly new homogenously-aspiring national identities. Along the years I feel sure that the same people who spoke vehemently against the impossibility of diversity of the Ottomans, toxicity of diversity of ex-Yugoslavia, are now fine and dandy with the idea of the European Union. Perhaps this is coming full circle with the realisation that co-existence is the normal state of being.

I still take pride in the religious tolerance of my people; and hope to see them under the same roof. Perhaps that is what the European Union is supposed to provide: one roof for all. Albanians behind any border are the least Eurosceptic of all. They want more EU not less EU. Europeaness seems to reinforce not threaten their national identity. Leave aside the toxic politics, intermingling of people is the natural state of being. When you add toxic politics to the normal state of being, exceptionalism and xenophobia are an inevitable product. But it takes time for toxic politics to intoxicate; and, in reverse, it takes time for social trust to be rebuilt. The good news is that in these time-consuming social processes, citizens can become agents for change to stem the unhealthy flow of conflict – provided they don't swallow the dictates of political expediency.

FEMINISM IS FOR EVERYBODY

Michael Vicente Perez

I first learned about feminism from a man. His name was Richard Haynes, a philosophy professor at the University of Florida (UF). It was my first semester at UF and I was working my way into the undergraduate philosophy major. Somewhere in his 70s, Haynes was a gentle man with a radical bent who approached philosophy critically and pragmatically. For Dr Haynes philosophy wasn't just about abstract speculation. It was, rather, a grounded effort to examine and address some of the most pressing questions of our time. Thus in addition to European classics like Aristotle and Descartes, Haynes introduced his students to the philosophies of critical race theorists, feminists and environmentalists. Through the works of scholars like Alain Locke and Catherine MacKinnon, Haynes compelled us to think about philosophy as a practical engagement with real world problems, even a prism through which we could understand ourselves and our relationships with others. Both racism and sexism were thus philosophical questions that, like any other issue in philosophy, required critical thinking and effective action.

I should say that Haynes wasn't the first to teach me the value of critical analysis for social life. About a year prior to my transfer to UF from a community college, I accepted Islam through the Nation of Islam (NOI). It was 1997 and I had been visiting the mosque consistently for months at my brother's behest. He had joined the NOI about a year before my first visit. Engaged in the study of America's black intellectual tradition, he found the NOI through college classmates and friends. Once he joined, my brother began raising questions I couldn't answer — questions which focused on my belief in God and how my lifestyle fit into that belief and religion more generally. These also focused on social issues including my perceptions of race and gender. Admittedly, I was stumped. I had never considered my religious beliefs as anything more than part of my taken-for-granted identity as a Catholic Cuban-American. Indeed, the two identities went hand in hand. Nor had I thought much about the problems of race and gender in any socially meaningful way. I knew, of course, that racism and sexism existed (my own experiences confirmed that). But I didn't really know how to think about these problems beyond the individual. I lacked both a framework and the tools for understanding inequalities as more than individual behaviours. Eventually, his questions frustrated me enough that I agreed to visit the mosque. There, in the heart of Liberty City, my questions found answers. And Islam was central to them.

Schooled in the Nation of Islam's Mosque No. 29, my first opportunity to think critically about the world was with a Qur'an in hand. As one of the 'Fruit of Islam', I learned Islam within a black radical tradition that brought questions of race, justice and the divine together. Indeed, my time in the NOI provided me with my first philosophical problem as a Muslim: if all humans are equal, why were America's black communities so impoverished? The answer to this question was the subject of countless Sunday sermons that linked Islamic ethics with social justice. From the central pulpit of the mosque, student ministers and the minister himself, Brother Rasul Muhammad, taught me that Muslims had an obligation to care for the poor and oppressed. Empowered by the principles of justice, freedom and equality, these teachers taught me how to think analytically about the conditions of Black America and the sickness of White supremacy.

Despite the problems with their approach (problems I learned as my critical skills sharpened), the essential point is not what the NOI taught me but how it forced me to think. As a radical black tradition concerned with social inequality, the NOI compelled its membership to think analytically about issues like race, religion and the struggle for freedom. Employing a critical hermeneutics of the Bible and Qur'an, for example, the NOI argued that race was a divine construction that explained the violence of European whites against the darker people of the earth. Turning the ideology of white supremacy on its head, the NOI claimed that whites were the inferior race whose propensity for violence reflected their nature as uncivilised 'devils'. Whatever its problems, this rewriting of racism brought the Qur'an and Bible into a complex theory of black enslavement under white hands. It was an analysis of evil in a world with God. Within the storefront mosque of Miami's Liberty City, I thus learned some of the basics of critical analysis: how to reason, how to examine assumptions, how to deconstruct texts, how to construct an argument and how to think critically. As I was becoming a

Muslim, in other words, I was also learning how to be analytical. The two were inextricably linked.

While in the NOI, I travelled extensively with my brother and some of the local members to learn from the movement's leader, Louis Farrakhan. In the late 1990s, we followed Farrakhan throughout one of his Florida tours. At home, we studied everything he wrote and said. For us, Farrakhan was a sage. His ability to weave sociological analysis with religious texts and attention to the plight not only of black Americans but of all 'Original' peoples of the earth inspired us to learn about everything he spoke about. One of those topics was the plight of black women. In 1994, he held a lecture in Atlanta, Georgia, titled 'A Nation Can Rise No Higher than Its Woman'. Although Farrakhan often spoke about the struggles of black women, this was the first time that he had prepared a lecture exclusively for women, and was the first lecture I heard in a religious context that examined the suffering of black women in terms of history, politics and God. It was also the first time I had to think about black women as a particular group with its own struggles in America.

Suffice it to say that by the time I reached Haynes' classroom, I was ready for the critical project of philosophy. For almost two years before arriving at UF, I had learned to think critically about religion, racism, gender and justice. Engaged in the intellectual and practical work of the NOI, the importance of critical analysis and praxis were firmly established in my mind. More specifically, the idea that critique and Islam went hand in hand was fundamental to my sense of what it meant to be Muslim. Thus when Dr Haynes assigned the work of radical feminist, Catherine MacKinnon, I was moved by the opportunity to further my understandings of gender, feminism and women's struggle. Like the NOI's critique of race, MacKinnon questioned the taken for granted world in which women were seen as inferior beings. And like the NOI's insistence on racial consciousness, MacKinnon argued that the critical perspective necessary for women to realise and challenge their oppression *as* women required a collective effort to think and act in concert. But the works of MacKinnon and other feminists I read pushed me further than the NOI had ever done. Whereas for the NOI women were to be honoured primarily for their motherly and domestic capacities, the feminist philosophers I read challenged me to consider the nexus between women's 'domesticity' and their oppression. From this perspective, I realised how the connection between women's bodies and the domestic realm were rooted in deeper ideas about the distinctions between women and men.

It has been almost two decades since I sat in Muhammad's Mosque or in Haynes' classroom. Yet what I learned from these two contexts was fundamental for my approach to the question of feminism and Islam. Whether in the religious context of the NOI or the secular space of the university classroom, the importance of thinking critically about issues of race, gender, oppression and justice remain essential to my approach to Islam and the world. Indeed, from my experience in both settings, the significance of a specifically feminist understanding of the plight of women and position of men has remained central to my perspective of Islam. This is because feminism, as I learned it, never troubled my sense of being Muslim. On the contrary, the analytical tools and goals of feminism complemented my vision of Islam as a religion serving the interests of justice. In the NOI, for example, I learned that addressing the situation of black women in America was inseparable from the project of Islam more generally. Whether in the community or the home, it was our duty as Muslims to challenge the forces of racism and sexism and create a more just vision of gender through the prism of Islam. In a similar vein, Haynes taught feminism not as an opportunity for theoretical speculation but as a pragmatic framework for engaging some of the problems women face within our society. As a Muslim committed to creating a more just society, feminism thus presented an opportunity to continue thinking about what I learned from the NOI: a truly just society is impossible without considerations of justice for women. In this way, feminism offered an opportunity for examining my own understanding of who I was as a man and how that fits into my ideas of Islam. It forced me to confront my own assumptions about gender and how Islam mattered for those presumptions.

For these reasons, the ceaseless debate among some Muslims about feminism and Islam are baffling. Not that there haven't been rich discussions about the problems with *particular* feminisms like *liberal* feminism, which often reflects the racialised perspectives of white middle and upper class women. But the ongoing attempt to exclude feminism from a meaningful debate about what Muslims believe and do in the name of Islam seems misplaced. Driven by simplistic reactions to modern imperialism or the problematic assumption of an essential Islam, the effort to limit feminism in discussions of Islam often precludes any serious considerations of what feminism actually offers both analytically and pragmatically. And in my view, this has not only complicated our ability to critically understand our own historical tradition but also its future.

Criticisms of feminism among Muslims are many. For some, feminism represents yet another instance of 'Western' imperial power. In both its discourse and practice, they claim that feminism works well with the interests of empire and functions to denigrate and subordinate Muslims and Islam. Others think of feminism as ideologically opposed to what are assumed to be essential ideas within Islam including gender 'complementarity' and the 'natural dispositions' of women and men. Still others argue that feminism stems from a fundamentally secular viewpoint and thus cannot work with a tradition constructed according to sacred texts and the imperatives of a divine moral order. Despite their variations, all of these positions share a set of assumptions that treat feminism as something *other* and therefore problematic. For the Muslim concerned with imperialism, for example, feminism emerges as a foreign project constituted by the racism of 'Western' superiority and motivated by the goals of colonisation. Those who think of Islam in essential terms also see feminism as an external other. For these Muslims, feminism reflects a coherent vision of gender that stands in opposition to the vision offered by God in Islam. In the end, none of these positions are adequate for their purposes. In essentialising feminism, they not only misrepresent what feminism is but also fail to account for the essentialisation of Islam the critique requires.

A thorough examination of these positions compels me to challenge the idea that feminism is antithetical to Islam and that its project can be reduced either to an imperial purpose or an external secular critique. I am informed by the work of a particular black feminist whose criticisms of feminism underscore both its resilience and promise for addressing some of the ongoing challenges we all face under the structures of sexism. While I am certain my points won't convince all Muslims of the importance of feminism, I do hope it will break down some of the tired clichés that continue to turn Muslims away from a critical analytical and political movement to end sexism both within our own lives and in the lives of those with whom we share the larger social world.

Of all the feminist writers I know, none has impacted my thinking more than bell hooks. This is not to ignore the works of other authors. Indeed, without writers like MacKinnon, Patricia Hill Collins and Judith Butler, to name just a few, my evolving perspective on feminism would be quite narrow, to say the least. But in all my readings of feminism, hooks provided a crucial voice in the discussions about what feminism can and should be. And understanding that voice today provides an important opportunity for rethinking some of the most cherished positions Muslims have taken against feminism. In particular, both her critique of feminism and its related definition offer a chance to consider how Muslims can benefit from the analysis and goals of feminism both within Islam and beyond.

Beginning with her work in the 1980s, hooks examined the meaning of feminism with a critical eye towards its particular methods of analysis and politics. In *Feminist Theory: From Margin to Centre*, hooks presented one of the early critiques of feminism that included issues of race and class. Feminism in the US, she argued, had gained popularity as a movement defined by the goal of women's equality (with men). Without diminishing this vision of feminism, hooks raised an important question about such an aim: in a world where race and class not only structure inequalities between women and men but also between white women, white men, black women and black men, what would equality look like? To whom should women be equal and why should that vision of equality represent the goals of all women?

Needless to say, introducing the question of race and class to the feminism of mostly bourgeois white women was a significant intervention. For me it challenged the basic assumptions of a developing movement that, for all its merits, failed to take stock of its own limitations. By privileging the situation and desires of mostly white upper class women, for instance, she underscored how many feminists ignored the circumstances and voices of other women. In so doing, feminism emerged as a very limited project. First, by ignoring the lives of black, Latina and poor white women, feminists limited the scope of their analysis. Theoretically, they impoverished their conception of who women were and the oppression they experienced by excluding the ways racial and class differences structured women's lives. Second, feminists' failure to think beyond the lives of upper class white women resulted in a politics limited to that position. Politically, feminists thus ignored the different possibilities for challenging sexism by reducing their aims to the situated perspective of upper class white women for whom equality with upper class white men represented the basis of their demands.

Despite her criticisms, however, hooks did not abandon feminism. Instead, she used her critique as the basis for transforming both the meaning and politics of feminism for women and men. This is clear from hooks' later work, *Feminism is for Everybody: Passionate Politics*. In this book, she insists on the continuing significance of feminism, which, consistent with her previous works, is defined as 'a movement to end sexism, sexist exploitation and oppression'. According to hooks, this definition of feminism is important for several reasons. First, it underscores the fact that feminism is not a movement against men. Rather, it positions feminism as a movement aimed at sexism, which finds expression in both the beliefs and practices of men and women. For hooks, defining feminism in relation to sexism is thus critical since it suggests that the problem for feminism is not exclusive to women and thus can't be the burden of women alone. It is, instead, a shared condition and, as such, requires a shared commitment.

Second, by linking feminism to sexism, this definition affords feminists a diverse set of positions from which to take up their own aims. Complicated by the intersections of race, class and sexuality, the conception of sexism will necessarily vary. Thus the definition of feminism as a movement against sexism allows – indeed compels – feminists to think, first, about the specifics of sexism they face and, second, to identify solutions from that particular experience of sexism. If sexism intersects with race and class, as it did for women working as domestic labourers in white women's homes, for example, then feminism's goal could not be determined in advance. It would have to proceed from the specific analysis of sexism in the lives of women living at this intersection. And, more importantly, its goals would have to be determined from that intersection. In other words, while ending sexism would remain the critical task, how it would end could not be imagined without attention to the lived experiences of these women's lives.

For hooks, the critique of feminism and its concomitant definition empowered us to think about feminism as a movement for everybody. And I cite hooks' work because I think she's right. Feminism *is* for everybody, Muslims included. But how does hooks' discussion address the criticisms of imperialism, secularism and essentialism offered by Muslims who wish to keep feminism at bay? Let's take each position at a time.

One of the key criticisms of feminism put forth by Muslims has to do with imperialism. From the times of European colonialism to the contemporary politics of the 'war on terror', some Muslims rightly point to the role feminists have played in the symbolic and material subordination of Islam and Muslims. Their examples are many and offer a compelling critique of the intersections between feminism and empire or, as Gayatri Spivak once put it, the politics of 'white men saving brown women from brown men'. During the US invasion of Afghanistan in 2001, for example, it was no secret that former First Lady, Laura Bush, and several feminist organisations rallied on behalf of the oppressed 'women of cover' living under the Taliban. Wedding the military invasion and occupation of Afghanistan to the liberation of Afghan women, the US government exploited the situation of these women—a situation, it should be said, the US was largely indifferent to during our proxy war against the Soviets and subsequent takeover by the Taliban prior to 2001.

Here we had a clear example of how the project of neo-conservative empire relied on the willingness of feminists to endorse a war in order to 'save Afghan women' not only from the oppression of the Taliban but, as we'd later see, their very own culture. This alone is insufficient for understanding the critique, however. Muslims concerned with empire also point to the very understanding of the feminist project vis-à-vis Muslim women to showcase not only feminism's imperial connection but also its imperial vision. Here the critique focuses on the universalising nature of feminism; that is, the notion that feminism can operate discursively and practically in all contexts and at all times. In her critique of feminism, for example, this is the position Asma Barlas takes up. For her, 'it is the very inclusivity of feminism – its attempt, as a meta and master narrative, to subsume and assimilate all conversations about equality – that I find both imperialising and reductive.'

The imperial critique, both in its material and epistemological manifestations, is significant and presents an important opportunity to think carefully about feminism as an attempt to address the problems of sexism. Yet both approaches rely on a rather limited notion of what feminism is and how it works. If we follow hooks' argument and take feminism as a critical analysis of sexism that includes the intersections of race, class and other 'ism', both aspects of the critique seem difficult to sustain. In the Afghan context, for example, the argument that feminism is reducible to what Laura Bush and her feminist supporters promoted fails to take the question of sexism as seriously as hooks would want us to. Whatever their intentions, in other words, the feminist effort to 'liberate' women through war in a country already ravaged by imperial powers (ours included) can hardly pass as a project to end sexism as defined by hooks.

There are two points to be made here. First, these so-called feminists ignored one of the key aspects of the movement they claimed to represent: women's voices. We heard little from Afghan women in the rush to war. Without their voices in the discussions, the analysis of sexism these feminists put forth excluded the very women necessary for the analysis. If these women were interested in promoting a feminist cause in Afghanistan, then Afghan women should have been included since, as hooks showed with poor women of colour in the US, their contributions are essential for the understanding of sexism. Second, pursuing a war that in many ways relied on the racist discourses and practices of the US vis-à-vis Muslims ('backwards', 'primitive' and 'tribal') and Islam could hardly represent a commitment to ending sexist oppression. Indeed, the invasion of Afghanistan and the US approach to Muslims more generally shows how racism combines with sexism to render Islam and its believers either tyrannical oppressors (men) or passive victims (women) in need of 'Western' liberation. In this sense, Afghan women faced a *dual* struggle. While in the local context, many Afghan women suffered the abuses of actors like the Taliban, who used Islam to explain their oppressive practices, in the international context, Afghan women were silenced by 'feminists' who used racism and sexism to execute their liberal mission at the expense of the very people they would ostensibly save.

Suffice it to say that treating the feminist role in the Afghan invasion as an instance of feminism fails to address the fact that feminism also challenges that very role. It also ignores the argument made by feminists like hooks that cast the project of feminism in terms of ending sexism, not promoting liberal notions of equality or capitalism. Either way, by defining feminism by what some feminists did runs the same risk as claiming Islam is what Muslims do in its name. A more critical approach would have to reckon with the fact that many feminists, Muslims included, opposed US liberal feminist support for a war that not only compromised Afghan women's desires but their very lives.

The second and third critiques of feminism mentioned above can actually be combined since they both depend on an epistemological distinction between feminism and Islam. Feminism, some Muslims say, is incompatible with Islam because it proceeds with a specifically secular epistemology that denies God as a source of divine, and therefore *true*, knowledge. Moreover, because feminism doesn't take the status of the Qur'an as divine or the vision of a sacred moral order into consideration, it thus represents an external perspective that is fundamentally incompatible with an Islamic one. Feminism is, essentially, distinct from Islam and must be treated as such.

Here the idea can be illustrated by way of the Qur'an. For some Muslims, if the Qur'an says women should inherit less than their brothers, then it is by divine order that they do so. Whatever feminists might say about this inequality, the divine status of the Qur'an means that the inheritance rule ordered by God is moral and must remain unchanged. Inheritance and the gendered order it constitutes, in other words, is not sexism or oppression. Rather, it is an order that is morally justified by its status as the word of God and cannot be challenged on a secular basis.

Such critiques have an obvious appeal. By identifying feminism as a secular Other, it creates the impression of an epistemological essentialism in which feminist ways of knowing are markedly different from Muslim ways of knowing. In particular, it suggests that because feminism does not proceed with the same assumptions a Muslim does – that God exists, that the Qur'an is divine, that Muhammad is a Prophet – it cannot productively inform those who use it to engage Islam as a textual and practical tradition. Feminists think in secular terms, Muslims think in Islamic terms. The two are fundamentally different and fundamentally irreconcilable. Thus Muslims will have to think about gender without feminism, which can remain within the secular world of the 'West'.

This approach is deeply flawed. Its greatest weakness is its reliance on a distinction that resembles the structure of Orientalism identified by Edward Said long ago. According to Said, Orientalism was much more than a stereotype of a place and its peoples. It was also a 'style of thought based upon an ontological and epistemological distinction made between "the Orient" and "the Occident"'. This distinction, Said further explained, serves as the 'starting point for elaborate theories, novels, etc.' In the argument above, the idea of Islam (and feminism) presented depends on the Orientalist assumption that Islam really is a distinct, essential entity complete with its own epistemology. Much like the Orientalists of old, it suggests that Islam is a coherent body of thought and practice informed by an hermetically sealed procedure of knowing and doing unlike anything else. Similarly, the argument assumes that feminism belongs to the 'West', which is essentially secular and therefore different. Here feminism is also bounded by an intellectual geography called the 'West' that is fundamentally different – Other – from Islam. Simply put, the argument rests on Muslims' acceptance of the Orientalist distinction. It treats Islam as its own system of thought and action. It does the same with feminism.

But why should we assume that Islam is *essentially* anything? And why should we assume that secularism is antithetical to Islam? Can we really examine 1,400 years of intellectual and practical traditions in terms of a singular way of knowing? More specifically, can we think about the religion of communities spanning much of the inhabitable world as a single tradition informed by an exclusive epistemology? Is it not the effect of Orientalism that leads us to think so? And is it not Orientalism itself that benefits from such forms of Othering?

Throughout history, Muslims have always confronted problems in the world that could not be addressed through religious means (Qur'an, hadith, etc.) alone. Whether the problem of government, the methods of agriculture, or the practice of medicine, Muslims have always relied on, or at least engaged with, ideas, theories and methods that were not explicitly found in God's words. Drawing on Greek philosophy, for example, some of the greatest Muslim thinkers explored the meaning of justice and the State in ways that combined Islam with other (secular?) epistemologies (al-Farabi, for example). Indeed, Muslim philosophers and scholars have considered the very question of God's existence through epistemologies that were not exclusively Islamic. Greek philosophy, for example, still pervades much of Islamic literature and informs Muslim thinking about some of our most basic understandings of God and the divine. And Greek philosophy did not take the idea of a monotheistic God or God's divine text as the premise for philosophical thinking. Should we therefore look back and reject anything Muslims thought or said simply because it was informed by an epistemology identified as foreign to Islam? Should all ways of knowing be proscribed simply because they proceed from an epistemology that does not demand belief in God as necessary for its purposes? I, for one, think not. To do so is both to reinforce the false dichotomy of Orientalism, which presumes an essential Islam, and to create a problem with secularism where none exists.

The essentialisation of Islam and feminism has other problems. At a basic level, it is difficult to sustain the critique of feminism's secularity if the feminist happens to be Muslim. In such a case, a Muslim feminist could take God's existence and truth seriously and still proceed to use the analytical tools of feminism to address questions of sexism and women's suffering.

Second, it's not even clear that feminism is really a secular epistemology. Feminism does not entail adherence either to atheism or agnosticism nor does it require the rejection of theism. What it does require is a commitment to the analysis and disruption of sexist oppression. This very well may be challenged by theistic claims about divine justice, for example, or conceptualisations of sacred texts that read differently from a feminist perspective. Again, the perspective here is not one that denies theism; rather, it is a perspective informed by the concern over human suffering constituted by sexism and its relationship to other forms of oppression including racism and classism.

If we reject the proposition that feminism's secular stance is sufficient for its dismissal, then we find little to object to. Remember, hooks defined feminism as a movement to end sexist oppression. It is thus a project involving the critical analysis of sexism and the development of particular strategies for challenging it by the people who live its pain. To reject feminism in Islamic terms could only proceed if the analysis and abolition of sexism contradicts what Islam requires according to God's word. But this too has certain problems. First, such a rejection would require identifying clear instances of divinely sanctioned sexism. Given that much of the sexism we find throughout the Muslim world has little to do with God or reflects more Man's words than God's, such a refusal seems hard to sustain. We know, for example, that women's seclusion in places like Saudi Arabia is actually a modern norm formulated in the context of rapid urbanisation, the emergence of the nuclear family, the expansion of petro-capitalism and modern constructions of Islamic law. While some Saudi clerics would like to assign this practice a distinctive Islamic origin, a more careful look betrays its façade.

Second, even in the most complicated instances of what might actually be sexism in the Qur'an, such as the infamous 'strike' verse (4:34), is it clear that God is *commanding* men to hit their wives? Here feminism could at least intervene by asking Muslims to consider whether such a verse actually requires us to follow it. The feminist imperative to challenge sexism, in other words, would raise the question of action, not meaning. This would compel Muslims to challenge the position that following this verse is incumbent on Muslim men *as Muslims*. In other words, where sexism may exist, feminism presents an opportunity for Muslims to engage it critically and strategically. In some cases, this may happen at the interpretive level (does verse 34 mean 'beat' your wife?), in others at the practical level (do I need to do this?). In either case, feminism helps Muslims think about the problem of sexism in ways we otherwise might not.

Third and lastly, it is unclear to me that the Islamic injunction to seek justice is in any way compromised by feminism's concern with sexism. If we accept that Islam is a practice that entails the relentless effort to end unjustified human suffering, and if we accept that sexism is indeed unjustified, then it seems prudent to consider some of the most effective means for thinking about its causes. For decades, critical race theory, political ecology, post-colonial theory and feminism (to name a few) have offered just some of those means. Together, they have presented advocates of justice with some of the most important analyses and solutions to the ills they've named. Racism, environmental pollution, the exploitation of the 'third world' and sexism have all been challenged by the theories and methods of these frameworks and, in many cases, they have aided Muslims in their struggle for justice. Malcolm X, for example, never shied away from the racial critique of white supremacy. Informed by secular notions of liberty and equality, not to mention the vision of human rights, Malcolm challenged the myth of US democracy by exposing the racist underpinnings of an apartheid system that privileged whites politically and economically at the expense of blacks. Moreover, when Malcolm engaged the question of capitalism, he never feared assuming a socialist critique. On the contrary, Malcolm always seemed willing to take on the tools of whatever frameworks existed for advancing the cause of justice as a Muslim. If Malcolm took up the question of sexism through feminism, would Muslims reject him? Is feminism that unique?

Moreover, when Muslims rely on feminist analytical tools like standpoint epistemology or social construction theory, are they no longer thinking like a Muslim? Is the secularism of feminism so tyrannical that Muslims cannot rely on it without becoming secular? The simple answer is no. Muslims rely on a variety of epistemologies and methods for addressing problems in the social world. And I think we are enriched by doing so. Thus neither the concern over sexism nor the use of feminism is antithetical to Islam. As Muslims, we can take on the question of sexism both in our tradition and practice with the tools feminism offers. Nothing about the struggle against sexism has to be taken in opposition to the belief in God or respect for the Prophet. On the contrary, feminism can aid us in our very thinking about

Islam in such a way as to provide interpretations and practices that align better with the vision of a just world required by Islam.

My intellectual upbringing in the NOI and the many classes I took with Haynes taught me a great deal. In the NOI, I learned about Islam and how to be a Muslim in America. I also learned the value of critical thinking as it informed not only how we were taught to think about religion but also how to think about the world and our relation to it. Racism, sexism, economic marginalisation and other forms of oppression were at the centre of the NOI's praxis, which linked their own theories of race, gender and Islam with real world problems. This was a formative period in my life and, in many ways, it laid the foundation for everything that followed. In philosophy class (and later anthropology), I learned more. Through Haynes' critical approaches, I expanded my thinking of the social and the divine. Indeed, the two were never far apart. How else could I thrive in this world with a God of justice and so much human pain?

For me, feminism was one of the analytical approaches and commitments (a commitment I'm still working on) I needed as a Muslim and, more specifically, as a man. And this is perhaps one of the greatest proofs of feminism's value: its transformative effects on the meaning of being a man in a world that, in so many ways, favours manhood. For this reason, I think hooks got it right. Feminism is for everybody. Not because it questions gender and sexism but because of the way it does so. Feminism is both a set of theories and methods of transformation borne of the desire for justice, a desire it happens to share with Islam. Rather than turn away from feminism, Muslims should engage it, understand it, critique it and, when possible, apply it. Doing so not only aids ourselves in challenging the ills that affect our communities but also aids feminism itself. By embracing feminism, in other words, Muslims can help rethink feminism in ways that make its approaches more suitable to our needs and the needs of justice.

READING ALOUD

Saulat Pervez

'Mama, books are boring!' My daughter announced one day when she was in third grade. Her statement flabbergasted me. After all, since my little girl was a few months old, I had been reading to her. Even before she learned how to walk, she enjoyed a tall stack of books that we would read together every single day.

When my husband and I decided to leave our Long Island suburbs for the bustling city of Karachi, where both he and I grew up, our daughter was only two-and-a-half and our son was just fifteen months younger. Although I had to give away many of their bulky toys, I made sure I packed as many books as possible – knowing very well that easy access to public libraries was a privilege I was about to lose.

Yet, in Pakistan, I soon discovered busy book fairs and random bookstores with reasonably priced tomes that I kept adding to our collection. And so our reading journey continued. Living in a bilingual world, of Urdu and English, meant that we would read books in both languages. When we sat with our books, my kids didn't care about their toys or television. They simply loved delving into the stories and worlds the pages opened up to us.

By the time my daughter began school, I also joined the same institution as an English Literature teacher for secondary graders. School gave us access to vibrant libraries tailored to each age group – thankfully, our school was very focused on providing reading material to their student body, purchasing hundreds of books annually when other schools would only buy a handful and keep even those behind glass-encased bookshelves like precious wares.

In teaching children how to read, our school employed sight reading methodology, relying on the Ladybird Key Words with Peter and Jane series. While I knew that my daughter didn't enjoy their recurring words and plotless narrative, the books worked amazingly: by the time she reached the fourth level, she could pick up any storybook and read it on her own! Both of my sons followed suit, retracing identical paths to become independent readers even before they reached first grade.

Once she outgrew picture books, I introduced her to chapter books through Enid Blyton's lovable character, Noddy, and his many adventures. We would sometimes find Magic Tree House or Magic School Bus books at a book store or expo and buy them immediately because chapter books were so rare to come by other than the Noddy series. More commonly accessible were abridged easy readers of classics such as Charles Dicken's *Oliver Twist* or Miguel de Cervantes' *Don Quixote* – made attractive with illustrations on glossy pages in very thin paperbacks.

There is, quite conspicuously, a great British influence in Pakistan – from books available to read to the widespread private educational system (not to mention the country's obsession with tea and cricket!). Many of the English teachers themselves graduated from convent schools, going on to study mostly British Literature at university. Hence, there is a strong emphasis on classics, which comprise the majority of books available at school libraries, especially for younger audiences. The more common American chapter books and school tales haven't yet made it there, although adolescent and adult American popular fiction are easily available at bookstores and school libraries alike (except for some strict convent schools, where even *Harry Potter* is banned).

Upon reaching third grade, my daughter was already a confident reader and I felt she could progress to the next selection offered by the school library. So, I began encouraging her to read Enid Blyton's subsequent series and full-length children's classics such as *Black Beauty*, *Charlie and the Chocolate Factory*, and *Heidi*, among others. Little did I realise that despite all the years of cultivating her reading habit, we were about to hit a big obstacle and, by the time we made it to the other side, I would have benefited greatly from the learning process.

Once the shock of my daughter's declaration that books are boring had settled, I realised there was a deeper reason why I had been so taken aback. I had, by now, left my teaching position and was immersed in researching early childhood educational theories of how schools can build thinking cultures through literary pursuits. My experience as a teacher had been enlightening. Through years of mundane, methodical instruction of English Literature, my students had come to expect a modified version of rote learning and were at first confused by my emphasis on making connections, thinking as a class, and analysing the text. They were also not used to higher order questions in tests and were frustrated that a hitherto 'easy to ace' subject had suddenly become challenging and required a different, unfamiliar level of studying. Indeed, I heard a fair share of 'Books are boring!' during those years.

As we proceeded through the semester, I found many students would fall behind on the reading assignments, naturally leading to low test scores. No matter how much I tried to energise them through questioning or prod them into completing their reading by giving 'pop quizzes' (a concept unknown to them), some kids continued to perform poorly in class. Others did well or achieved average marks. I tried holding extra classes to help them, but there were always a few who never got over the fence, so to speak.

After my years of teaching, it was these kids that stayed with me, propelling my interest in researching how to make learning successful and how to enable students to develop cognitively from an early age. Just as every teacher struggles with the divides in their classroom – between the children who understand the material effortlessly and the ones who are unable to keep up with the class despite intervention, and everyone in between – I was haunted by those students for whom I failed to make a difference.

A few days after her pronouncement, I was intrigued to see my daughter reading a book during the early morning, bumpy rickshaw ride to school. When I questioned her about her earlier assertion, she countered, 'But this is a lot of fun! And I have to return it to my friend today!' After a quick check, I discovered it was a Mary Kate and Ashley Olsen mystery. Suddenly, things began to connect in my mind. Obviously, there was a vast difference between *Heidi* and a Mary Kate and Ashley Olsen mystery. So, I realised, when my daughter said 'Books are boring!' she was only referring to certain books. It occurred to me that perhaps the vast gulf between classics and modern chapter books was too much for her to cross independently.

For my own literary sustenance, I had initiated a Book Club with three other English Literature teachers in Karachi. I now remembered that one of them had once mentioned how much her students enjoy it when she reads aloud to them. So, I went to the library and checked out *Black Beauty* and began reading it aloud to my daughter and son. I was surprised to find that every night they became so engrossed in the story that they would beg me to continue reading. An otherwise slow read suddenly became exciting! Next, we read *Little House on the Prairie* together, followed by *The Lion, the Witch, and the Wardrobe*. Inevitably, I would not be able to complete the read aloud from cover to cover, leaving them to finish the last third of the book on their own.

Over the years, I saw a number of benefits of this strategy: suddenly, they started reading E.B. White, Roald Dahl, and C.S. Lewis on their own. My daughter never quite took to Enid Blyton but my son devoured her numerous series. She enjoyed books such as *What Katy Did*, *Ballet Shoes*, and a host of tales centred on horses and ponies. In addition, my daughter began reading with expression and would often be found reading things aloud with affectation. Watching her, I was thankful that I had successfully helped her overcome that particular obstacle.

More importantly, as an educator, I understood that the only way to navigate the divide between the books she wants to read and the books I want her to read is to read aloud to her. This realisation led me to think of the multitude of students I had taught who insisted that books are boring. Was this the answer to their disenchantment too? Besides, what does 'boring' mean anyway?

And, so, I began researching reading aloud. And, what I discovered astonished me. For instance, in 1985, the American Commission on Reading's report, *Becoming a Nation of Readers*, presented among its findings that 'the single most important activity for building the knowledge required for eventual success in reading is reading aloud to children.' The commission backed up its conclusion with research that indicated reading aloud in the home is an essential contributor to reading success, and that reading aloud in the classroom is 'a practice that should continue throughout the grades'. In other words, reading aloud is indispensable in the classroom, and not just in the early years when kids are learning how to read. After all, isn't that what happens? As soon as children start reading independently, parents expect them to sit silently and read. While there are some who can naturally climb the rungs from picture books to chapter books to novels, others get stuck on the way. The colourful illustrations start disappearing, replaced with longer and longer text, with very few sketches here and there. The child with her youthful exuberance might give it a try, but it seems to be taking greater effort, and isn't so much fun anymore as the simple, rhythmic text of picture books. And yet, parents and teachers alike, continue to drum louder and louder: Read, Read, Read! Books are our Friends! Readers are Leaders!

All the while, they are oblivious to the struggles the child is facing alone, until he gives up. His bright mind calculates that it's so much easier to play games on the computer, to sit back and watch television, to go out and play. Who needs books? They are boring, anyway. And, so, the books that have weathered decades' and centuries' worth of critical acclaim are cast aside and become blameworthy in her mind: something is wrong with the books which makes them 'boring'.

Somewhere between elementary school and middle school, we lose our potential readers. These could very well be readers who could go on to read not only thick page-turners but quality literature too, but the system fails them. Without the hand-holding necessary to guide them through, they become lost in the maze of reading, unable to recognise that what they term 'boring' is really the difficulty they are experiencing in mastering a certain skill.

Another piece of scholarly research that intrigued me was carried out by Betty Hart and Todd Risley at the University of Kansas. They published their findings as 'Meaningful Differences in the Everyday Experience of Young American Children.' Their study showed that a four-year-old American child born in a professional family will have heard 45 million words, a child from a working class family 26 million, and a welfare child only 13 million. While each will begin school at the same time, there will be a pronounced divide in learning. When you adapt this research to a bilingual city like Karachi where private education is pretentiously in English, then you can imagine a similar rift among children of families where both parents prefer to speak in English to their children, only one parent speaks English, or neither parents are fluent in conversational English. Hence, when these children begin school together, their familiarity with the English language will vary to the extent that teachers will have a greater burden to teach them the English language. Further, with parents not proficient in English, the responsibility for developing a love of reading will also fall on the shoulders of the teachers.

Until teachers accept this responsibility, and carry it out as the single most important activity ... throughout the grades, students will continue to blame books rather than understand that they are the ones struggling to traverse the increasingly challenging world of words. Unfortunately, in their race to complete the syllabus, teachers often neglect supplemental reading aloud or sustained silent reading in their classrooms and, as a result, are saddled with years of trivial lessons on grammar, comprehension, and vocabulary.

Perhaps the biggest obstacle to the successful teaching of English literature is the fact that English is the second or third language of the student or teacher and an overall linguistic weakness makes comprehending the text difficult. As a result, too much focus is devoted to grasping difficult vocabulary and dismantling paragraphs in an attempt to comprehend the literal meaning of the story, so much so that its intended message and deeper implications are neglected. In addition, students may be unfamiliar with the culture the story is set in, which makes it even harder for them to relate to the story. They often complain that the book is boring and the lessons drag on. In such circumstances, students get easily distracted and are unable to take any pleasure in the study of literature.

Language undoubtedly is a tremendous challenge. We demand our students excel in English even though many of them come from homes where the spoken language is the mother tongue. Just as schools have managed to overcome this conundrum by exposing students to the English language from an early age, students must be acquainted with literature from an early age. Reading aloud is a useful tool to achieve this creatively. When students are used to listening to entire books, they will not feel as intimidated by the task of reading an entire book for literature class. Their ears would be trained to the English language with varying sentence structures, an assortment of words, and multiplicity of expressions, making the act of reading easier. Their overall attitude towards books would be positive since they have already experienced the pleasures of reading through reading aloud.

Interestingly, in the absence of widespread literacy, Pakistan has historically had a vibrant tradition of oral story-telling. Throughout the history of the Subcontinent, poetry, literature, tradition, genealogy and history itself were transmitted orally. Values, morals and religious education was communicated through folklore and folk tales. People gathered in villages and town centres to be raptured by great poems of Bullah Shah and tragic folktales such as *Heer Ranjha* and *Sohni Mahiwal*. With the advent of modernity, oral story-telling took on a new form: radio broadcasts. 'The entire family would sit around this magical box', notes Samina Parvez, 'and avidly listen to their favourite programs, including dramas, music and radio shows ... Radio educated the people and played a pivotal role in shaping their minds. On the lighter side, it was a great entertainer too'. Listeners would be mesmerised by the stories of Saadat Hasan Manto and Sayeed Alam and plays of Bano Qudsia, Jamiluddin Aali, and Ashfaq Ahmed.

Even though literacy was common in the urban centres, books and libraries, unfortunately, were not. When my mother was growing up, this was a particular dilemma. People would loan books to one another for short periods of time – but how could so many members of a family read it so quickly? One person would read it aloud while everyone else sat around and listened attentively. Without knowing it, they were reviving the age-old tradition of oral storytelling, modified for their time and space. Poetry recitals, called *mushairas*, continue to be popular public and private events to this day in Pakistan and among the diaspora.

Today, the medium of instruction in Pakistan's private schools is English and the texts studied for English literature are widely from foreign cultures, Britain in particular. Not only does this pose problems with comprehension, it may also be a turn off for many students. However, by identifying commonalities between the culture depicted in the text and local culture and building on the students' existing knowledge, experiences, and ideas in order to inspire interest in the text, any cultural marginalisation may be minimised. Similarly, differences can be explored to help students engage with the narrative. Discussions that focus on textual themes inevitably have universal appeal.

To teach reading without thinking completely defeats the educative purpose: reading is a thinking activity. It involves the use of critical thinking (decoding words, phrases, sentences) and creative thinking (using imagination, empathy, problem solving). Fluent readers, having a mastery over words, can reason from language and extract contextual meaning whereas poor readers suffer from, what Robert Fisher calls, 'cognitive confusion': they regard reading simply as a process of decoding isolated words and focus on proper pronunciation. Hence, they 'may consider a passage of random words as easier to read than a coherent story'. As a result, poor readers are not able to fully apply thinking while reading to understand the text. On the other hand, good readers 'are actively engaged in a problem-solving activity, striving for "cognitive clarity" by seeking meaning from words'.

The question arises: how do we empower discouraged readers to become enthusiastic and fluent bibliophiles? The answer simply lies in supplemental reading aloud. Although some people may be naturally inclined towards reading, this does not mean that others cannot be taught a love of reading. In classrooms filled with students with different strengths and interests, reading aloud can help the linguistically weak student gain better comprehension skills while that scientific whiz kid, otherwise a non-reader, can learn to enjoy fiction. I decided to try this out in a classroom setting. To help young children transition from picture books to chapter books, I started going into second grade classrooms to read aloud Noddy books. Likewise, I visited a third grade classroom consistently for over a week and read aloud *Charlie and the Chocolate Factory* in its entirety to them. Most of the students were familiar with the story because they had watched the movie. As I continued reading the text to them, the students became increasingly captivated by the story, and would be visibly thrilled whenever I showed up. Their English teacher invited me back into the classroom a few months later to read aloud a chapter of their textbook (an abridged and accessible version of *Don Quixote*) because the kids missed me so much. Sometime later, I would be greeted by these youngsters, smiling broadly, waving enthusiastically. I didn't know their names, I only recognised some of their faces, but in their minds we were forever linked by the books we had delightfully enjoyed together.

Reading aloud truly empowers the teacher to impact each student in her classroom – not just in terms of developing a fondness for reading in her student context, but also in sowing the seeds for higher order thinking skills and reflection as a habit. Indeed, when children are exposed to consistent reading aloud, they are able to develop cognitively, with improvement in their fluency and reading habits. Students can listen on a higher language level than they can read, so reading aloud makes complex ideas more accessible to students and exposes them to vocabulary and language patterns that are not part of their everyday speech. This, in turn, helps young people to understand the structure of books when they read independently. We know that fluency in conversation, richness in vocabulary, depth in comprehension, creativity in composition, all stem from one single factor: reading. Instead of telling students to read, it's high time we show them the pleasures of reading.

My daughter recently started her college education; she has grown to become an avid reader, far exceeding me in her reading speed and enthusiasm. Due to the mastery she has gained over the years of the English language, she was able to seamlessly transition into an American high school once we returned to the States, and took Advanced Placement English Literature in her senior year. Her leisure reading skills – which taught her to comprehend text, extract meaning, improve her writing, and refine her cognition – have helped her in other humanities subjects too.

As I watch her confidently tackle *The Death of a Salesman*, *The Great Gatsby*, and *The Sun Also Rises*, among numerous other titles she has lately studied, I feel a heartwarming joy that I did not fail her. But, at the same time, I can't help but wonder: what if we could reach many other little girls and boys all over the world, those who are not particularly inclined towards reading for whatever reason, show them the wonders of books through reading aloud just for fun, and over time empower them to not only learn how to read, but *want* to read? In doing so, we can go beyond chasing educational outcomes and instil what books truly teach each and every one of us: emotional intelligence, universal values, reflection, tolerance, compassion and most importantly critical thinking. Thereby, hopefully, making the ultimate difference: contributing towards a more peaceful world.

HIJABI DATING

Ayisha Malik

'Terrorists don't wear vintage shoes.' At least not according to Sofia Khan, the heroine of my novel, *Sofia Khan is not Obliged*. Because she knows, just as well as the next person, that a terrorist would not be wearing a pair of teal, snakeskin, peep-toes. What else, after all, could she have said to the man on the tube, who quite dismissively presumed she spends her time Googling chemical formulas just because she wears a hijab? As a rule of thumb, it's a pretty basic assumption to make, but given the world's occurrences I think it's safe to assume that common sense isn't that common nowadays.

Sofia's a plucky, somewhat foul-mouthed, book publicist who's on her way to an important meeting and has been caught rather off-guard by Mr. Racist. This, as well as having broken off her engagement with her fiancé – who, by the way, wanted her to live with his parents and a hole-in-the-wall, and please, what year do you think this is? – distracts her from paying attention in her meeting (she's busy figuring out how to doodle a house with a hole-in-the-wall). So distracted in fact that she ends up being asked by her boss to write a Muslim dating book. You know, to expose the underworld of furtive hand-holding and chaperoned dates. Sofia reluctantly agrees and so begins the sequence of events that will unravel a contemporary love story, while also unravelling some home truths.

As a hijabi Muslim I've been asked some pretty weird questions in my time. For example: 'Do you have to wear your hijab in the shower as well?'

What's a girl to do? Eye-rolling isn't very Muslim and then you can't blame a person for asking. Anyway, the last thing you want is for people to think that you never wash your hair properly. I blame the media (it's always a safe bet). If they didn't bang on about how we're all bombing things, perhaps we wouldn't want to harp on about the fact that actually, some of us have very different past-times. For example, some of us like to write.

'Excellent! More diverse writers – that's what we need. Do you want to talk about forced marriages? The oppression of the hijab? Honour killings...that's a big one.'

Er...

'Can I just write about normal stuff?'

'Normal? What do you mean, normal?'

Apparently we don't have similar trials to our non-Muslim counterparts, such as: should I text him back now or in a few hours? Do these skinny jeans make my arse look fat? And sometimes, just sometimes: isn't this Brexit and Trump thing a nightmare? Of course we're all concerned about exposing the horrors of some practises that take place in the name of our religion and culture, but occasionally, it's not so much about saving the world as it is the small, everyday struggles of having to live in it. Or in the case of Sofia Khan, dating in it.

'Do Muslims date?'

'Erm, yes.'

'How?'

'With great bloody difficulty.'

'Is that because your parents have already chosen someone for you?'

Cue: attempt to stop your eyes from rolling.

'No. Because Muslim men are arseholes.'

That's not fair, of course. Only some of them are. (As are some Muslim women, obviously – though perhaps the ratio isn't quite 50:50). When you've had several conversations where your life is reduced to unimaginative assumptions to do with arranged or forced marriages it can become quite boring. But you can't blame the public for that (return to my earlier point about the media). So, when people ask what inspired me to write *Sofia Khan*, I tell them: life.

To be entirely truthful, writing the book was partly an act of catharsis because in life there are plenty of things that piss me off. It just so happened I was able to write about these things and then get paid to have them published. I'd tried to write novels before, giving up usually around the ten-thousand-word mark. Perhaps because I was so keen to reject the adage of writing what you know I ended up writing things which always felt a little hollow. I gave up. I decided to embrace the adage, along with the peaks and troughs of what it's like to date when you're a practicing

Muslim. How else was I meant to answer questions about why I choose to live the way I live? And not just by non-Muslims:

'Beta, why don't you get married now?'

'Well, Auntie number three-hundred-and-twenty-six, I'm trying, but it's not like it was in your day.'

Because we can all agree that when it comes to making a long term commitment the game has changed considerably. In fact, it's a new one entirely and everyone's a little sketchy on the rules.

The multi-faceted life of an everyday modern British Muslim is overlooked on such a gross scale — when considering how much more attention the not-so-everyday-British-Muslim gets — that I began to wonder whether people would be interested in reading about it. Because another thing I knew was that my experience, and those of countless other Muslim women — specifically the dating experience — wasn't available in literature. It's no secret that people who read a lot have a greater capacity for empathy and understanding. Studies confirm this. So does personal experience. After I read *Jane Eyre* I'd think twice about judging a person for the way they looked. *Wide Sargasso Sea* had me re-assessing the entire notion of the mad woman in the attic — she could be any one of us. (I, myself, am probably an attic short of being one.) *Little Women* taught me it was okay to be bookish and obscure. By the time I was in my twenties I was brimming with empathy (though perhaps still substantially lacking in understanding). I'd managed to find myself in life but still hadn't found myself, truly, in literature.

The beautiful thing about literature is it encompasses us all. The reader — wherever you're from and whatever you believe — is transported into a world where they become that protagonist and live a life through their emotionally turbulent glasses. The problem I found was that there just weren't enough characters like Sofia Khan in literature. You show me a Muslim hijabi in fiction and I'll show you a female jihadi who's gone to fight with ISIS. The great heroines from my literary life: Elizabeth Bennett, Bathsheba Everdene, Isabel Archer, Cassandra Mortmaine, and of course the eponymous and more contemporary Bridget Jones, always managed to be only almost completely relatable. The likes of Liz and Cass might get away with it, because, let's face it, we Muslims hadn't quite taken over the country at that time, but the heroines of Bridge's time should surely know better.

I have to confess here that I've had a life-long love affair with *Bridget Jones' Diary*. Bridget was a definitive icon: the modern British woman navigating her way through the concrete jungle in the pursuit of love, optimum weight and happiness. She juggled men, career, family and friends, and spent her days reconciling the emotional turmoil of being independent and yet wanting to get married and settle down. But here's the thing: she drank alcohol. A lot of it. And she had sex. She complained that she never had enough because she was always single, but Bridge, trust me, you were way ahead of the Muslim game. (Incidentally, no-one really talks about the fact that there are a growing number of Muslim men and women, unmarried in their thirties, and still abiding by the tenets of no sex before marriage. Not even a little sex. Like, phone sex. But perhaps that's another story.)

So, the familiarity of Bridge's dating tribulations always stopped short at worrying about whether or not to wear big pants on a date. I've never had an occasion for *genuinely tiny knickers*. Because as a practicing Muslim the only person seeing my genuinely tiny knickers would be me, and perhaps my mum when she accidentally walks into my room while I'm getting ready for said date. For we all know that dating in Muslim-land is a lot like dating back in the eighteenth century. Except strapping men don't come galloping on horses to court you anymore. There's no such thing as courting, in fact. There's a forty-five-minute journey on the Northern line and a coffee in Costa. Maybe a cookie if you're lucky. When was the last time you read about the heroine who had to sit in the house, waiting for a potential *rishta*, to serve samosas and chai to people she will never see, or want to see, again? Or when her friend is dating that white guy? Not to mention the black guy who she can't marry, because heaven knows that the darker the skin colour, the greater the evil. It's hard to come across these trials without them being linked to tales of oppression, or used as crass comic set-pieces without nuance to pander to pre-set ideas of what it is to be a second generation British Muslim; or, most significantly for me, without a woman rejecting her religious values in order to become the enlightened Westerner we should all aspire to be. Because God forbid a Muslim woman have an opinion, much less a choice in how she lives.

Enter Sofia Khan, created to subvert expectations and right all misperceived wrongs. Actually, Sofia as a character is quite wrong herself;

she smokes like a chimney, swears like a sailor and only stops short of drinking like a fish. Unless that drink is tea. She is Pakistani after all. For me, Sofia is the manifestation of your typical modern-day hijabi. She can be reduced to a certain type – robust in her opinions and her use of foul language – but is also unique, as indeed, wonder of all wonders, all hijabis are. (Goal number seven-hundred-and-ninety-eight: to scrap the idea that hijabis and their experiences are the same.) But she was also a vehicle to express the many, many frustrations that Muslim British women feel nowadays – whether that's do to with the dating pool (or lack thereof), or the perpetual misperceptions surrounding our everyday lives. Even more than that, she's the type of Muslim woman who will probably throw the samosa meant for a potential husband in his face, should he piss her off.

I wanted her to be the samosa-throwing type, along with the smoking and swearing type, because somehow hijabis become less human for virtue of a piece of material wrapped around their head. They inhabit a space that is either reserved on a pedestal or in a kitchen. Because they are holy they must also be homely. Or they are homely when they're at home, and not quite so holy when out of their parents' sight. The idea that they could be anything in between seems extravagant. Sofia's penchant for prayer and a cheeky fag might feel like a bit of a disconnect. In the grand scheme of things her misdemeanour is relatively quaint, yet at the same time, within the sphere of the Muslim community, quite outrageous. Not because she's a Muslim who smokes, but because she is a Muslim woman who smokes. There's a scene at the beginning of the novel where she's sitting in the garden with her dad who's puffing away, happily, on his cigarette. She sits, having to be satisfied with the second-hand nicotine being blown her way (a metaphor for her dating life, if ever there was one). There's the introspective acknowledgement of the double-standard in which a man is free to smoke whenever he wishes yet Sofia, at the age of thirty, must always do it behind closed doors. In so many ways, Sofia is on the cusp of change and becoming a grown woman, and yet she recognises there are hurdles to overcome in order to fully realise this evolved status. What has that got to do with dating, though? I'll come to that in a bit.

One thing Sofia refuses to change, however, is the fact that she wears a hijab. This piece of material is a point of contention throughout the novel, not least by her own mother who thinks it's going to stop Sofia from finding a husband – her hair, after all, is her one beauty (my not-so-subtle homage to *Little Women's* character, Jo). So, Sofia sighs and eye-rolls her way through her mum's constant jibes, while showing her work colleagues that not only does she have to put up with racist shit on the street, but similar kind of shit from her mother in the house. The idea that a woman might choose to wear a hijab when none of her family members do seems absurd, and yet it is not, by any means, an anomaly. But reconciling cigarettes and scarves isn't something Sofia struggles with, that's an issue for the people around her.

Except when it comes to dating. One of the love interests in the book gets out a cigarette on one of their dates and Sofia contemplates asking him for one, except she's wary of his judgement. Why? Because she likes him. The constant rearranging of virtues Muslim women still feel compelled to do in order not to be judged by their peers, or have potential husbands put-off by such outlandish behaviour is depressingly rampant. The accidental pursuit of love doesn't come easy, and weighing up just how much of one's true character you should be showing is all part and parcel of the dating game. It just so happens that in this balancing act Sofia shows that while we are free in many ways, there are limitations to this freedom. That limitation, apparently, is deciding whether to get the Marlboros out. You just have to ask yourself:

'What is the line between compromising and compromising oneself?'

It might not seem like a big deal – it's not as if smoking is something to be proud of – but look closely and that double-standard is just one of many that we're expected to accept, even when deciding on the biggest commitment in life.

Sofia's friends too have about ninety-nine relationship problems, but at least a hijab ain't one. There's Fozia who's with a man who refuses to commit because Foz is divorced and his parents don't approve; then there's Suj, her Sikh friend who's in a relationship with a black man and promises that the next time she sees him will be the last, because she doesn't want to be the reason her dad has a heart attack; and of course there's Hannah, the doctor who's inconveniently fallen in love with a married man (but that's okay because at least he's allowed more than one wife). It just goes to show that we're not all the same. It's easy to view Muslims as this homogenous group with the same ideals and notions – living parallel lives

— but Sofia's group of friends give (or should give) lie to this impression. Each scenario opens up its own issues, but of these perhaps polygamy is the most interesting. Why would an intelligent, educated woman, consign herself to such a fate? I've spoken to women who wouldn't rule out a polygamous marriage because, for those who are career-driven, it would allow them time to focus on their ambitions.

'Men can be demanding. I wouldn't need to shave every day.'

And then there's the tick-tock of the biological clock. If you can't find Mr. Right, Mr. Married will have to do. There is a flip-side to this, though — if it is a choice made by a woman who knows what she wants, then why should it be frowned upon? Hannah's friends throw each other surreptitious glances when it comes to her decision; they go along with it because, well, she seems happy, and isn't that the end-goal? In fact, the support network goes to show how royally buggered a person could be were it not for the friendships formed on the back of bad dates. No-one can deny the unique bonding experience of talking about the guy who says 'availabe' instead of 'available', or the one who can't be bothered to spell goodnight properly (Nyt Nyt. 'Lazy with words, lazy with life'). A few of the incidents in the book were gathered from friends and people I know, purely for entertainment value, but what transpired was that through all the dating pitfalls, even though quite a few tears have been shed, they've mostly been tears of laughter.

Speaking of tears, you couldn't possibly talk about Muslim dating and not talk about the parents. They're meant to be the model upon which we make our marital decisions. This might account for why so many of these decisions are messed up. I remember speaking to a friend's mum once — we have little heart-to-hearts now and again. She told me about her husband and how unsuitable they were for each other; she was the life of each party and he was an introvert; she loved to laugh and he always took a while to catch the joke. When he died though she felt the grief of his loss.

'There wasn't anything between us,' she said. 'But there was something.'

It was probably the most poignant thing I'd heard an Asian woman say about her husband. Forty-two years of marriage reduced to a vague feeling that didn't seem to have a word; something between love and a hard place. Sofia's parents are your typical, immigrant, disgruntled couple, living in a marriage of inconvenience. You never can tell if they love each other, and they often don't seem to like each other very much, but they do know each other. Their lives are made up of routine and familiar habits; its day-to-day running like a well-oiled marital machine. Sofia finds herself reflecting on her parents' marriage, as well as their expectations of her, while writing her book. I myself find it's difficult to date without observing the ebb and flow of the accusatory glances my mum might've thrown at my dad;

'You; you brought me to this country. I had to live with your damn mother and sisters and didn't manage to get a life until they decided that you had to choose between them or me. You chose me.'

In the end you come to realise that not all love stories are the same. Some end up happening years after the marriage takes place. Sofia's dad just happens to realise that you can't put a price on the woman who remembers when you need to take your medication. Even if sometimes you're not quite sure what that medication is.

While the above scenario might be familiar to many second-generation immigrants, Sofia recognises that being in a marriage which is a 'combination of resilience and resignation' should hardly be life's aim. What's the point in your parents having emigrated if it doesn't mean more options for you? Wasn't it all done for a better life? Better for who though? When Sofia's dad is taken ill her resolve to stay single rather than marry the wrong man begins to waver. How are you meant to stick to your guns when there are wires stuck to your dad's chest? I've seen a lot of people get married to please their parents – add a parent who might die any day now to the mix and you'll be sure to hear wedding bells. What is it about the potential ending of life that induces people to, metaphorically, end theirs? But then love is illogical, and when it is for the love of a parent, maybe it is that much more poignant.

Perhaps never more so when faced with questions about your sexuality. As the research for her book continues Sofia meets a man online. Abid is impossibly beautiful and, rather bewilderingly, interested in her. They exchange several emails before they decide to meet and when they do she's not quite sure what to make of the non-glitch of a date. How could something, and someone, so perfect be within reach? Of course, if it seems too good to be true, it usually is. She ends up bumping into him one evening outside Heaven. And not the afterlife kind. Abid wasn't used to remark on whether homosexuality is a sin in Islam or not. Rather it was to question the effect of our inability to talk about it in the community. Everyone is scampering around, looking to complete half their *deen*, while amongst them there are people who are living an incomplete truth.

The reception to *Sofia Khan is not Obliged* has been overwhelmingly positive. Most of the Muslim women who have contacted me have just been delighted to have a character in literature who finally reflects their daily experiences. The non-Muslim readers enjoyed an insight into another culture as well as the dating spectacle to which any woman could relate. Actually, a lot of men – one of whom is my editor and publisher – have enjoyed it because apparently it's funny. (I mean, not all men. One guy seemed a bit put-out in his Amazon review, telling me that I paint all Muslim men with the same negative brush – I wonder if I ever went on a date with him?) And of course there were the people who found it annoying. Ah, well, you can't win 'em all. But many people (especially non-Muslims) think that it's just the kind of thing that should be on television because finally, miracle of all miracles, we have a Muslim character who transcends the boundaries of religious identity. Who'd have thought that having a shared humanity would be such a novel idea; that a woman's Muslim-ness could become incidental and that she could appeal to the basic emotions we all have? It's probably why my publisher wanted me to write a sequel – *The Other Half of Happiness* – (because we're all adults here and know that finding a partner isn't the sum of all our dating parts, but just another variable to confuse matters).

Most importantly, though, when I was writing Sofia Khan, she was a symbol of hope – and one for Muslim women in particular – because it's no secret that the road to marriage, quite literally, is paved with man-holes. It is the hope that you don't have to negotiate your beliefs in order to find happiness and that, limited or not, there is always a choice in the decision you make. Short of that, you can always get the Marlboros out.

TWO BOOKS AND AN AUNTIE

Ziauddin Sardar

Most South Asian families have one. An Auntie Ji, who is not really a member of the family, but everyone's Auntie. On the Subcontinent, they serve as marriage brokers and go-betweens, and keep the neighbourhood well-oiled with gossip. Amongst the Asian diaspora in Britain, the universal Auntie Ji performed an additional function: she served as a local moral guardian who kept a beady eye on the young. During the 1960s and 1970s, when the British Muslim community was finding its feet and mosques were few, the neighbourhood Auntie was a powerful figure. She would visit the households of her district judiciously, dispensing religious and social advice, occasionally giving Qur'anic lessons to children, and serving, when necessary, as a marriage guidance councillor. The Auntie Ji of Clapton Pond in East London, where I grew up, was called Auntie Rashida. A tall, dark woman, she was, in the company of other women, an exceptionally graceful and tender person. But when it came to men, she was transformed, approaching with the menace of a tough, no nonsense matriarch. Men would tremble before her; and she treated them with unreserved contempt. Among my mother's friends, she had a reputation as a religious scholar, holding weekly religious classes for women in her house. Once a week she would visit all the households of the neighbourhood, taking tea and reading the riot act to deviating husbands and neglectful fathers.

My first encounter with Auntie Rashida was a memorable one. One night, on returning exhausted from a conference of Muslim students, I brought a young woman home. It was long past midnight; the lights were off and everyone was asleep by the time we reached the door of our flat. I had forgotten my key and so had to ring the doorbell. The sound reverberated around the tower block in which we lived and seemed to meet itself in unending echoes. We waited. The pregnant pause was interminable. A light went on, and my mother, affectionately known as 'Mumsey', opened the door wearing her white nightgown. I introduced my companion to Mumsey, my eyes fixed to the ground. Mumsey looked at me; Mumsey looked at her; Mumsey turned to me again. The complexion of her face slowly merged with the whiteness of the nightgown. Then she collapsed.

The following morning, I woke up late. My companion had already departed, but in her place another woman was awaiting me. Sitting next to Mumsey at the dining table was Auntie Rashida. The Inquisition had been summoned, the condemned man would not even receive tea, let alone a hearty last meal. In the ordeal to follow Auntie Rashida would be prosecutor, judge and jury, all rolled into one.

Auntie Rashida motioned for me to sit opposite her.

'It has come to my notice', she pronounced looking directly at me, 'that you ... Well, let's say, you have not exactly been following the Straight Path.'

'But Auntie Rashida, nothing happened,' I sputtered my innocence. 'She needed a place to stay for the night so I brought her here.'

'Do you know what the Islamic punishment for *zina* is?' she got straight to the point.

'*Zina*? What *zina*? How can you possibly accuse me of Adultery? At worst I am guilty of allowing a sister to rest her tired head upon my equally tired shoulders. What's wrong with that?'

'So you admit you touched her. That is only the beginning. What happened next?'

'Nothing. Nothing happened.'

'Islam considers *zina* not only as a great sin but also as an act that opens the gate for many other shameful acts, which destroy the basis of family life, which lead to quarrels and murders, which ruin reputations and property, and which spread physical and spiritual disease.' I could hear the rumbling roar of civilisation as we know it collapsing in rubble about me as she spoke.

'But Auntie Rashida, nothing happened.' I was shouting, 'Nothing happened'.

'Don't shout,' Auntie Rashida replied in her usual soft tone. 'I can hear you perfectly.' She allowed a silence for the dust to settle over the wreckage of departed civilisation before continuing. 'The punishment for *zina*,' she leaned forward, raised my chin with her index finger, and looked straight into my eyes, 'for someone like you who is not married is a hundred lashes and one year's exile from home. For a married person it is one hundred lashes followed by stoning to death.'

'What is the point of giving someone a hundred lashes if they are going to be stoned to death anyway?' I muttered miserably.

'The idea behind this punishment is not that it should be given but that it should serve as deterrent, like nuclear weapons: they are there as deterrent; they maintain the balance of power. No one in their right mind would want to use nuclear weapons. And no sensible judge would actually carry out the punishment for *zina*. Indeed, it is quite impossible to prove in a Shariah court as it requires the testimonies of four reliable and pious Muslim witnesses to be given at the same time. The witnesses must have seen the guilty persons actually committing the offence.'

'So how can you accuse me without any witnesses?'

'No one is accusing of anything.' Auntie Rashida was emphatic.

I breathed for the first time in what seemed an age of the world, breathed deep like a drowning man suddenly breaking the surface of the water.

Auntie Rashida had no need to pause for breath, she was borne along by Inquisitorial fervour. 'There are various degrees of *zina*. The Prophet, may he be blessed a thousand times, said: "The adultery of legs is walking towards a woman with unlawful intention; the adultery of the hand is touching and patting a woman that is not lawful to you; and the adultery of the eyes is casting passionate glances towards a woman."' Now she paused, gathering a mighty menace about herself, drawing in the full force of prosecutorial solemnity, exhaling the majesty of the law: 'Now, you did touch *this* woman, didn't you?'

I covered my face with my palms in shame.

There was quiet, the dull, heavy laden sepulchral quiet of doom. It seemed eons before the calm, austere voice of judgement reached across the dust-filled void. 'As a punishment, I want you to read this book.' Breaking the spell Auntie Rashida rummaged in her capacious hand bag. She withdrew a book, placed it on the table, and gently pushed it towards me.

I picked up the book and read aloud. '*Bihishti Zewar* – *The Jewels of Paradise* – a discussion, by section, of everything that women need to know about beliefs, legal points, ethics and social behaviour, child rearing, and so on. Complied by the Reverent Hazrat, Sun of the Scholars, Crown of the Learned, Maulana Hafiz Muhammad Ali Sahib.'

'But this book is for women', I commented perceptively. 'What good will it do me?'

'I was given this book on my wedding day. I entered my husband's home with the Holy Qur'an in one hand and the *Bihishti Zewar* in the other. It has helped me in my spiritual development. It will help you too, provided you read it diligently,' Auntie replied with a tart edge to her voice.

The reprieved man exulted in his freedom. The reprieved man gloried in his liberation from the rack of the Inquisitorial Matriarchate. The reprieved man nursed the wounds of trauma. He did not immediately read the book either.

But Auntie Rashida was not the kind of woman, prosecutor, judge, jury, executioner or Inquisitor to let her pronouncement go that easily. She would ask, during the suddenly more frequent visits to our home, how much of the book I had read. Justice delayed, they say, is justice denied. But justice diligently pursued, persistently harried, dedicatedly enforced by the Chinese water torture of matriarchal persistence with its soft but blatantly unsubtle repetition, let me tell you, is certain, inevitable, unavoidable, a force of nature none can resist nor evade. So *Bihishti Zewar*, also translated as *Perfecting Women,* it had to be. The final drip, which fell with the murderous power of a tidal wave and swept me to compliance, came when Auntie Rashida pointedly suggested I read the book aloud to my parents – 'after all', she rightly said, 'it is essentially an oral text, written to be read aloud, discussed openly, taught in groups.' Of a sudden, I began reading the book, to myself, as conspicuously and openly as I could during every waking moment, while performing every possible task and many that, in tandem, appeared humanly impossible.

Written at the beginning of the twentieth century, *Bihishti Zewar* is one of the most influential texts of twentieth-century Indian Muslim reform movements. It follows the classical Islamic model of *adab* – or etiquette – literature. Conventionally, such books, encyclopaedic in nature and known under the general rubric of 'Mirror for Princes', were written for kings and rulers; the best-known being Al-Ghazzali's *Book of Counsel for Kings*, written (although the authorship is disputed) by the famous twelfth-century philosopher and dealing with qualities required in kings, the character of viziers, 'the art of the pen' and the functions of secretaries. Many of these works, such as *The Qubus Nama* (*A Mirror for Princes*) by the eleventh-century Prince of Gurgan, Kai Ka'us ibn Iskander, also contain rules from everyday behaviour: how to speak, eat and sleep properly, how to 'take one's pleasure' with decorum, how to find a wife, marry and make love with due etiquette. Most such works begin with a statement by the author explaining himself and his reasons for writing the book. *Bihishti Zewar* begins with the statement: 'Here I, Ashraf Ali Thanawi Hanafi, contemptible and worthless as I am, declare my purpose in writing this work.' In Islamic parlance names, and the titles included in them, are a mode of communication. 'Ashraf Ali' is his real, given name. 'Thanawi' provides us with an indication of where the author comes from: when still in his mid-thirties he retired to a small rural town called Thana Bhawan in the United Provinces of India, where the book was actually written. His house became a magnet for visitors – the visits facilitated by a new railway line that passed through Thana (meaning police station) Bhawan. His faithful followers came to believe the train tracks had been laid down with the sole purpose of taking visitors to the learned scholar. By describing himself as 'contemptible and worthless', Thanawi displays, right at the beginning, the hallmark of traditional scholarship: humility. He does not use the title of 'Maulana', the conventional designation in the Indian Subcontinent for religious scholars; or 'Sheikh' the standard Arabic label for the learned members of the ulama. But he does describe himself as 'Hanafi', indicating his faithfulness to one of the five principal Schools of Islamic Law and the one that predominates in India; at the same time thereby dissociating himself from the rival school of reformist religious scholars, the Ahl-e Hadith, whose members reject the Schools of Law and adhere directly to the Qur'an and the traditions of the Prophet Muhammad. To read the author's opening is to be given an orientation, a route map with convenient markers of the territory contained in the following pages. What we are about to read, we have been told, is set firmly within a specific tradition.

There is another appellation Maulana Thanawi might have added: Deobandi. He was an alumni of the famous madrassa in Deoband, India. The Deoband movement emerged after the 1857 Indian revolt against

British imperialism. Many veterans of the uprising came to the conclusion the battle should now be fought through education. The old Islamic seminaries had all but disappeared, what was needed was a new school to revive the tradition of Islamic education and resistance. The idea of establishing a madrassa for teaching religious subjects was that of a well-known Sufi saint: Haji Muhammad Abid, who lived ninety miles northeast of Delhi, in Deoband, and was to be the honorary patron of the seminary. On April 14, 1866, when enough funding had been collected, Darul-Uloom (The House of Knowledge) Deoband was established under a pomegranate tree. The school attracted eminent teachers; many continuing their struggle against the British through warfare. Soon, Deoband acquired a reputation as a reformist institution that actively resisted British imperialism. Maulana Thanawi was from the second generation of Deobandi scholars – his anti-imperialist credentials were well established.

As I perused *Bihishti Zewar*, I found, immediately following his self-description, Maulana Thanawi's declaration of reasons for writing the book:

For many years, I watched the ruination of the religion of the women of India and was heartbroken because of it. I struggled to find a cure, worried because that ruin was not limited to religion but had spread beyond to everyday matters as well. It went beyond the women to their children and in many respects even had its effects on their husbands. To judge from the speed with which it progressed, it seemed that if reform did not come soon, the disease would be nearly incurable. Thus I was ever more concerned.

Thanks to divinely granted insight, experience, logic and learning, I realised that the cause of ruination is nothing other than women's ignorance of the religious sciences. This lack corrupts their beliefs, their deeds, their dealings with other people, their character, and the whole manner of their social life. Their faith is barely spared, for they speak many words and commit many deeds that verge on infidelity ... their faulty beliefs lead to faulty character, faulty character leads to faulty action, and faulty action to faulty dealings that are the roots of anxiety in our society.

This concern, I found, led Maulana Thanawi to produce an encyclopaedic, self-help manual for paradise. *Bihishti Zewar* contains almost all a traditional Muslim woman should know: from the alphabet to advice on letter writing; from how to talk, to how to walk and lay down; from hints for household work to the correct pronunciation of Urdu words; from the stories of Prophets and Saints to the fundamental beliefs of Islam; from customs deemed sinful to customs considered legitimate; from how to get married, have sex, bring up children, to how to behave properly. The book, full of quotations from the Qur'an and the traditions of the Prophet, is crammed with lists of dos and don'ts. Not surprisingly, a great deal of the advice found in *Bihishti Zewar* is of a universal nature and eminently sensible, such as:

Do not oppress anyone.

It is very bad to tease an animal or to beat a cat or a dog.

Act respectfully before your elders.

Treat those younger than you with love and affection.

Consider no one contemptible.

Regard yourself as less than everyone else.

It is a great sin to make fun of others.

Whatever you say, say the truth.

A great deal of the material is gleaned from the classic books of etiquette, such as Maulana Thanawi's advice on how to behave in company:

No one should sit in the place of a person who gets up from a gathering to do something and is expected to return. That place is hers by right.

Do not sit between two women who are deliberately sitting together in a gathering. Of course, there is no harm if they invite you to join them.

Do not act as if you are in charge of a gathering. Sit down whenever there is a space, just as the poor would do.

If you have to sneeze, cover your mouth with a cloth or with your hand, and sneeze quietly.

Stifle a yawn as best you can. If you cannot, at least cover your mouth.

Do not laugh loudly.

In a gathering, do not extend your feet in anyone's direction.

On the subject of how to eat and drink:

Say 'Bi'smi'llah' (In the name of God) before eating. Eat with your right hand. Eat from the side of the dish nearest you. If several kinds of things are served, such as several kinds of fruits or sweets, you may choose whatever you like and eat what your heart desires.

Take melon slices, dates, grapes, or sweets one at a time. Do not take two at a time.

When you eat something such as raw onions or garlic, rinse out your mouth to get rid of the smell if you are going to sit in company.

Be considerate of a guest. If you in turn are a guest, do not stay so long that you begin to burden your host.

And, on the subject of dealing with other people:

Do not squander the money God gives you. Refrain from spending money unless there is a genuine necessity.

People who are forced to sell their goods in distress should be considered people in need. Do not take advantage of them. Do not force them to lower their price. Either help them or buy their things at a suitable price.

Do not harass poor debtors. Either give them extra time or remit part or all of their debt.

It is wrong to refuse a request to repay a debt if you have the means to pay.

Much of this advice is freely mixed with Indian Muslim folklore: 'If you have a frightening dream, spit three times to the left and repeat three times: "I seek refuge in God from Satan, the Cursed," then turn over and mention the dream to no one. If someone is suspected of casting an evil eye wash her face, both arms up to the elbows, both feet, both knees, and her private parts. Collect the water and pour it over the head of the person afflicted, and, Almighty God Willing, that person will be cured.'

In proof that I was not only a reprieved man but one diligently observing his repentance by fulfilling the entire letter and spirit of his remedial punishment I once addressed my father according to the prescription in *Bihishti Zewar*: 'Respected father, sir, the *qibla* and Kaaba of your descendants, the object of service from your dependents, may your lofty shadow never vanish. After salutation with endless respects and exaltation, I beg to submit ...' It was not a success.

In similar vein, I found it easy, at the outset, to dismiss *Bihishti Zewar* as an archaic, conservative book; another formula for punctilious observance of prescribed duties taking its readers to paradise by numbers. But the more I read the more paradoxical it became. Gradually, it became clear to me this was not a traditional but a modernist text. Traditionally, women are not seen, addressed nor included in the mainstream of Islamic teaching; but *Bihishti Zewar* insists women should know what has traditionally been

TWO BOOKS AND AN AUNTIE

the preserve of men in mosques, courts, schools, and Sufi groups. There could be only one conclusion; that it was meant as an instrument of cultural transformation. Moreover, despite the fact it is clearly addressed to women, the teachings are aimed at all. The aim is to instil a reformist disposition based on moderation in all things, modesty in all aspects of life, and strict self-control in all spheres. The inscrutability of Auntie Rashida's judgement and her intransigent insistence that I read this book were starting to make sense.

At the end of *Bihishti Zewar* the learned Maulana thoughtfully provides a list of 'forbidden books'. It includes well-known texts such as the *Thousand and One Nights* and the *Tales of Amir Hamza*, and all books of poetry. When I came to this passage I recoiled. Historically, the Inquisition had led to the Index, the list of forbidden books, but it had never occurred to me Auntie Rashida might be that kind of Inquisition. I read the list over and over again, becoming more and more perplexed. Something, suddenly, was not at all right. Something did not fit, let alone make sense. Whatever worthy instruction I might gather along the way, how could Auntie Rashida have led me to this denouement? Was not Auntie Rashida herself a great devotee of Urdu poetry – as indeed were my parents? Did she herself not devour Urdu novels, including those on the forbidden list? Had I not seen many of these forbidden texts on Auntie Rashida's bookshelf? After her tidal wave of judicial urgings, it seemed, she was leaving me marooned amidst mixed messages, more perplexed than ever. What, exactly, was she trying to tell me?

The question intrigued me. More than that, it became an obsession. This most imperfect culmination to the perfection of women was a hellish problem I kept turning over in my mind in search of some resolution. Unable to satisfy myself, I determined to resort to intrigue. One day, when I knew Auntie Rashida was out addressing a women's meeting, I decided to visit her house. Her husband was home; indeed, he was always home – some strange illness had led him to give up his teaching job and confined him to a rather cushy armchair. I made some excuse, poured him a cup of tea, and began to browse the bookshelf. Yes: Auntie Rashida had been reading all those books Maulana Thanawi had explicitly forbidden. One in particular had been thumbed numerous times: page after page underlined, annotations in the margins, passages flanked by mathematical signs. I interpreted an $\sqrt{}$ sign to mean Aunty Rashida agreed with the passage; $\int$

indicated she was trying to integrate the passage with what she already knew; and Σ signified she was trying to summarise the arguments. What was the meaning of this calculus? Was this the key to explaining the nature of the judgement she had laid upon me. What I held in my hand was no instructional manual; it was a novel. I tucked the book under my jacket and slipped out of her house.

Mirat ul-Arus – *The Bride's Mirror* – is claimed by many to be the first Urdu novel; it was certainly the first Urdu bestseller. Published in 1869, almost half a century before *Bihishti Zewar*, it is the story of two sisters: Akbari (Big) and Asghari (Small). Akbari is bad tempered, uneducated, not very pious and in the final analysis a failure. Asghari is literate, competent, pious, patient and finally successful both in this life and the Hereafter; a fictional representation of the perfect women *Bihishti Zewar* aims to produce. It is, as its author Nazir Ahmad suggested, a syllabus, in the narrative form, for the instruction of women.

So why would Maulana Thanawi forbid *Mirat ul-Arus*?

Like Maulana Thanawi, Nazir Ahmad was deeply religious with a distinguished religious ancestry. He learned Arabic and Persian from his father and studied at the Aurangabadi Mosque in Delhi. Later, he attended the Delhi College to learn Urdu because his father had told him that 'he would rather see me die than learn English'. He joined the British colonial administration, probably causing much anguish to his father, became a deputy inspector of schools and went on to serve as Deputy Collector in the Revenue Service. Often referred to as 'Deputy' Nazir Ahmad, he also wrote what many considered to be one of the finest novels of Urdu literature: *Tabahtun Nisa* (*The Repentance of Women*), which is set in Delhi at a time when an epidemic of plague was raging. I read it, with great empathy, while studying for my Urdu 'O' level. Like a detective forensically piecing together the elements of a crime, I began to consider possible motives for the Maulana's disapproval of the Deputy. Clearly, it could have something to do with the fact he has seen Nazir Ahmad as colluding with the Christian English to the detriment of Muslim Indians. The fact Nazir Ahmad equated Islam with other religions would also have been problematic for the Maulana. His mockery of certain religious figures, like the Maulana himself, could not have helped matters either. But these reasons, in themselves, simply did not convince as sufficiently compelling motive for *Mirat ul-Arus* to end up on the forbidden list of *Bihishti Zewar*. Whatever their differences, both men reached the same conclusion and were allied in proposing that it was women who would eventually usher in Islamic reform: paradise, after all, as Prophet Muhammad said, lies under the feet of mothers.

Yet there is a crucial parting of the ways. Fitting the evidence together, I at last found the crux of the matter. For all that women were the means to true reform, the gatekeepers of paradise, it was the realm and sphere of their activity that so completely divided the two works. Maulana Thanawi was determined that women be confine within the walls of the family home; Nazir Ahmad wished to liberate them. Maulana's women are independent but docile, deferring to men; Ahmad's women are capable, dynamic and tower over the men in the novel. And this led on to the ultimate heresy, the idea that women could be better than men. Here was the clear anathema for Maulana Thanawi.

In Islam, Nazir Ahmad writes in the introduction to the novel, there is no distinction between men and women. Women have the same faculties as men and can become as learned and famous. Moreover, this is a seminal point in the structure of the message of Islam, one mouthed but seldom acknowledged, mouthed only to be significantly and emphatically neglected. The Qu'ran explicitly and repeatedly addresses itself to 'the believing men and the believing women', 'the believing women and the believing men'. This form of address is used whenever the Qu'ran commends a specific operative principle, an aspect of its moral and ethical framework to be enacted by the community. But, when we look at 'the common practice' we discover that 'no value is set upon women', as the Deputy wrote. Indeed, the practice is deeply entrenched: 'public opinion and the custom of the country have made a retired life behind the purdah obligatory and incumbent upon women, and in these days the observance of this institution is more rigid than ever,' he writes. His novel serves to elaborate and reflect upon the social consequences. Strict observance of religious ritual as conventionally understood becomes not merely a regimen, but in practice a prison; by the very act of following this routine of strict observance a pattern of life and thought is established that denies the very essence of the message. What was true in the time of the Deputy remains in force in many Muslim societies, continuing to be internalised as the 'real' ideal by those of a pious, observant persuasion. It is not only a matter of men believing women should be confined, even if they are to be educated in their confinement. The very worst of the matter is the millions upon millions of Muslim women, educated or un, who have internalised this idea, who observantly and scrupulously imprint this ideal on their children by indulging and pampering their sons, inculcating the double standards that are to last a lifetime, fostering the restrictions that confine the outlook, ambition and destiny of their daughters and ensuring this way of being passes down the generations as the ultimate recessive gene. How could the Deputy not be correct? The marginalisation of one half of the entire Muslim community more than halved the possibility of vibrant revitalisation. If the basic institution of the Muslim world, the family, was deformed by this engendered imbalance, then all other institutions would be affected: neighbourhood, community, society, nations as a whole were part of the ramifying chain reaction, distorted in its wake. The most educated, most observant, most pious women were the most punctilious in teaching their children the manners, morals and ethos of Islam in its gender truncated variant of limited female aspiration. To change the circumstances and mind-set of women, therefore, would be a fundamental shift. It would energise the remodelling of the entire fabric and structure of Muslim existence then, now or at any time in the future. Nazir Ahmed's pertinent question was, sadly, timeless: with the route to reform confined 'while living in purdah, how are you to acquire' the capacity to transcend your boundaries? He proposed the only possible answer, education; but not the kind of 'bad education' one finds in *Bihishti Zewar*. Instead, the Deputy's argument that women must seek real education suggests his preferred answer lies in the kind of education that promotes knowledge: women must seek learning. With that the Deputy is off a new trajectory: 'And now I am going to tell you an amusing story, which will show you what kind of troubles are brought about by a bad education.'

In the novel, the badly educated Akbari is a model of how to do everything wrong. Asghari is a much more rounded and complex character. She transforms her father and discreetly takes over the affairs of her father-in-law and brother-in-law while building the career of her husband, Muhammad Kamil. She encourages him to accept a modest apprenticeship at the courts then move to a slightly better post while looking out for a better one. God's will alone, she tells him, will not get him a better position: nothing can be gained without his own efforts. When he begins to meander from the path of virtue, she travels alone to a remote place, compels his bad companions to flee, and reshapes his life to her own virtuous specifications. In the conclusion of the novel, we discover Asghari has left quite a legacy behind: 'the things which she achieved under these conditions — for all that she was a woman — will no doubt remain in the world as memorials of her to the last day; but unfortunately I have not the leisure to set them down in writing'. But we know that she has left a mansion, a mosque, a caravanserai, and a number of charitable trusts in Delhi. Despite all this Asghari, in my view, is problematic: she cannot totally free herself from men, constantly consulting her father and her father-in-law. Nazir Ahmad too had his limitations — the nineteenth century world in which he was writing.

A few days after I had purloined *Mirat ul-Arus*, Auntie Rashida cornered me.

'Young man,' she said in her usual soft tone, 'when exactly did you decide to become a thief?'

'When I saw a copy of *Mirat ul-Arus* on your bookshelf.'

'Islam permits the theft of books,' she acknowledged with a smile.

'Why did you not give me *Mirat ul-Arus* straight away to read?' I asked.

'Because, without reading *Bihishti Zewar* you could not really appreciate *Mirat ul-Arus*. Both books are concerned with perfection and aim to reform Muslim societies. Both are problematic. But together they suggest the same sources can give rise to totally different ideas on reform.' Auntie Rashida paused. Her smile evaporated slowly and she became rather solemn. 'I am too set in my old ways,' she said. 'But we all look to young people like you to come up with more meaningful notions of reform.' She looked straight into my eyes. 'Now go out,' she said with some determination, 'and reinvent tradition'.

I have been following Auntie Rashida's orders ever since.

ARTS AND LETTERS

SHORT STORY: DRIFTING BARBS *by Muddasir Ramzan*
SIX POEMS *by Mohja Kahf*
TURKEY AND KASHMIR *by Perzada Salman*
PROBLEMS OF A BROWN GIRL *by Safeena Razzaq*

SHORT STORY

DRIFTING BARBS

Muddasir Ramzan

While relishing a cool evening walk in the countryside, Meehan and Aimer stopped at a clearing along the path, nestled between rice fields that lay dormant after harvesting. Children, who had created a make-shift playing pitch, were rushing towards garments, mostly *Pheran*, which they had taken off and collected to serve as wickets; some put them on, and some ran off clutching their retrieved clothes in their hands. The scene reminded Aimer of the days they too played cricket in their neighbourhood. All the family members would join in, even the elders, and their neighbours, too, would come and take part.

'Those were golden years. Why did we grow up?' Aimer sighed.

'Yes, life was good then.' Meehan too was lost in childhood memories. 'Worldly gloom is directly proportional to growth! The more you grow up the more you lose any taste of happiness.'

'That's right.' Aimer replied solemnly.

While they walked they remained engrossed in discussing their lives, oblivious to their surroundings.

'Have you ever thought what you'll do?' he continued.

'About what?'

'Getting a job?'

'Well, I'm realising it's not easy to get a government job. I had no idea it would be so difficult.'

'Yeah but Meehan, the next stage of life will start soon for us, just as soon as we get a job.'

'What – you mean getting married? Having children and working ourselves into the ground to provide for our family. Maybe after years of hard work we might save enough money to build our own house – miles away from parents and brothers. Great! And then we die. Our lives are mapped out for us whether we like it or not.'

'Life is nothing without a job here. Even girls won't give you a second look. You'll get offers from a good family only when you have a decent job.'

'Haha! Maybe; everyone is after money and good family status here. This money shit - earning money to barely live! Whoever created this concept of money needs hanging. Have you ever thought what it would be like if we were free from the concept of earning money?'

'Dream on... Life without money is not possible in this day and age. Come on, let's walk back home now.'

'I mean it. There's got to be a world that's beyond making money. I dream, therefore I live.'

There is triviality in their seriousness. The boys are not worldly but they still dare to dream, even though they hide their aspirations shyly. One tries to fly, the other is pragmatic.

Aimer put on his warmers' cap. 'Don't you feel cold? You can put your hands in your trouser pockets.'

'Ok, but I'm not thinking about the cold.'

'There is no one here today, maybe because it's such a chilly evening.'

'Yeah, see these trees? They were laden with fruits and leaves just a few days ago, and now they're bare. It's late anyway.'

'Hmm it is late; we shouldn't be here at this time.'

'What're you doing tomorrow?'

'Nothing, there's a strike tomorrow, remember?'

'Oh! The seasons change like our nation. One day it's peaceful and the next the blood of innocents paints it red. Winter is almost all year round. I wish we could do something for our 'azadi'!'

'Join the mujahideens if you're serious,' Aimer joked.

'No way. Why should I?!'

'Why talk of freedom then?'

'Is joining the freedom fighters the only way to liberate ourselves?'

'I don't know. We've never been tortured by the army. Why bother. We're good like this, what are our elders doing? See the rich people! Do they ever care about it? They only fool the poor... Do you hear the sound of footsteps?'

Both silently looked around but could see and hear nothing, only the whispers of the night.

'It's nothing, you fear too much. Put on some music.'

Meehan laughingly began singing along to the Bollywood song 'Soncha Hai' as they walked back home: '... *Duniya mein hai jang kyun, behta laal rang kyun, sarhadien hai kyun har kahin, soncha hai ye tum ne kya kabhi, soncha hai ki hai ye kya sabhi, soncha nahin tou soncho abhi.*'

'Why did you put it off?'

'Don't you see, someone is behind us ...?'

Looking back they saw uniformed men loaded with pouches and guns shouting at them to stop. In the dim light they froze, their eyes searching for any other civilians who could help them, but there was no one around. They were quickly surrounded by soldiers shouting angrily as if they had caught a couple of militants.

Suddenly the serene landscape became surreal and their confidence faltered.

'We are civilians, sir,' Meehan tried to assert, while glancing at Aimer to reassure him.

They are frisked. '*Saley* stand straight! Show your identity cards.'

Aimer hurriedly handed over his identity card but Meehan fumbled while searching his pockets... 'Shit! I forg... my wallet...'

They were then separated and questioned.

Meehan was marched to a nearby poplar tree where he was frisked again. All the while a gun pointed at him. Aimer was dragged over to where a soldier was sitting on a huge stone, behind some apple trees. In the darkness they lost sight of each other.

'I'm just a student. I live locally, in that town over there. Ask anyone who lives there. I was in a hurry leaving the house and forgot my identity card; we're just taking a walk.'

Other members of the military gradually faded away.

'*Lagta hai tujhe seeda karna padega*, you're working for militants?' barked the soldier questioning him.

'Sir I am telling you I'm a student.'

Half an hour later, Aimer and Meehan were brought to the same spot. They could hear the pounding of each other's heartbeats and begged to be released.

'Don't come this way again,' an officer yelled and told them to return directly to their homes.

They didn't give Aimer's identity card back to him and said the boys would have to return to the military camp tomorrow to collect it.

In silence they walked and, half-turning their heads every few steps, hastened home.

The road seemed too long as they stumbled, still terrified, over the long bushes and small trees in their path.

Aimer broke the silence: 'Thank God! They could have killed us in this lonely place. I told you to always carry your identity card. They would have had to let us go straight away if you'd had it!'

'If that would have been the case they would have freed you and questioned only me. They do this to everyone. Relax, ok. You should get your parents and elders to help you get back your ID.'

'No, don't mention this to anyone; I'll make a new one.'

'But why? If you want I'll speak to you parents.'

'No don't … don't tell anyone about this, I don't want any trouble for my family.'

'Ok. Hey, don't worry about your identity card. They've probably got loads that they've snatched from innocent people like us.'

'You know what that army man asked me "were you here to meet some girls"? I wanted to say yes but I stayed silent, he then asked me if he could find a girl here.'

'Now you can't say that we've never been tortured by the army. Relax, don't run like this, we're safe now. We'll be home in a few minutes.'

They tried to erase the fear from their faces as they entered their homes.

Meehan greeted Aimer's father, Uncle Kamal, who emerged from his house when Aimer walked in. Aimers' parents quietly considered Meehan to be far more sensible, brighter and with a more promising future than their own son and they were glad the two were friends. Abu Kamal greeted him back and asked Meehan to stay the night but he politely declined.

Just a few yards away Meehan entered his own home. His mother asked, as she always did, why he was home so late. As usual he answered, 'I was with friends'.

'Some men with long beards came looking for you.'

'Who were they?'

'I don't know. They were in hurry, they said they wanted to speak to you.'

'Maybe they're from the mosque.'

He sat down with his family to eat the evening meal. His father Ab. Faraz asked him, as he often did, about his future plans but without waiting for an answer he immediately started talking about other matters. This relatively new, strangely serious attitude was beginning to worry Meehan's parents. Without talking much to anyone he went to his room and started writing a list of life goals. He always made endless plans, trying to imagine what could come in the way of his dreams and how he may resolve these obstacles. Fear and logic seem unending when you're constantly living for the future. With so much going on around him it was proving more and more difficult not to feel the impact. That evening's incident was fresh in his mind.

His father had told him once that most of what is important to our lives happens in our absence. Meehan felt that his life was already caught in the web, a web not dissimilar to that of many other youngsters of his homeland. He was fiercely proud of being Kashmiri, but he realised too how disastrous it is to live with an identity that is interned. He thought back at all the significant events in his life, most of which were related to his family's circumstances. He wished dearly that he could lift his family out of financial difficulties but he recalled how helpless he was when his family needed support. They had been through bad times, but to survive one has to struggle. He spent hours lost in his thoughts, contemplating his future, preferring to remain alone with his dreams than confront his reality.

The next morning, Meehan woke up early. Because there was a strike he lay in bed, just messing about on his laptop. After a while he became restless and went to the window: outside he saw snow and with a joy he hadn't felt in a long time he ran outdoors. Flakes of snow whirled effortlessly before his eyes and settled in a thin soft layer on roofs, the tops of trees, and every surface around. It was the season's first snowfall and was earlier than expected and heavy. After lunch his father asked him to help in freeing tree branches and trunks from snow.

Soon Aimer joined them and after finishing the task, their hands were shivering with cold. They came indoors and Meehan's mother made some hot tea and brought them Kangris.

Eventually they were alone to talk.

'Is everything ok? You seem stressed,' asked Meehan.

'I fought with AB last night. You know yesterday, what happened, it shook me up. I just wanted to sleep and not think about it. When she called, I wasn't in the mood to talk. So I didn't answer but she then kept calling and when I answered she freaked out, and we had a massive fight.'

'Don't worry; she'll call you when she's calmed down.'

'I'm fed up with this relationship. I've had enough. She's changed. She's not the same girl I met at college, she's like a different person.'

'I don't know Aimer; you do what's right for you but it's better if you don't involve me.'

Meehan was wary of handcuffed relationships: he knew too well how words, if not used correctly, turn into venom, and the way in which misunderstandings always seem to rule. The constraints of social conformity were suffocating. Wherever he tried to search for understanding, instead people seemed to be clamouring to find offence. At a recent wedding, the elder brother of the bride became furious over his little brother's innocent remark, 'who are you to me?' he had shouted. He couldn't see his own faults, only those of others. How harshly he had spoken to the young boy. Words seemed to always be exploited to create misunderstanding, which grind us down and ruin our relationships. If only words could be used more cautiously.

From the window, he could still hear the noises of children excitedly playing in the snow, making snowmen, hurling snowballs at each other outside. He watched, mesmerised.

He turned to Aimer: 'Let's go out again. Wait a second while I grab my camera. I want to take photos of the kids playing in the snow.'

Aimer stood up: 'I'll go get my jacket.'

SIX POEMS

Mohja Kahf

Here It Is

Here it is Ramadan
and I forgot to pray
I can think only of you

Here it is iftar
and I forgot to eat
I'm banqueting on a joy
that's not on this table

Here it is nightfall
and I forgot to switch on the lights
There is a whole chandelier
brilliant in my ribcage

Here it is sunrise
and I've forgotten—
what is it

I am to do at dawn?
Oh yes: Slip away,
die,
and come back to life—
Here it is

delivery

i am driving down US40
toward the mail stop when
the radio says jews
were stoned by their former neighbours

in a german town the day
a concentration camp opened there &
they had to march
through the gated entrance.
former neighbours, how could they,
how? i turn
into the treeless strip
mall wondering if i am connected
to every place & time instead
of occupying
this lane only. in which i am
not german or jew but arab
american & enjoy
a recent model car & prowl
for parking space in asphalt
america. yet even now
i prowl hungry somewhere in the world,
filthy, & somewhere i am cruel.
bosnia or rwanda is it now or
syria these days. i pull
the hand brake up & cross
the parking lot & double
glass entry. how in every age
they tear my flesh
& i a child
of god. then i ground-ship
several packages for $11.49
& drive home never
having met the gaze
of another
human in the whole
delivery.

The Shining Genji

I don't know what I expected
The Shining Genji maybe, charming,
writing to me, poems on fine parchment,

teaching me twelve-kimono'd taste

Yes, I expected you on my horizon
Like a Prophet of God
Like a Wizard of Oz
To whisk me to wherever is Not Kansas

To seize me up, three times, perhaps,
and command me, "Read the Signs!"
I expected you any moment to arrive
filling my field of vision,

striding across the blue divide
I am always expecting you
and I expect you no less, no less
Now that you have died

The Pleasure That It Is

In Ramadan, we spoon,
innocent as children
We sleep with the door wide open,
hammocked in Ramadan-time,

its slow-ticking day, its blink-quick night
In Ramadan, we know that this,
your hand under my breast, the splay
of legs, the parted lips,

is not a prelude to anything:
It is the pleasure that it is—
another one of Ramadan's
shy unbounded gifts

Ramadan S&M

Coffeeless and sleep-deprived, I stagger
into the first day with my face
tripping over my shoes

Ramadan, why you do me this way?
On the second day, I'm haggard
and horny and bad-breathed,
needing a drag, and a drink,
a boot leather taste in my mouth
Ramadan, what I ever do to you?
The body whines its need:
If I can't have bread and sex and chocolate,
let me at least have sleep
But even against that refuge,
Ramadan raises its whip
Hour after hour on the rack of Ramadan,
day after captive day,
the appetite is dulled
down to its last whimper
The wooden will goes limp,

and discovers the resolve that lives
under its surface whims
Ramadan, you sado-masochistic
driver, don't make me love you
in the final stretch,
in my triumph of Self
mastery

All in Good Dying

'*People are asleep; when they die, they wake.*' – Prophet Muhammad

I can see dying young,
cocksure, laughing,
sweaty and slick between the thighs
I can see dying old,
steady and bemused,
unfazed by Azrael,
his large muscular wings
folding heavily over me
I can see dying for a cause,
Syrians sniped in the street for protesting,

SIX POEMS

Rachel Corrie under a bulldozer,
trying to save a Palestinian home,
a Chinaman on Tiananmen Square,
an American on Normandy Beach,
his weapon clutched tightly to his chest

I can see dying without a cause:
Virginia Woolf, pocket full of rocks,
stepping into the stream of liquefied consciousness,
Carolien Heilbrun in her armchair
calmly choosing her time to go,
people who party in a hurricane,
secret sufis longing to be overwhelmed
by something greater than their selves

I can see dying from slow disease, in pain for months,
like Edward Said, seeing it coming,
with time to make goodbyes, arrange affairs,
the liberating knowledge of my imminent mortality
allowing me to do exactly what I need to do
I can see dying unexpectedly
in mid-street or mid-air
with no warning to loved ones,
no way to prepare

I can see dying clearly,
its luminous eyes,
its face like a nun's
uplifted, full of serenity,
its promise of final knowledge

Dying, I could be all women, fuck a thousand men
from Solomon to Bogey
There would be no sordidness to it
or messy moral issues, because – well, I'd be dead

Dying, I could be in many places at once
instead of having to fly in a steel box for fourteen hours,
my shoulders pressed against my seatback

with my front neighbor's head nearly in my lap
Like the Starship Enterprise Transporter,
dying would know all the blackhole backroads
through the time-space continuum
I could materialize in Syria,
my ancestral fascist homeland,
without having to pass through border police
Dying transcends politics, especially fascist politics

Dying is smelling the fajitas sizzling
on the hotplate of an amoeba family
living in the lining of my stomach cilia,
being able to open the ninety percent of the brain
that humans don't use, perceiving,
at last, worlds within worlds

Dying is understanding in a flash the enemy
you fought against all your life
Dying is discovering in one burst of insight that all this,
our busy lives, this whole important cosmos,
is a mote on the tip of the eyelash
of a sentient being shaped approximately like the rings of Saturn,
a mote she flicks off with a careless movement
in her last moments of REM sleep before waking for dinner
with other Saturnine sentient giants

All this is illusion; the only real
is what we think illusion:
the hunger that a certain music makes us feel,
the half-formed poetries that flicker through us waking,
the calling out in love to other beings
whom we imagine that we know

Dying is living here and there,
bits of me, little pods I let loose
stuck in my daughter's hair,
a poem under some shrubs I let grow wild,
the tiger lilies I planted getting thicker

SIX POEMS

Dying, I wouldn't have to try so hard
to not run out screaming "I can't take it anymore,"
this being cut into a thousand living pieces,
consciousness chopped and tossed into history,
into wars, on opposite sides, limbs splayed across continents
like livers and spleens flopped on a chopping board,
squirming inch by inch to draw themselves together
into one sewn-up mattress flesh of a human being,
into the single unit of self we are allotted

Dying, I could be all things at once

Dying, I could be nothing
and what a relief that would be,
to lie on the beach being Nothing,
being vacuumed up into the Universe's Navel:

Whoosh

Hello, dying
You are beautiful
Always be with me

TURKEY AND KASHMIR

Perzada Salman

Turkey – 1

I'm Europe with a sense of deprivation
I'm white
But not quite
I will look back as far as I can
I will look back till my eyes begin to bleed
Indeed
Because I'm Europe with a sense of deprivation
I'm white
But not quite

Turkey – 2

Pasha – ambitious, short-sighted
Pasha – poor, poor Pasha
Like a hopeless romantic
Did not think it through
What he could or could not do
Paradise found was paradise lost
For all those who accost,
Fire, just fire, not desire –
Ire, ire, ire

Kashmir goes blind – 1

I can still see, mother
I can

I can still be, mother
I can
They don't know
I have your eyes
Big, blue, beautiful
Like Dal*
I can still see, mother
I can
I can still be me, mother
I can

Why do you ruin your eyes?
Big, blue, beautiful
Let's stand by the window
The breeze is green
The mountains, azure
The bonfire, red
No one's dead
See, I can still see, mother
I can

(*Dal Lake)

Kashmir goes blind – 2

The man said,
"Look into my eyes,
I'm dead behind them."
The valley replied,
"Death had left your eyes,
A long, long time ago."

Kashmir goes blind – 3

Eyes
Red, swollen

Like a morphed Kafkan image

Eyes
Gunk-laden, moist
Like Manto's clean woman

Eyes
Questioning, flummoxed
Like a bleeding Ghalib couplet
Eyes

PROBLEMS OF A BROWN GIRL

Safeena Razzaq

There are moments when someone relates an anecdote from their younger years and it feels as if they had a window into your childhood! The embarrassment or discomfort of that moment comes flooding back, capturing a memory that could have been from many years ago. Edinburgh-based artist Safeena Razzaq captures exactly those emotions except instead of words she expresses such toe-curling, hilarious, and often infuriating moments through illustrations. Growing up as a Muslim girl in Britain, she knows exactly what it's like to be the only brown girl in the village. She's fielded all the ridiculous questions about faith and tradition you can imagine. 'Do Muslim women take their hijab off when they go to sleep?' 'You really fast for thirty days – how can you still be alive?' She brings to life the tactless and prurient questions of nosey relatives who seem to live their lives delighting in gossip and scandal-mongering about extended (usually female) family members: 'Aunty Anjum told me she saw you talking to a boy at the bus stop this morning'. And heaven help a Muslim brown girl if she smiles while texting in full view of her parents: 'who are you texting? A boy? No? What's so funny then? You better not be doing any of that sexting mexting!'

Although she specialises in printmaking, it is Razzaq's illustrations that fulfil her desire to create art that tackles social and political issues. Creating awareness through wry humour has proven a disarming and subtle way to confront difficult or awkward situations. The inspiration for her work comes from personal experiences and incidents that many Muslim women will undoubtedly relate to. She uses her sketches to reflect on and contemplate aspects of her own journey, navigating cultural confusion and her struggle to locate her identity and feel empowered both as an individual and as a brown Muslim woman within our patriarchal global construct. Her imagery draws on sensitive and controversial aspects of Muslim family life in the UK although she could be a woman in any context who seeks to subvert the generational norms that seemingly confine her. Her 'Brown Girl Problems' series will resonate with many second and third generation women whose origins lie in the Indian subcontinent. But, as well as making us laugh, we can all relate to the message in her illustrations: the universal quest to look within ourselves and find the light of our own being. www.safeenarazzaq.com

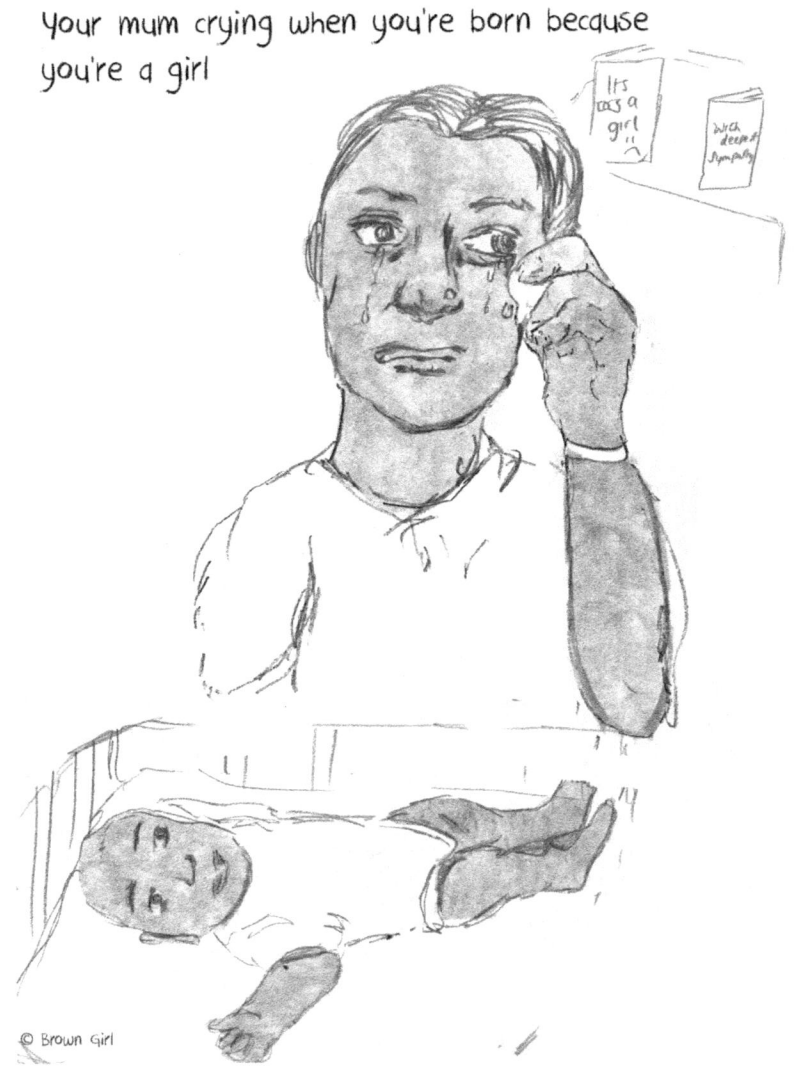

PROBLEMS OF A BROWN GIRL

Thinking you look rock n roll when you get your nose pierced but really you just look more asian...

© Brown Girl

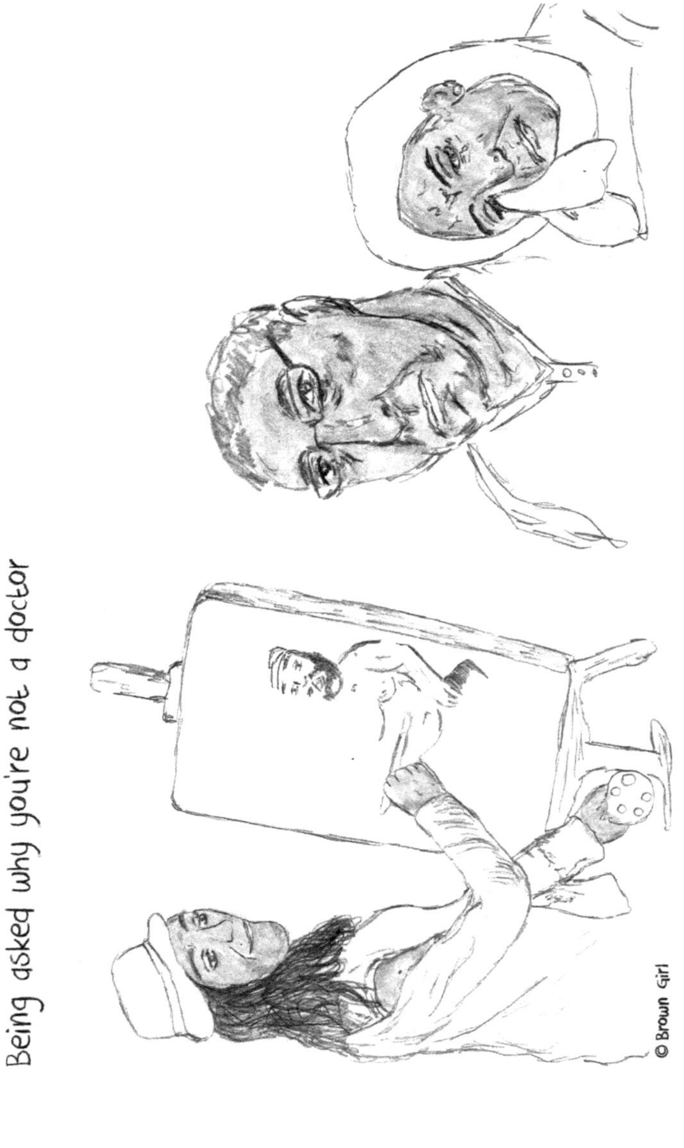
Being asked why you're not a doctor
© Brown Girl

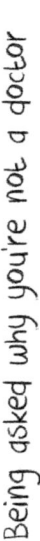

PROBLEMS OF A BROWN GIRL

Having to lead a double life.

What my parents think I do...

What I actually do...

© Brown Girl

Not being able to walk with a guy without asian people talking and telling your mum he is your white boyfriend.

PROBLEMS OF A BROWN GIRL

REVIEWS

HIJABISTAS *by Nadiah Ghani*
SOVIET TERROR *by Aysha Garaeva*
SELF-REFLECTIONS *by Hannah Kershaw*
HOLY IGNORANCE! *by Hassan Mahamdallie*

HIJABISTAS

Nadiah Ghani

Growing up in Muslim-majority Malaysia, I became accustomed to battling with the identity I chose to uphold – that of the unveiled Muslim woman. There is a local term coined especially for us unveiled girls: 'freehair'. It is a label to stigmatise and differentiate us from the veiled girls. Being a 'freehair' girl, I have also had my fair share of feeling displaced in a community that can be uprightly religious depending on occasion and location. Born and bred in the city, I was encouraged but never forced to don the hijab or dress like a 'proper' Muslim by my religious yet fairly moderate parents. But because of my 'freehair' identity, I had an especially difficult time in public schools and colleges, where the hijab was never quite made compulsory for Muslim women but there existed an unspoken rule that, somehow, you had to cover your hair or risk becoming a pariah.

Thus began my initiation into being coerced to don the hijab when I entered public secondary school, and later, public university. To describe my experience as a nightmare would not be an exaggeration. Islamic Studies, a subject made compulsory for all Muslim students, was not my most hated subject, but undoubtedly my least favourite. That disinclination, however, did not stop me from excelling, consistently scoring A's that put me on par with my veiled sisters, if not better, and trumping the stereotype that 'freehair' girls possess only a shallow knowledge of Islam. It was still my least favourite subject because of my *ustazah*'s glaring eyes on the first day of class and her outright snarky comments addressed to the 'freehair' girls. This was to be followed by a sermon right after, about 'the women of hellfire' – that we would be hung by our scalps in damnation, never to get even a whiff of Paradise. When that did not work, I remember being pulled aside by other *ustazahs* in hallways and corridors (we did not have an *ustaz* or male religious instructor though I'm curious as to how a man's approach would have been). I remember the awkward, deafening silence that greeted me whenever I entered a classroom, the unkind, judgmental stares by eyes that followed my every movement. I remember not looking forward to school, my fear of bumping into any *ustazahs*, and most importantly, I remember my tears of despair. In the end, I did cover up for much of my schooling years because the pressure was too much for a teenager to bear and also because I was beginning to be ostracised by my peers. Unfortunately, even after donning the headscarf, the way I dressed became a point of scrutiny – my trousers were too tight, my sleeves not long enough, and my tops too suggestive of my curves. From then on, I have struggled and skirted around the issue of dressing like a 'proper' Muslim.

Relatives were, and still are, somewhat subtle in their attitudes and demeanour towards my unveiled self. My parents never demanded I veil. However, I doubt that a day has gone by that my mom and my grandmothers have not prayed to God to bestow me with *hidayah* (guidance) so that I might one day wake up and reach for a scarf. This, along with the inevitable and always expected comments of, 'You look so much prettier all covered up' on those religious occasions that require me to don the headscarf. Mostly, my family remain subtle in their indignation, likely believing that it is up to my parents to reel me in, and, because I am unmarried, it is therefore my parents' sins to bear. But not everyone manages to keep their thoughts to themselves. Coming from a large extended family mainly comprising girls, I was unaware that anyone was keeping track, or doing a countdown along the lines of *And Then There Were None* when it came to the number of unveiled girls in our family. It was when my cousin veiled up after marriage that an aunt pointedly said to me, 'And now we have one!' Her remark cemented my position as the black sheep among my rather conservative relations.

Reina Lewis, *Muslim Fashion: Contemporary Style Cultures*, Duke University Press, Durham, NC, 2015

When I obtained a scholarship to pursue my PhD in the UK, I jumped at the opportunity to escape the suffocating atmosphere back home. In fact, as bad as it sounds to admit this, part of me looked forward to not identifying with my Muslim identity and blending in into what I imagined as the secularism of the West. Amidst my excitement a friend even advised that perhaps it would be best not to announce to people I meet that I am Muslim. I had almost zero idea what England, and the rest of the West would be like for me as a Southeast Asian Muslim woman. My experience of leaving the motherland had only been within the confines of Southeast Asia. However, when I was told not to announce my Muslim identity to the world, I became conflicted. On one hand, I was more than happy to not be judged for my (non-) religious appearance. Yet at the same time, despite not having the stereotypical appearance of a Muslim woman, I am still very much a practising Muslim and have never felt ashamed or afraid to announce my beliefs to the world. It inadvertently opened up my eyes and warned me that I was about to leave the cocoon of my 'safe' Muslim-majority country.

When I set foot in London, I was pleasantly surprised to see Muslim women and men everywhere, going freely about their daily lives. My previous fears about London had been misplaced and unjustified. Of course, things look less rosy through my rose-tinted glasses as reality sets in with the passage of time and particularly since the EU Referendum, but I am definitely not wrong to think that London is a city that celebrates multiculturalism and multi-religious beliefs. On the streets, Muslims dress vibrantly in the fashions of the Middle East, South Asia, Africa and even Southeast Asia. What is even more interesting is the distinctive hybridity of British Muslim fashion that has come to prominence as a result of the growing Muslim demographic.

Many of my own early misconceptions about Muslim fashion have now evaporated. I admit that I once equated Muslim fashion with religious dogma. As more and more Malaysian Muslim women start donning hijab and experimenting with modest fashion and countless ways of veiling, I eventually learnt the new hipster term *hijabista*. I witnessed the growth of Malaysian celebrities donning the veil and reinventing themselves as *hijabistas*, not to mention the immensely popular hijabi lifestyle icons who dominate social networks like Facebook and Instagram. Similarly, in the West, modest fashion that was almost unheard of a decade ago has been estimated by Thomson Reuters to be worth $224 billion globally in 2012 and is projected to grow to $322 billion by 2018 – in itself larger than the combined clothing markets of the UK at $107 billion and Germany, $99 billion. It is hardly surprising then to see major fashion companies in Europe competing to fill the gap in Muslim fashion. With Londoner Mariah Idrissi becoming H&M's first Muslim model in a hijab in the international brand's 'Close the Loop' video campaign, the buzz over Muslim fashion in Europe is at an all-time high.

All this make Reina Lewis' *Muslim Fashion: Contemporary Style Cultures* a timely and much needed analysis. Lewis is Professor of Cultural Studies at the London College of Fashion, University of the Arts London. She spent the last ten years researching Muslim fashion and other faith-related modest fashion. This project is documented in her exploration of print media, online networks, designers and consumers. In 2013, Lewis edited *Modest Fashion: Styling Bodies, Mediating Faith,* which explored modest fashion in peoples of diverse faith. *Muslim Fashion* focuses solely on modest dressing in the Muslim world, exploring the various contemporary factors that shape Muslim style within Western modernity, particularly in Britain, Western Europe, North America as well as Turkey. She approaches the tropes of Muslim attire from the perspective of fashion as opposed to a dogma; and showcases how Muslim designers, bloggers, magazine editors, entrepreneurs, store assistants and shop owners are rewriting the fashion narrative for Muslim women. She moves back and forth between Islamist politics, fashion history, the structural logic of fashion magazines, conventional modes of Islamic knowledge production and transmission, and case studies involving garments, images, media, people and spaces as well as other theoretical approaches. The end result is an expansive scholarly output that does not merely describe an emerging lucrative niche market, but also historicises, theorises and analyses the development of Muslim fashion in Britain.

At the beginning of the book, Lewis makes clear that she is not a Muslim, enabling her to 'eliminate the nuances of spiritual and political judgment often faced by coreligionist researchers'. Her non-religious observation fuels *Muslim Fashion* as an intellectual enquiry rather than a benchmark of orthodox, heterodox, correct or authentic Muslim affiliations of practices. Unsurprisingly, validating hijabi fashion as an 'object of intellectual enquiry' soothed the reservations of her respondents – Muslim women who were not just about promoting their brands, blogs or magazines, but rather more keen to contribute positive information about themselves as Muslims.

Lewis positions the book by stating that its strapline could have been 'Muslim fashion: underrepresented in the style media, overrepresented in the news media'. She puts faith and fashion in the same frame, with shopping, fashion and veiling as indicators of Islamic modernity and commercialism. Through this she sets out to challenge mainstream media's stereotypical images of Muslim women shrouded in black as well as the overuse of images of veiled women as resisting or being incompatible with Western modernity. In treating hijab and other Muslim modest clothing as fashion, the central idea of the book is that 'Muslim fashion needs to be taken seriously as fashion', and hence, instead of focusing on the oft-studied issues of alienation and extremism among young Muslim men, she seeks to place emphasis on young Muslim women in 'their engagement with mainstream fashion to communicate their ideas and aspirations about modern Muslim identities to coreligionists and to majority non-Muslim observers alike'. For that alone, her work is remarkable in proving that a discussion on Islam does not need to become stuck on stereotypes of violence and radicalism.

Particularly engaging is Lewis' discussion of emerging contemporary modest fashion as the by-product of 'youth subculture'. Young women are revealed to be part of an emergent and hybrid cross-faith transnational subculture of modest fashion appropriating and transforming commodities from multiple intersecting fashion scenes. This would explain the high visibility of young British women clad in the latest lines from popular retailers such as Primark and Topshop while incorporating hijab fashion to declare their faith. They symbolise a collaboration of collective religious and national heritage, all the while trouncing the stereotype that Muslims are incapable of fitting into the British body politic. As an immediately visible symbol of religious dress, the hijab is seen as an assertion of religious identity in much of the non-Muslim majority world. Unsurprisingly, Muslim women are prime targets in public debates, with their actual or presumed dress practices becoming a flashpoint of controversy. Their ability to fit in with the rest of the Western modernity is fetishised and they play involuntarily central roles in deliberations over citizenship and national belonging.

As informative and exquisitely researched as the historical, geographical and theoretical context of the book is, the later chapters captivated me completely. Literature review and theoretical framework comprise the bulk of the data analysis, offering personal narratives and anecdotes from case studies that the reader is able to relate to and engage with. The chapter, 'Muslim Lifestyle Magazines: a New Mediascape' lays bare the conflicting demons of the mainstream and minority fashion industries. Here, Lewis compares the pressure faced by Muslim lifestyle media with the development of lesbian, gay, bisexual, transgender and queer (LGBTQ) lifestyle media that emerged in the early 1990s. In an almost barren minority publications scene, reader expectations are at an all-time high, relentlessly seeking affirmation and points of identification unavailable from mainstream media. The appeal, however, serves as a double-edged sword, with conflicting demands from readers making minority lifestyle media the hardest and most contentious to produce. Her exploration of how hijabis and modest fashion designers utilised digital and communication technology to create new understandings of modest fashion is equally fascinating. It is an ode to Muslim women and their DIY success in using social media and the blogosphere, without conglomerate or corporate funding. This success, coming from a group frequently portrayed as defenceless, powerless and unable to fit into a wider secular society, makes it even more poignant and inspiring.

Lewis also offers qualitative accounts of Muslim employment experiences in British high street stores and the participation of Muslims in the British fashion industry. The young women featured in the case studies shatter stereotypes of ethnic minority Muslim women being largely unemployed. Instead, they are fluent in English and with a voracious appetite for the latest trends in British fashion. What's more, many work part-time in the retail industry while studying at university, or saving up to do so. The job often turns out to be the beginning of a career in retail buying. The girls act as 'unofficial' brand ambassadors, especially to other hijabis and bridge high street sensibility with ethno-religious sociality. The decision by Lewis to refer to 'Muslim' and 'Muslim modest fashion' as opposed to value-laden 'Islamic fashion' as well as the inclusion of the category of 'modest fashion' is laudable and demonstrates her insight into faith and fashion. It is also consistent with the book's objective not to arbitrate on what is 'correct' Muslim fashion. Hence, despite the book's cover depicting two very stylish hijabis, which may or may not give the vibe of advocating hijab as 'proper' Muslim attire, the concept of choice is prevalent, highlighting that for these young women, understandings of religious identity are voluntarily achieved rather than ascribed or prescribed.

Of course, the choice also includes taking the veil off. And Lewis gives some weight to the sensitive issue of de-veiling to redraw the boundaries of modest presentations. So, for unveiled women like myself, it is heartening to read that there is an audience for Muslim modesty and Muslim identity that is not underwritten by the hijab. A half-century after Islamic revivalist movements began touting the hijab as the pinnacle of Muslim piety, removing the veil is now an alternative marker of religious engagement for a new generation of women. Many contemporary dejabis (hijabis who removed their veils) chronicle their journey of de-veiling as 'a form of pious practice' and to stop wearing hijab is to commit to a version of Islam as a religion that, 'aside from its essential core, is about interpretational diversity'. Nevertheless, the act of de-veiling will inevitably get negative attention on dejabis, as attested by former hijabi/current dejabi blogger Winnie Detwa when she went public with her de-veiling. Detwa's switch required her followers to 'expand their definition of hijab and modest fashion to include her new bare-headed presentation'. Despite the initial backlash from the Muslim community, Detwa's continuing popularity sheds light on the availability of an audience for an alternative version of Muslim modesty.

Stemming from the negativity surrounding dejabis and the belief that the hijab is the 'litmus test' of being a 'true Muslim', Lewis's conclusion in *Muslim Fashion* deeply resonates with me and I expect many others. The Muslim fashion industry has come a long way from being almost invisible and non-existent a decade ago. Muslim fashion blogs started by Muslim women for Muslim women, spurred by the unavailability of fashion guidance and products for those who wanted to be stylish, fashionable and religiously observant, have proliferated. The field of hijabi fashion has grown so exponentially that hijabi dressers are increasingly able to see their styles validated and accepted as a daily religious practice.

Yet, there is an irony here, particularly for someone like me. The hyper-visibility of veiled women means that the unveiled or de-veiled women have now become near-invisible and under-investigated. The more exponential the growth of modest or Muslim fashion becomes, the more invisible unveiled girls like myself will be as we do not fit into the 'marketable' Muslim image. This was exactly how I felt in all the years I existed as an unveiled Muslim in Malaysia. We remain outliers, outsiders, non-visible, yet still very much Muslim at heart.

SOVIET TERROR

Aysha Garaeva

The 1930s were marked by tragedies that to this day strike terror and grief in the hearts of descendants of those few who lived to tell their tale. Political repression, collectivisation, dispossession and forced relocation to Siberia was the norm. 'Death journeys' were the cruel destiny for millions of residents of the multinational country called USSR. Images of mothers holding their dying babies, dead bodies thrown into rivers, hungry and wretched elderly people and children continue to haunt. There are not enough pencils to fill enough sheets of paper with enough adequate words to describe the horror of these times. Those who survived the hell would come together to meet on the banks of the Angara river. Peasants and Leningrad intellectuals, declassed people and criminals, Muslims and Christians, pagans and atheists, Russians, Tatars, Germans, Chuvash - congregate on the banks of the Angara daily, struggling to defend their right to live in the harsh conditions of taiga.

The trauma of dispossession did not spare my ancestors, who at the time were peasants in Georgia. As a child, I would pester my grandmother, asking her to tell me stories about the old days and what life was like back then. Every evening, when the lights went off I would ask her to tell me about the same thing. I would prick my ears and listen avidly until I fell asleep. It was from my grandmother that I first heard about dispossession, or 'dekulakisation'. The Kulaks were a category of peasant farmers who owned land and hired labour. My grandmother's uncle, Piri bey, was from a wealthy family. He and his two siblings, the Julfayev brothers, owned a huge farm with a great number of cattle and with many workers. But the relationship between the workers and their employers was different from that of landowners and serfs. They operated more like one extended family. The Julfayev brothers cared about the welfare of their workers, ensuring that they could provide for their families and helping them out whenever necessary.

When rumours about dekulakisation began to spread, the Julfayevs were warned that they should divide their property between the three brothers so that it did not look like accumulation of wealth in the hands of just one. But the concept of individual property ownership was completely alien to their values and their notion of family so they refused. The result was that when officials came to their village they nationalised everything. Their house in which the entire extended family lived was turned into a school. Each member of the family was forcibly taken to the Georgian capital, Tbilisi, where they were placed in echelons that transported them to Kazakhstan. A week long journey ensued during which no food was provided and the only stops were to throw away the dead. Diseases such as typhoid ravaged those suffering in the insanitary vermin-ridden conditions. Upon their arrival in Kazakhstan they were afforded no relief, and were simply dumped on the ice and left to fend for themselves. Weakened by malnutrition and disease, they had to build cribs for themselves.

Guzel Yakhina, *Zuleykha Opens Her Eyes*, ACT, Moscow, 2015

While many died on the train, even more died in Kazakhstan. Dead bodies were left in the forest because the soil was so icy that it was impossible to dig a hole. When Piri bey felt that he would not be able to endure the nightmare existence any longer he begged his relatives not to abandon his body and to at least try to bury him.

After he died, his wife, Gozel hanum found herself alone with three young sons. At night, when the cold became unbearable, she covered her children with a goatskin she had smuggled with her from Georgia. In the morning she would hide it, so that officials would not take it away. Her burden eased a little, when relatives from Georgia came and helped two of her boys escape. One of them was now almost blind. After three years, she also managed to run away with her remaining son. Her first destination was Astrahan, a north Caspian city. From there she stole onto a train and finally reached her home city, Marneuli, where an emotional reunion with her family awaited.

These stories that my grandmother told me gripped and horrified me in equal measure. I still am unable to comprehend the immeasurable suffering my relatives and others endured. How did they find the strength to wake up every day and strive for life, for mere survival in such cruel conditions? It moved me to hear how my ancestors survived such hideous times with dignity and courage. I promised myself to never forget these victims of Stalin's regime, the 'big terror' and I continue to devour every book, film or any material that links me to this past. So when I started reading *Zuleykha Opens Her Eyes* I was transported back to the stories my grandmother told me and felt the memories of my forefathers being brought to life.

In her novel, Guzel Yakhina sets out to describe the lives of people in exile, in particular the lives of women. Zuleykha is our protagonist, our everywoman whose experiences, attitude to her deteriorating situation, reluctance to die yet rejection of life in these hellish conditions encapsulates the torment of the times and the dangerous vulnerability of women. With bristling eloquence the nightmare unfolding in the containers transporting people, packed like cattle, to harsh and cold Siberia is startlingly vivid. She also conveys the desperation and despair of those eking out an existence on the banks of the Angara river – no aspect of dekulakisation is ignored.

Zuleykha is a richly-layered character who becomes the contested site for emancipation. Even before being forcibly transported her life is abysmal. She lives in a village with her tyrannical husband and temperamental mother-in-law who treat her no better than a slave with endless beatings, insults, humiliation and abuse. But Zuleykha endures it all, accepting her lot as mere trials of a woman's life. This daily hell ends and the real one begins, when collectivisation in the face of Ignat Ignatov came to her village. This hell is different, it is solid and uninterrupted. She inspires respect and pity but she is more than a victim. Her character symbolises the ugly misogyny that is the fate of many women, but there is one underlying theme that shook me and encompasses the pain of Stalin's great terror: betrayal. Yes, the novel is both about courage and cowardliness. About how much one can sacrifice to survive and how worthless someone becomes when morals and humanity are lost.

Yakhina creates her own space where Tatar ideology, identity and originality are torn. Here are a people who have lost their sacredness and no longer sound like a beautiful melody in the heart. All this is ripe for dismantling. In a world were ridiculing religion, traditions, customs has become a trend, Yakhina just keeps up with the trend. She understands all the rules of manipulation, perhaps a throwback to her years working in Moscow's PR world. Everybody knows how readily central government besmirches others at whim, especially religious minorities.

The novel undoubtedly has an ideological slant, but it cannot be labelled anti-communist. Yakhina inflicts pinpoint strikes on key symbols of the Tatar culture. In the framework of dekulakisation, she also subverts the symbolic foundation of the Tatar people. Murtaza, Zuleykha's husband, for example, is depicted as a stereotypical tyrant and his mother, whom Zuleykha mockingly calls Upyriha (100-year-old blind woman) is no better than her son. It feels like these two characters are intended to caricature Tatar people as patriarchal and backward. Ammunition is also aimed at two pillars of traditional families: the mother as a guardian of the home and the husband as a provider for the family. Both are intentionally humiliated by Yakhin, whose distaste for patriarchal structures denies any value in hierarchy, applauding only the horizontal. Murtaza is killed by Ignatov, who later becomes the beloved of Zuleykha. But there are no mournings of a widow. Ignatov represents the generation that gained power and made mass terror in the 1930s possible, simply by obeying the orders of the regime. Ivan Ignatov, the killer, the criminal - this is who 'innocent Zuleykha' falls in love with. Is this what the title of the novel refers to? Is this what is meant by Zuleykha opening her eyes?

In Siberia, Murtaza and Zuleykha's son is born. Yusuf, deprived of his father's influence, becomes an educated and sophisticated young man. He speaks French, studies medicine and is a skilled hunter and fisherman. Upon breaking all connection with his ancestral heritage he realises his full potential. He is free from the prejudices of religion, ethnicity, tradition – all supposed enforcers of patriarchy. Yusuf does not ask his mother about his biological father, he is not interested in his national and religious background. French is more important and more necessary than Tatar, art is more important than faith. Ultimately, in order to further his career,

Yusuf takes Ignatov's surname, and changes his name to Joseph. He bears the surname of his brutal father's murderer. What irony.

When I began reading Zuleykha I hoped to learn more about the victims of the Stalin regime, remembering the stories my grandmother used to tell me and which I cherish to this day. Yakhina's novel did more than that, it left me asking: what is a man without his roots? How far can one go in pursuit of success? How much can one strip away identity, principles, morals and beliefs before they find they have stripped away all sense of self?

SELF-REFLECTIONS

Hannah Kershaw

Dear Infidel is Tamim Sadikali's first novel. And it is quite an achievement. It is subtly written and permeated with moments of comedy as well as tragedy; and tackles looming political and social issues including responses to terrorism in the West and the treatment of Muslims in Britain. Sadikali doesn't hold back, encouraging the reader to face up to crucial but difficult questions. Should Muslims feel obliged to condemn acts of violence by supposedly Islamic groups hundreds of miles away? Can Muslims and non-Muslims in Britain not only coexist but be mutually respectful of each other? Indeed, what does the future hold for Muslims in the West? Although an intensely political novel, it also touches on issues that many readers, regardless of race or religion, will empathise with: tumultuous marriages, painful family reunions, and personal and professional failure.

Tamim Sadikali, *Dear Infidel,* Hansib, London, 2014

Although *Dear Infidel* incorporates multiple generations, from first-generation migrants to young children, it focuses on five main characters who are the 'middle' generation. Office worker Aadam gradually becomes disillusioned with life in Britain and vehemently opposes the War on Terror. His wife Nazneen takes an often rational political position but spends much of the narrative pining after a non-Muslim ex-boyfriend. Aadam's brother Salman is more religious than the others and is pessimistic about the future of Muslim and non-Muslim relations. Their cousin Pasha enjoys a successful career and, of the group, is the most keen to assimilate into British society. Finally, Aadam's other brother Imtiaz is in many ways the family 'loser'; unmarried, awkward and addicted to pornography. These second-generation Pakistani characters offer a multitude of perspectives on what it means to be both British and Muslim.

Part One of the novel explores the characters' lives and how they negotiate their everyday interactions in Britain. Spread out across the UK, the extended family comes together for Eid ul-Fitr celebrations at the modest northwest London home of Arwa and Zakir Walayat, first-generation Pakistani migrants to Britain and Pasha and Imtiaz's parents. Far from a joyful reunion, tension builds throughout the day as family members debate pertinent topics such as 9/11, the War on Terror and Muslim integration in Britain. Pasha feels that Muslims must assimilate into British life and be grateful for the freedoms offered. Salman, in contrast, feels he cannot truly belong, expressing his temptation to migrate to a more orthodox Muslim country that can provide a religious society but with 'Western' comforts. Dubai is his first choice: 'the East served up on a Western plate' he wryly notes. In contrast, Aadam craves the apparent plurality and tolerance of Canada. As the argument peaks and the group disbands, tragedy strikes and family feuds are left unresolved.

Dear Infidel is eclectic in its structure, and the narration moves between the third and first person as the characters experience flashbacks that offer insight into their pasts. There are several recollections of Nazneen's time at Red Rocks in Colorado with her non-Muslim boyfriend, Martin. Frustrated at her often meek husband, she misses the excitement and confidence of her previous relationship. Yet Martin's refusal to accept her renewed Muslim faith is shown as an unbridgeable divide between the couple. His desire for Nazneen to live a secular lifestyle and her wish to engage with a religious and cultural identity frames her difficult path from carefree student to half-regretful wife. Nazneen's struggle to let go of the past is both frustrating and captivating. Her non-Muslim ex-boyfriend is exciting but sexually aggressive, yet she is largely indifferent towards her polite, cautious and attentive Muslim husband. Whilst the novel's structure can be confusing, it is fast-paced and the characters are multi-dimensional and textured.

Sadikali is rather good at capturing quotidian forms of racism and Islamophobia. The novel opens with Aadam at an office meeting with a client, meeting a new trainee analyst for the first time. When Aadam introduces himself, the analyst asks what his name is short for. Nothing, he responds, Just Aadam. The analyst feels 'short-changed', uncomfortable at being presented with a Pakistani man with a British-sounding name.

Incidents like these are peppered throughout the novel, and they draw attention to everyday forms of racism occurring in unremarkable environments such as the office or on the bus. Sadikali's settings for these moments of tension and strife are recognisable to both non-Muslim and Muslim readers. Potentially minor on their own, these incidents gradually build a picture of life in Britain where a non-white, Muslim identity is constantly under scrutiny and suspicion. Later in this same scene, Aadam is reprimanded by his boss for 'gawping' at the TV screen in the lobby, which is beaming footage of an American news channel discussing the death of an American solider in Iraq. His boss, George, asks: 'what the hell did you think you were doing back there?' George then makes it clear that their relationship is professional, suggesting that outside of work, he would have no interest in conversing with a Muslim man: 'I have my views and no doubt you have yours, but when you're here, you stay focused'. Through such experiences, Sadikali highlights the discrepancy between multicultural rhetoric and the microaggressions that Muslims experience on a daily basis. The characters cannot escape the bombardment of Islamophobic and racist rhetoric through media forms, from seeing monkey noises directed towards a black footballer on the television to hostile interviews with Muslim 'experts' on the radio. If any reader approaches *Dear Infidel* with the idea that Britain floats in a post-racist, egalitarian bubble, they will certainly be challenged.

The novel builds to a crescendo in Part Two, when the family come together for Eid celebrations. The atmosphere changes and the scene feels tense, almost claustrophobic. On one end of the spectrum is Salman. Determined that his children will maintain their faith in a secular country, he buys his son Tamir a Qu'ran. Disappointed and preferring to play with his toys, Tamir angers his father, who hits him and storms out of the house. When Aadam claims that he doesn't feel an affinity with Britishness, and even hates 'their' country, Pasha retorts with: 'This country is a haven for Muslims…There's complete freedom of worship here – even Muslims criminals get halal food in prison. Just how much more do you want them to give?'. Unlike Pasha, Aadam feels that both Muslims and leaders of the US and Western European countries must take responsibility for 9/11 and the bombings in Madrid: 'Terrorism? Just what does that word mean? If you and I were in Baghdad at the start of the war, with the city being pounded from the air, wouldn't we have been terrified? What a fucking stupid word. If some madmen ever do let off bombs on the Underground, Britain will have no right to be outraged'.

Acts of terrorism, Aadam believes, are an expected consequence of the carnage that has been inflicted on Iraq by Western powers. Western countries, therefore, are naive to believe that there will be no consequences for their citizens during and after the war. Sadikali does not use this lengthy section of the novel to preach a personal perspective, nor does he try to neatly summarise a singular Muslim position towards terrorism and Western society. Instead, the passage offers a kaleidoscopic picture of the diversity of opinion within Britain's Muslim communities. Even family members who share the same economic background and upbringing approach the challenges of life in Britain from vastly different perspectives. Sadikali illustrates the heterogeneity of the Muslim experience and so counteracts ongoing attempts in media and everyday discourse to contain and summarise the 'Muslim perspective'.

Although contemporary politics is at the forefront of the novel, one of the most intriguing characters, who in fact distances himself from the debates, is Imtiaz. Whilst the other members of the family function relatively well in society, being married or holding down respectful jobs, Imtiaz is a true outsider. His isolation derives not from extreme views or involvement in terrorism, but because he is addicted to pornography. Unable to form any genuine relationships, he becomes infatuated with the women in pornographic magazines. His Muslim identity is of little consequence to him and he spends each day simply trying to survive his addiction to sexually charged, taboo women. Imtiaz has to negotiate family pressures to find a Muslim wife, but the lure of 'the West' is irresistible to him. Although the other family members are somewhat assimilated, Imtiaz is unable to integrate his Muslim values with a Western lifestyle. Instead, he is trapped in an unending cycle of shame and lust.

In its representation of women, however, the novel falls short. White women in particular are either portrayed as voiceless sex objects to be used by men or as stubbornly ignorant of cultures and religions that deviate from their own beliefs. Aadam, for example, is aggressively grilled by a white woman at a bus stop about the existence of God, and Imtiaz's radio plays an interview in which a Ms Petiffer relentlessly interrogates Dr

Qasim about Muslims in Britain. In contrast, Nazneen is in many ways dynamic and is the only female Muslim character explored in any depth, yet a majority of her narrative is spent thinking about men. On the whole, her character is somewhat underdeveloped in comparison with Aadam or Imtiaz, for example.

However, Sadikali's ability to scrutinise the depths of his characters' minds is certainly one of his strong suits. If the title, *Dear Infidel,* suggests that the novel is directed at a non-Muslim readership, then he does indeed challenge a reader's preconceptions and insists on an understanding of Muslim identity that is varied and dynamic. But for me, the title reads more as the first line of a confession, written furtively in a diary. Indeed, there are no characters who are exemplary in their lives as Muslims in Britain; they each have moments that they are ashamed of, which they regret, and which they admonish themselves for. We thus have a novel that not only speaks back to Islamophobia but speaks out about the challenges involved in negotiating both Muslim and British identities. There are no conclusions on offer. But that is precisely the point.

HALAL FOOD FOUNDATION

Halal Is Much More Than Food

The Halal Food Foundation (HFF) is a registered charity that aims to make the concept of halal more accessible and mainstream. We want people to know that halal does not just pertain to food – halal is a lifestyle.

The Foundation pursues its goals through downloadable resources, events, social networking, school visits, pursuing and funding scientific research on issues of food and health, and its monthly newsletter. We work for the community and aim at the gradual formation of a consumer association. We aim to educate and inform; and are fast becoming the first port of call on queries about halal issues. We do not talk at people, we listen to them.

If you have any queries, comments, ideas, or would just like to voice your opinion - please get in contact with us.

Halal Food Foundation
109 Fulham Palace Road,
Hammersmith, London, W6 8JA
Charity number: 1139457
Website: www.halalfoodfoundation.co.uk
E-mail: info@halalfoundation.co.uk

 @HFF_UK

 Halal Food Foundation

HOLY IGNORANCE!

Hassan Mahamdallie

On the day in February 2003 when a million tramped through London against the impending war on Iraq, I happened to be one of the first protestors to arrive at Hyde Park, which was the end-point of the march. My job had been to steward the very front, co-ordinating a long chain of yellow-bibbed volunteers: Muslims, CND members, socialists, Christian pacifists, trade unionists, arms interlinked, all in furious high spirits, stretching every sinew to keep the monster march inching forward. As I approached the area of the park where the rally was to take place, I was taken aback at the sight of the black *shahada* emblazoned flags of Hizb ut-Tahrir (HT) planted on either side of the stage. Which was annoying, given that they had not been on the march itself, indeed they had been handing out leaflets as we assembled on the Thames Embankment with the absurd headline 'DON'T STOP THE WAR – except through Islamic politics' along with a *fatwa* forbidding Muslim participation in the march as *haram*. The HT flag-wavers had obviously jumped on the tube as the march set off, ridden to Hyde Park and opportunistically installed themselves in the prime location by the stage, so as to catch the lens of the forest of news cameras covering the biggest demonstration in British history. Before long, however, the HT members had been persuaded to remove their flags out of sight of the media. They ended up as miniature dots on the horizon, far away figures on the edge of the crowd that packed out the park that day.

    Sadek Hamid, in his authoritative and enlightening new book *Sufis, Salafism and Islamists*, describes HT's doctrine as 'political literalist Salafism'. In February 2003 its aggressively rigid stance proved, in the face of events in the real world, to be its weakness. Its 'uncompromising ideology and methodology' wrapped in the vague promise of a re-born

Caliphate, shattered in the face of a genuine mass movement, its behaviour reinforcing the growing perception that it 'was merely a talking shop'. One ex-HT activist later admitted to a journalist that the February 2003 Stop the War protest 'did overthrow some of the arguments of HT — that they hate Muslims, that they demonise Islam. If so, then why is everyone out there (on the march)?'

> Sadek Hamid, *Salafism, Sufis and Islamists: The Contested Ground of British Islamic Activism*, I.B. Tauris, London, 2016

However, what is clear from reading Hamid's book is that HT's subsequent drift into irrelevancy (at least in the UK) was not unique, but indeed emblematic of the challenge facing all the competing Islamic reform movements at that time: whether they would succeed in decisively shaping the religious identity of young British-born Muslims (what it meant to be a good Muslim) and the nature of faith-based activism (the place of Islam in British society).

Hamid's book concentrates on four trends and their principle organisational expressions: the 'reformist Islamist' Young Muslims UK (YM), Hizb ut-Tahrir (HT), the Salafi-oriented Jamiyyah Ihya' Minhaj as Sunnah (JIMAS) and the neo-Sufi 'Traditional Islam' network (TI). Each one articulated their own view of 'the problem' and their distinct pathways to 'solutions', and each sought power, authority and authenticity through interpretations of Islamic texts, history, and teachings.

In short, the reformist Islamists sought to re-awaken and then train 'a righteous community' that would provide 'a dynamic nucleus for the Islamisation of society'. The radical pan-Islamists set out to build a vanguardist authoritarian party that would lead the masses towards the *Khilafah*. The Salafis laid claim to be the authentic home of those who wanted to believe in a pristine Islam'. The Sufis (rather cleverly) combined an emphasis on transmission-based traditional scholarship and individual spiritual growth alongside a duty to be socially engaged. Hamid describes the arc of development these formations traversed; emerging from the roots laid down by the immigrant generation of Muslim intellectuals and activists of the 1960s and 70s, followed by growth and consolidation over the next two decades, then fragmentation due to internal and external factors, and finally their latter-day attempts to re-establish and re-orientate themselves in what is a very different world to the one that gave birth to them.

One surprising insight slowly emerges as Hamid's narrative unfolds: that the challenges testing the mettle of Islamic 'reformism' bore more than a passing resemblance to those simultaneously confronting 'reformist' politics in the 'secular' sphere (if we can make such a separation for argument's sake). Even though most of those involved in latter-day Islamic reform movements would argue, to differing degrees, rejection of 'the West' and its project, in reality, most had unconsciously accepted its parameters as a given, or had consciously come to terms with it. As Hamid notes, conventionally Islamic movements wished to capture state and apply Islamic law in its totality. But nowadays, they are more pragmatic. They seek representation at government levels to influence policy and legislation. And, in general, they accept that the nation state is here to stay, and democracy and constitutional framework is the best way to reconcile tradition with modernity. And they are happy to borrow from the West – but selectively.

But the close of the twentieth century proved to be an inauspicious time for 'pragmatic, gradualist' visions. During this period, the old European social democratic parties, including Britain's Labour Party, were grappling with the conundrum of how to survive as reformists in an era of economic decline. The collapse of the Soviet Union and end of the Cold War, instead of ushering in 'the end of history' had opened an era of instability not experienced since the 1930s. The effects of the free-market, including de-industrialisation, the driving down of wages and standards of living of workers was eroding the reformist's traditional base of support. The majority responded by dumping their core values and de-camping to the centre ground in the hope of capturing new voters. Those who succeeded, however, soon found themselves despised managers of austerity, increasingly hedged in by new political formations from both the far left and extreme right. Reformists of every stripe, in a climate of stable economic expansion can demonstrate their ability to deliver progress. But in less favourable circumstances, they are prone to crises of legitimacy and relevance. (Thus, five years into his premiership Tony Blair effectively abandoned his domestic agenda, lured by the fatal delusion that he could secure greatness as the liberator of the Iraqi people).

Towards the end of *Salafism, Sufis and Islamists* Hamid pinpoints how currents in Britain's Islamic reform movement found themselves vulnerable to charges. They had become irrelevant to the majority of young, generally working class, Muslims, effectively abandoning them to face deep-rooted social and economic problems within their communities and intensifying Islamophobic discourses without. YM was accused of reproducing the elitism and nepotism of Jamaat-e-Islami of Pakistan. HT was viewed as out of touch with the day-to-day concerns of British Muslim communities and its vision of a *Khilafah* was seen as a utopian mirage. The obsession of the Salafis with doctrinal differences with other Muslims and their isolationist outlook had little appeal for young Muslims. The TI Sufis were seen as too 'other worldly' and too focussed on personal religiosity.

Hamid does not rush to judgement, instead, quite correctly, he seeks to inform the reader in a scholarly fashion. His former career as a grassroots community activist allows the reader access to 'insider views' – first-hand accounts of key individuals involved in shaping the contours of Britain's Islamic reform movement. However, in the final reckoning, Hamid judges that 'no single trend has yet offered a detailed vision for betterment of the Muslim communities in the present or future'. It must represent an uncomfortable perspective for those who claimed leadership of Britain's Muslims, that after nearly four decades of activism, campaigns large and small, raging debates, splits and realignments, personal sacrifice, organisations built from scratch, propaganda of the word and deed, they had very little evidence of tangible change to point to.

What of future prospects? Will an increasing hostile climate drive Muslims towards the existing groupings, infusing them with new recruits and energy? This is a possibility. However, it is also possible that the continuing process of state 'racialisation' of Muslims may produce Muslim-centred Black Nationalist organisations, similar to the Parti des Indigènes de la République (PIR) in France. It is also entirely possible that politicised individuals and groups will bypass existing networks in favour of building their own alternative structures. The contemporary landscape is being rapidly re-shaped by new spaces, organisational methodologies, structures and networks that the established players may have difficulty relating to.

These gathering points tend to be driven by new technology, social media platforms, and have decentralised, horizontal and collaborative cultures, are porous in membership and ideologically eclectic and diverse. Not an easy fit for organisations that have been mainly built around vertical hierarchies and exclusive memberships defined in opposition to those around them. Hamid convincingly argues that, if they wish to survive:

> the Islamic trends would better serve their communities by jettisoning exclusionary, supremacist apologetics that compare Islam with other faiths and world views. A more fruitful approach would be to offer an increasingly sophisticated engagement with the diverse intellectual and philosophical currents that define modernity by drawing upon the historical richness of Islamic civilisation and learning from other faith traditions and world views. Rather than engage in rhetorical shadow boxing or moralising, the trends should positively contribute to pressing global and local debates about the relationship between faith and reason, secularism, public – private distinctions of religion, social pluralism, social exclusion, human rights, economic justice, peacemaking or the potential ecological disaster facing the planet.

He also draws attention to another change in the landscape: the past decade has seen an increasing flow of young activists into artistic and cultural fields of production. They have constructed their own 'New Muslim Cool' on the way, much to the discomfort of those Islamists who fancy themselves as versions of the Saudi Committee for the Promotion of Virtue and the Prevention of Vice.

Hamid highlights two major challenges facing not just the Islamic currents, but the wider Muslim community. The first is the need to tackle entrenched inequalities to release untapped potential; principally dismantling the barriers facing Muslim women, including their widespread exclusion from religious institutions and power structures. Sexism and institutional discrimination have been challenged by generations of women activists and leaders, but largely without wider support. The second is what Hamid describes as a lack of intellectualism. He argues that 'whilst most value Islamic scholarship, very few people in the various trends engage in critical thinking about their religious heritage, history, science or contemporary ethical debates'.

But critical thought is outside the domain of Salafis, Islamists, and others of their ilk. They may have changed outwardly but the mind-sets are firmly entrenched. Most of the shock horror things we hear about Islam comes from this quarter. What is clear is that a lot of this rubbish masquerading as 'authentic' Islamic tradition needs bagging up, throwing in a skip, taken to a landfill site and burying in a deep hole. A brief example will suffice.

In July 2016, the BBC Asian Network ran a story on the development of the Inclusive Mosque Initiative in the UK and abroad. It was recycled by the international press last year, due to the success of the group's activities in the intervening period. Step forward 'Imam' Adnan Rashid, head of the London-based HT allied Islamic 'think-tank' The Hittin Institute. According to his web profile Rashid is a very learned man who believes 'that Islam is a way of life which promotes modernity (in all of its positive manifestations) and provides realistic solutions for all problems facing mankind'. He describes himself as a historian, 'human-rights activist' and 'supporter of peace/justice'. He told the BBC that as far as he was concerned the issue was cut and dried: 'The orthodox values of Islam are very clear. Muslims already believe in things that have been established for them for centuries and they are not going change. The Qur'an is not going to change, the prophetic position is not going to change. Muslim thinking and practices are not going to change. So I don't know what the point of this mosque is.' Thus, no change could possibly be made.

You couldn't make it up. The head of a think-tank, someone who regards himself as a scholar, a senior researcher, a historian, a human rights activist and supporter of peace and justice. God help us all. Perhaps Oliver Roy is right, the world is indeed in the grip of the crazies who worship at the altar of 'holy ignorance'.

ET CETERA

THE LAST WORD ON AFRICAN CHIEFTAINCY *by Henry Brefo*
THE LIST: TOP TEN RELATIONSHIP BREAK-UPS
CITATIONS
CONTRIBUTORS

LAST WORD

ON AFRICAN CHIEFTAINCY

Henry Brefo

Not many people know what it feels like to grow up as a black man in Brixton. It's a lot like growing up as a Pakistani in Bradford. Everywhere you go people want to talk to you about the riots and the issues and the 'race problems'. You get used to becoming a barometer for the latest bout of hand-wringing about integration and marginalisation. Such a worry isn't it? All those young black men drifting into anti-social behaviour and criminality and not treating their women right. Sound familiar? Now the debate has moved on to my Muslim brothers. It's your turn to be in the spotlight as the contested focus of society's anguish. You'll grow accustomed to the profiling, just as we did, but that's not to say that we're fine with it. But hey, if you're a Muslim black guy, or worse still a Muslim black guy living in the US, phew you certainly got a lot on your plate.

The wearying conflation of identity persists, oscillating between my race and heritage, depending on who is asking. As it turns out I'm not only black but also of African heritage. Specifically, my family are from Ghana, where my mother continues to reside. My formative years in the UK were spent in the care of my grandmother, who was as matriarchal as she was an empowered African woman. I was never sure if the family structures that were conveyed by my heritage had succeeded in defining me so I set about discovering ways to understand my place and space in the framework of those traditions. This desire to delve into the legacy of my history became a late passion, because I first needed to situate the concept of belonging in a wider context of lived realities.

It occurred to me that developing my interest in African literature would enhance my insight. I devoured everything I could find and became intrigued by the complex relationships that are played out in the imagined world of African writers. The debate on African literature endlessly redraws discursive boundaries in an attempt to either redefine or reinforce the make-up of African communities. The scene would be all too familiar. A renowned writer would develop his plot by exhorting common and emerging textual trends as transgressive. Ben Okri, the eminent African writer, instigated a virtual brawl with his brushed criticism that 'African writers are largely read for their stories about slavery, colonialism, poverty, civil wars, imprisonment, female circumcision – in short, for subjects that reflect the troubles of Africa and black people as perceived by the rest of the world'. The minutia of everyday existence was apparently not of sufficient interest to captivate readers, consigning African writers to a 'literature of suffering and heaviness', instead of an artistic expression.

I became attentive to the development of fictional writings and studies about African societies – from the post-colonial era to present – and noticed that the view of Africa has undergone a shift in its narrative structure and aesthetics. The homogeneous village scene and imagery that once pervaded post-colonial narratives has slowly given way to an urbanised cosmopolitan drama with the diaspora at its core. The militant tone of the 'Africa writes back' generation to a large extent has been moderated by a modish blend of narratives from the diaspora and the African continent. This is not to say that canonical narratives that reflect 'the troubles of Africa and black people as perceived by the rest of the world' are still not fashionably penned by some writers. Instead, this trend of writing about the 'human theatres of adversities' is being balanced with accounts of everyday struggle as opposed to long lasting historic suffering.

In 2014, a fortuitous set of encounters led to the setting up of Afrikult., an online forum for people to connect, explore and expand knowledge on African literature and culture combined. My co-founders and I were motivated by the existence of an ensemble of young writers all fine-tuning their instruments of expression to the vibrations of contemporary experiences. Their work, whether set in the diaspora or on the African continent, evokes gripping scenes of everyday experiences and it was this normalcy we wanted to bring into mainstream consciousness. *Black Sister's*

Street by Chika Unigwe is set in Brussels and speaks of the horrors of migration. Tendai Huchu's *Hairdresser of Harare* takes us back to the continent to confront the tragedy of bigotry. Whereas NoViolet Bulawayo and Pede Hollist pose perennial questions on the metaphysics of belonging and identity.

Not only has there been an emergence of works that present universal themes, but there is also a distinctive aesthetic appeal. In *Harare North*, the author's take on language is remarkably adventurous and existentially playful, endowing his characters with an authentic simplicity. Chimamanda Adichie may be largely celebrated for her elegant command of narrative, yet it is her ingenious lyrical flow that finally conquers our appreciation for her work. And not to forget Teju Cole, the young man with the clairvoyance of a painter, and a magician's touch that conjures words into colourful portraits. Emboldened by this seeming rebirth of the culture and arts in Africa, I looked to the entwined social structures that the literary narratives were bringing to the fore and their impact on the path of development.

People ask me what my postgraduate research is about and when I oblige them with a response, telling them that it's looking at Chiefs and Development in Africa, it always elicits a mixed reaction. Some stare blankly at me searching for the politically enlightened response. Others simply nonchalantly mime 'cool' and quickly divert the discussion onto a plethora of unrelated topics. Just as African writers historically wrested with the indifference their stories of everyday life in Africa once elicited, I felt a similar attitude towards chieftaincy being projected by those I would disclose my interest to.

For many it is not so much as to whether chieftaincy holds any real value at all, but rather the mere mention of it evokes images of a distant and obscure African past. As history and memory has it, the road to this African bygone cuts through deep thickets of strange customs and traditions, meandering along gullies of vile mysticism and primitive vices. It is after all where darkness reposes in the heat of eternal youth. Joseph Conrad was less verbose in his description, simply characterising the continent as the 'heart of darkness', which quickly became a catchy and commercially-friendly description that still plagues Africa.

In the same breath, most argue that restoring Chieftaincy will drag Africa back to its heart of darkness. Similar to 'orientalist' depictions of Arab chiefs and their harems, representations of African chiefs in popular culture heavily feature the African chief as a lionised demigod, ruling over his pride of primitive 'tribes' in accordance with the law of the jungle. One has to look no further than the 1986 television series *Shaka Zulu*. In *Shaka Zulu*, we are confronted with an ambitious young man who rises amongst his people to become the founder of the Zulu nation as a consequence of his military genius. The tale of *Shaka* is narrated to us by the British doctor Henry Francis Fynn, whose intimate reflections as recorded in his diary presents a towering image of a 'degenerate and pathological' monster. Throughout the narration Fynn takes the high moral ground, and never loses sight of his paternal responsibilities towards the godless Africans. It is Fynn who takes up the mantle of the 'white man's burden' to administer Western medicine, when traditional African medicine fails to save lives; Fynn who introduces Shaka to a God beyond himself. Nonetheless, Fynn's narration stands out in its extravagant depiction of Shaka Zulu's irrational brutality and ferocity for carnage. Shaka beams on screen, wide eyed, like a rabid beast only motivated by cruel instincts. His heathen soul is incapable of love, depleted of all tender emotions.

Fittingly, he only recognises complete submission to his authority. All those around him are nothing but his slaves and no one dares to challenge or disagree with his wishes. With the exception of Dr Fynn of course, whose wise paternal counsel serves as a harbinger of the tragedy that befalls him. However in the midst of his butchery, the tale of colonial domination and annexation is subtly weaved in as almost a necessary but arduous decision to end Shaka's reign of terror. Consequently, Fynn's diary provides good grounds for the expansion of British rule in South Africa. The television series brilliantly vindicates colonialism and perverts Africa's complex systems of traditional rule, amid its stratified hierarchy of democratic practices. Creating a Manichean allegory where Western values and traditions stand tall in the frame of Francis Fynn as the force for good; the Africans, meanwhile, are represented by the exploits of the evil Shaka Zulu who is beyond redemption.

Such accounts of Shaka Zulu have been heavily contested, especially within academic circles. Nonetheless, they comfortably sit within a tradition of representation – of an 'innately African leadership troupe' – inimical to ideals of democracy and progress. Besides his military accomplishments and success in war, all of which are well recorded in the annals of history, the Zulu King was an effective politician. On many occasions he employed diplomatic measures to forge alliances or win over his rivals as opposed to crushing his enemies to submission.

Widely accepted distortions of this kind have severe implications. They reconstruct the history of memory whilst normalising inaccurate perceptions of the target group or 'subject'. This is particularly perceptible through discourses around 'other' cultures such as the portrayal of Muslim sexuality, which continues to mythologise orientalist designs by inscribing on Muslim bodies western fantasies. For example, the attire of Muslim women probably stands as one the few remaining frontiers of cultural resistance. It is of little wonder, that it is paradoxically reinterpreted within the context of binary patriarchy. Here, the race to 'emancipate' the Muslim female is re-enacted as a contest between men of different cultural logic: western liberator vs Muslim fanatic.

My desire to seriously embark on a study into my own tribal past was ignited while listening to a lecture on African politics at the School of Oriental and African Studies. It came in the form of careless criticism weighed against African chiefs by one of my British classmates. After condemning the institution of chieftaincy as undemocratic, uncivilised and hell bent on primitive customs, he casually called for the abolishment of the system, with no regard for its function or importance to the so-called 'Africans' on whose behalf he claimed to have positioned his sentiments. This was met with resounding applause, and a nod of approval from the lecturer. I was incensed. Prior to the incident, I must confess to harbouring an internalised and damaging perception of the African past, despite my consumption of literature from the region. But in that moment I was tired of hearing my culture, traditions and values be so swiftly relegated at the expense of a Western approach.

With just a little investigation into the history of my forefathers – the Akan, a meta-ethnic group believed to have migrated from the Sahel to coastal West Africa, residing in the southern region of Ghana – I discovered their system of chieftaincy, which challenged my thinking around notions of civilisation, particularly the view that civilisation is the preserve of the West. The Akan political structure, for example, is organised around a decentralised system of governance. The state's administration is divided into separate realms of authority (central and local), represented by a range of departments with different functions. The central apparatus of the state's administration comprised the King, Chiefs, the Queen Mother, Inner Privy and Council of Elders. Together they represent the office of government, charged with the task and responsibility of maintaining law and order and promoting national welfare. It might seem reasonable to assume that the King wields absolute power, but the reality is quite the contrary.

Fitting with the Akan custom of 'hierarchical democracy', the King is closely fastened to bureaucratic systems of checks and balances, which limits his claim to absolute power. In this way power is not concentrated in the personhood or office of the King alone but shared across the political spectrum. Yet, having in place a decentralised system which requires accountability, does not necessarily eradicate coercive practices commonly associated with hereditary governance. The nineteenth century Ashanti King, Asantehene Nana Mensah Bonsu, is known to have passed exorbitant taxes and carried punitive exactions against his subjects. In response, his people demanded his removal from office. He was summarily deposed and banished from the capital Kumasi. To regulate the power of office holders, the Akan political culture makes provision for popular participation within decision-making and extols democratic values. This is encapsulated in the old adage *ka bi na meka bi*, loosely translated as 'you say your bit, I say my bit'. Nonetheless, what the case of Mensah Bonsu reveals, is that no political system is perfect and requires careful handling to bring it in line with changes within a given society.

This is what the institution of chieftaincy in Ghana today is striving for. The structure of governance aims to avoid unnecessary power struggles by working in partnership with the state to enhance the deployment of development resources to local people. Given the important and necessary function that the model of chieftaincy fulfils, it is rather baffling that many, including Africans, are content to see it buried in the heap of colonial misrepresentation. Perhaps the emancipation of Africa stands incomplete without decolonising the history of memory, and in that we must revisit and adapt African solutions to African problems. Whether it be through showcasing literature that decolonises the African mind or by denying the authority of those elites that deem traditional pre-colonial structures such as kinship and chieftaincy to be the 'problem', now is the time for deculturalisation to be brought to reckoning and permanently dismantled.

THE LIST

TOP TEN RELATIONSHIP BREAK-UPS

In the words of Echo and the Bunnymen, nothing ever lasts forever. Relationships are precarious creatures, causing joy, pain and wonder almost at the same time. They plod along (un)comfortably or explode onto the scene with searing intensity before disappearing as suddenly as they arrived. Relationships can be enduring but more often than not they fracture catastrophically, unleashing unpredictable consequences to cause despair, destruction and if you're lucky, eventual growth. Here's our top ten relationship break-ups of all time – in the increasing order of their earth-shattering importance and magnitude on heartbreak Richter scale. Get your popcorn ready, sit back and take a ringside seat because let's not pretend that everyone's guilty pleasure is the full-on spectacle of a relationship in mid-meltdown (except your own).

1. The Break-up of One Direction

Ok, so a break is not necessarily a break-up but it's definitely a sign that the path of true love is not running smooth! First there are the photos of him hanging around with a different crowd. Then he's changing his look, tweeting stuff that couldn't possibly have been approved by his management team. Cheating rumours follow him around like a dog on heat and public appearances go randomly off-script. There's no denying… something is amiss… The squeaky clean image looks like it's about to crack and before you know it the sound of millions of pre-pubescent hearts breaking has drowned out all other noise on social media. Zayn Malik may not have been the first member of a boy band to announce his shock departure, sending legions of Directioners into an inconsolable frenzy, but his was a seismic eruption in the volcanic and instantly forgettable world of online news. The boy from Bradford had been the iced sugar glazing on the bitter cake of Muslim infamy greedily consumed by the Western media gaze. Reality TV made a youngster of mixed Pakistani-English heritage an international superstar of stratospheric proportions. A young Muslim man who hails from a city held up as a bellwether for the UK debate on immigration, integration and radicalisation, threw off the shackles of superficial entertainment conformity and set about carving his own path in the music industry, on his own terms. There is some solace for the devastated tween hordes, however — it may be a while but the inevitable boyband reunion tour is always something to look forward to.

2. The Brangelina Split

When news broke that Brangelina were no more, couples looked up from their smartphones in a state of shock at the sensational celebrity news, gazed into each other's eyes, possibly for the first time in months, and wondered whether love had died. If Brad and Angelina can't make a marriage last, with their beautiful faces and perfect rainbow family, what hope do we mere mortals have? There was mischievous speculation from some quarters that the split had been precipitated by Brad's fits of jealous rage at Angie's growing closeness to former British Foreign Secretary William Hague. However, the once Tory Leader rushed to defend the reputation of the glamorous actress and strenuously denied such scurrilous allegations. As well as jet-setting around the world making films and advocating for refugees in her role as Special Envoy for the UN High Commissioner for Refugees, Angelina is mother to six children, three biological, three adopted, with Brad. She also now needs to find time for her recent appointment as visiting professor at LSE, teaching a course with the aforementioned William Hague of which there shall be no further comment. Brad's previous relationships include marriage to the bland but lovely Jennifer Aniston who he was already married to when he met Angelina on the set of *Mr and Mrs Smith* (2005) — a film about two freelance assassins who find their latest assignment is… each other. Any suggestion of a relationship overlap is hotly rejected. Ange's love-life has been rather more edgy: she and ex-husband Billy Bob Thornton reportedly carried vials of each other's blood around their necks in a grandiose display of affection. How ridiculously romantic.

3. Prince Charles and Diana

Who can forget that heart-stopping moment when the late Diana, Princess of Wales fluttered her heavily mascara'd eyelashes and declared to a gripped television audience: 'there were three of us in this marriage, so it was a bit crowded.' That interview with Martin Bashir in 1995 for BBC Panorama further compounded the end of the myth of the fairytale marriage of Prince Charles and his young wife. The marriage had been beset by rumours of infidelity since the publication of a sensational biography of the Princess by Andrew Morton, which had also been published in the *Sunday Times*. The modern-day arranged marriage had seemed doomed from the beginning when a duty-bound Prince steeped in the constraints and stifling pressure of protocol and pageantry characteristic of a Royal upbringing, agreed to a match with a young Lady Spencer, barely out of her teens and idealistically believing that this was her 'happily ever after'. In an awkward interview with the couple after their engagement was announced, Diana's reply to the question of whether they were in love was a rapid 'of course' followed by Charles' infamous words 'whatever "in love" means'. The Princess spun the narrative that Charles had never been entirely faithful, flaunting his relationship with a former flame, Camilla Parker-Bowles, who he would eventually go on to marry. The couple were instructed to divorce by the Queen and they did so in 1996. Diana renewed her own pursuit of love, notably a two-year relationship with a Pakistani surgeon, described to be 'the love of her life', that would no doubt have been greeted with victorious celebration in Pakistan had it culminated in marriage, or better still, with her embracing Islam because we all know how much Muslims love a conversion story! It wasn't meant to be, however, and Diana tragically died in a car crash, alongside her Egyptian then-boyfriend Dodi Fayed.

4. Puma/Adidas Discord

We've had Cain and Abel, the Milliband brothers, Romulus and Remus, the Gallaghers, but who has heard of the acrimonious feud between two brothers that led to the founding of Adidas and Puma? The Dassler brothers ran a thriving sports shoe company in the sleepy German town of Herzogenaurach, operating out of their mother's laundry room. It was the 1920s and the two lived together in a state of uneasy disharmony exacerbated by the fact that their wives detested one another. The younger Adi was the artisan who designed and crafted the shoes while his extrovert older brother Rudi was the salesman. In their spare time they were members of the Nazi party. The family-run business was catapulted into the big time when they succeeded in persuading African-American Olympic gold-winning runner Jesse Owens to wear their shoes. It was from this moment that the tensions between the two families boiled over. During a Second World War bombing raid, when Adi and his wife were climbing into the air raid shelter already occupied by Rudi and his family, the younger brother was heard to mutter 'The dirty bastards are back again,' referring to the Allies, but Rudi was certain that the remark was directed at him. He suspected his brother and sister-in-law of getting him conscripted and blamed them for his arrest for desertion and subsequent arrest by Allied forces for being a member of the Gestapo. The level of suspicion and antipathy between the two siblings had plummeted to extreme depths. While Rudi had suffered his ordeal at the hands of the military and occupied forces, Adi had built up their business and in 1948 the company assets were split. Adi named his business Adidas. Rudi retaliated by building a factory on the opposite side of town and calling it Rudi, before eventually renaming it Puma. As the sole employers in the town, the Dassler brothers' feud sucked in everyone and divided allegiances along company lines. Local businesses served only those loyal to one business and not the other, marriages across Puma/Adidas lines were unheard of as inhabitants of the town took sides with entire families across generations working for one or the other brother. Herzogenaurach earned the nickname 'the town of bent necks' because it was necessary to check to see which shoes a person was wearing before speaking with them or allowing them into your shop. When the brothers died they left instructions to be buried at opposite ends of the cemetery. It was only in 2009 that a symbolic football match between two teams of workers from Adidas and Puma declared an end to the 60-year-long feud.

5. Brexit

Where to even begin. To fend off trouble from the euro-sceptic rabble in his own party and shore up his own position, Prime Minister David Cameron decided to gamble with the future of forthcoming generations by inviting the great British public to vote on one of the most complex and intricate matters of our lifetime: the UK's relationship with Europe. As if it wasn't enough to absolve himself of the responsibility for taking difficult decisions, something that governments were ironically once created to do, Cameron unleashed a hornet's nest of Machiavellian skulduggery and hate speech that left the country more divided and fractured than ever. Self-serving characters such as Michael Gove and Boris Johnson decided to treat the whole affair like a scramble for the election of School Head Boy in a cuckoo-nest plot gone awry, laying bear their selfish contempt for anyone other than their own ego. The Leave campaign triumphed on a miasma of misinformation fed to an electorate disillusioned by the tangible marginalisation felt by communities who were told to direct their ire towards Johnny Foreigner and let years of Tory austerity firmly off the hook. Legitimate concerns about the EU became drowned out by deeply unpleasant xenophobic rhetoric, emboldening racism in vague yet impassioned calls for 'we want our country back'. Swathes of tax-paying Europeans residing in the UK were plunged into an unhappy insecurity as shocked 'leave' voters, including the vacuous Johnson, struggled (and continue to struggle) to understand the implications of their actions while defensively maintaining it was not a vote on immigration. The end result is a continued limping on into the unknown, except this time with an unelected Prime Minister, an opposition too busy sniping at their twice-elected leader and all the while attracting the ridicule of the rest of Europe (or envy, depending on who you speak to).

6. Bangladesh's Divorce from Pakistan

When winner of the Great British Bake Off Nadiya Hussain took television viewers on a journey to the birthplace of her parents, Bangladesh, courtesy of the BBC, she placed a spotlight on one of the least known South Asian countries. The lush green landscapes and casual modernity were a surprise to many. Bangladesh has relatively recently acquired an identity of its own. Formerly known as East Pakistan, it had formed the east wing of a newly independent Pakistan up until the liberation war in 1971. The movement for freedom had been bubbling for a while, provoked by prolonged ethnic and linguistic discrimination as well as a lack of representation in Pakistan's government. It took the government's disinterested response to a cyclone in 1970 that devastated swathes of East Pakistan and killed at least half a million people, to make a split inevitable. Civil disobedience was followed by armed resistance. The Pakistani army, led by President Yahya Khan, attempted to crush the rebellion with a savagery that shocked the world and resulted in the deaths of possibly as many as three million people. But atrocities were committed on both sides: Bengalis took revenge on Urdu-speaking Biharis who were viewed with suspicion due to their ethnic and linguistic links to the Pakistani army. The scars of the split have yet to be fully healed both in Bangladesh and Pakistan. But these days internal feuds and dynastic politics has undermined the fledgling secular democracy and enabled a break-down in law and order and a rise in extreme Islamist ideology.

7. Partition of India

It was in August 1947, exactly 70 years ago, that India won independence from two centuries of British colonial rule and Pakistan was created. The struggle for sovereignty had been a bitter and bloody nationalist battle that lasted three decades and resulted in the deaths of many, with some estimates putting the figure at around one million casualties and countless more injured. The carving up of the former colony into Hindu-majority India and Muslim-majority Pakistan signalled the end of the British Empire as a dominant force in global geopolitics. While the road to independence had been hard-fought, its execution was chaotic. Pakistan was incomprehensively cut into half with a hostile, foreign land mass separating its two parts. Whether the concept of Pakistan was ever meant to evolve into reality or was instead intended by Mohammed Ali Jinnah of the Muslim League to leverage pressure for greater Muslim autonomy for Muslims within a loosely federated India, is still being debated. What is clear, however, is that a hasty British withdrawal after the Second World War, which left the former colonial power economically weakened and with little appetite for clinging on to its increasingly insubordinate Empire, created an unprecedented upheaval. British officials hurriedly drew up the borders for the two countries and what ensued was one of the greatest migrations of people at that time. One million lost their lives and ten million abandoned homes and livelihoods after finding themselves on the 'wrong' side of a border. Partition was a tragic and devastating period in the history of South Asia despite the joy of liberation from the British. Some would argue that the break-up of India was one of the greatest calamities to befall the region, with the continuing brinkmanship over Kashmir a perpetual threat to world peace.

8. Break-up of the Ottoman Empire

Founded at the end of the thirteenth century in Turkey by Osman Gazi, the empire was at its most formidable in the sixteenth and seventeenth centuries with Suleiman the Magnificent at its helm. It had expanded into a thriving political dominion reaching as far as Europe, Asia, North Africa, the Caucasus and the Horn of Africa. Robust, free-flowing trade routes serviced learned and sophisticated societies. However, by the end of the nineteenth Century the Ottoman Empire was routinely described as the sick man of Europe. The rest of the continent had entered the age of industrialisation and the Habsburg and Russian Empires in particular were proving a menacing military threat. Nationalist uprisings in Eastern Europe and the Middle East led to the weakening of the regime. While its military machine remained stuck in its golden era, other powers were utilising advances in technological warfare to inflict a series of definitive defeats on the Ottomans towards the end of the 1800s. By this time the Ottoman Emperor was a mere figurehead as regional power brokers plotted, schemed and undermined the regime. A process of reform and modernisation was triggered, but was not enough to steer the Empire off the path of fragmentation. The Arab revolt and loss of territory to the allies after the First World War cemented the fate of the Empire. The emergence of an independent Turkey was followed by the re-drawing of the world map to create the Balkans and Middle East as we recognise them now. The break-up of the Ottoman Empire and what took its place is widely considered to have created the fissures and dislocations due to disregard for ethnic, linguistic and tribal ties, that set the foundations for the tensions we see in that part of the world today.

9. Shia-Sunni Split

Media commentators love to blame the Middle East's problems on the Sunni-Shia divide. To such an extent that for the unschooled observer it is often a shock to learn that Shias constitute only ten per cent of all Muslims while Sunnis make up the remaining 90 per cent. So who are these two groups and why is their seemingly irrevocable enmity taking up so many newspaper column inches? The answer is actually relatively simple. Islam's ancient schism came about almost immediately after the death of the Prophet Muhammad in 632 CE. In typical mosque-committee elbows-out style the big split was over the matter of who should succeed as leader of the Muslim community. Sunnis support the appointment of Abu Bakr, trusted advisor, companion and also father-in-law of the Prophet, as first Caliph. Another group had formed around Ali, who was the cousin and son-in-law of the Prophet. They felt terribly betrayed, believing that succession should follow the bloodline and that Ali was the best candidate. A movement grew around Ali and called itself the Party of Ali, or Shia. Ali eventually became the Fourth Caliph, presiding over a five-year period that was one of the most tumultuous and bloody in the history of early Islam. After his assassination in 661, his sons Hassan and Hussein, also grandsons of the Prophet, lay claim to the succession but were denied. The Shia fought for what they considered the brothers' right to rule but Hassan was poisoned in 680 and Hussein died in battle a year later. The cruel treatment of the Shia at the hands of the Sunni Ummayad dynasty formed the basis for the rituals of grieving and celebration of martyrdom that are an important part of Shia tradition. We think it is time to kiss and make up, and bygones be bygones!

10. Antarctic Breakdown

The Antarctic conjures up images of treacherous feats of survival undertaken by romantic figures from polar history such as Ernest Shackleton and Captain Scott. This breathtaking land mass of ice diverges in geography from its Northern opposite: the arctic consists of pack ice in the winter that melts in the summer months, offering a (still harsh) environment in which the Inuit peoples survive. The Antarctic, however, has long been regarded as a relatively stable and unchanging ice shelf so it is with increasing horror that glaciologists have been watching the ice at both poles appear to be breaking up due to climate change. The break-up of the Antarctic is particularly alarming and with frightening expected consequences. Contrary to the claims of climate change deniers, experts warn that the melting of the ice caps will raise sea levels to such an extent that cities such as London and New York will be submerged under water as well as considerable parts of Holland and Bangladesh. The idyllic paradise island destination the Maldives is already at threat from sinking. In 2009 the country's president convened an underwater cabinet meeting during which he signed a paper demanding cuts in carbon emissions in an effort to highlight the precarious future of the archipelago and called for decisive action at the UN climate change conference that was about to take place in Copenhagen. The break-up and melting of the polar caps and any subsequent rise in sea levels is destined to have a disproportionately adverse impact on developing countries in the southern hemisphere. Burma, Bangladesh and India can expect stronger cyclones, East Africa could face a prolonged drought, and Indonesia would face drastically reduced rainfall. A truly earth-shaking split!

CITATIONS

Introduction: The Relations Matrix by Samia Rahman

Zygmunt Bauman's *Liquid Modernity* is published by Polity Press (Oxford, 2012); and *Globalization: The Human Consequences* by John Wiley (London, 2013). Ayisha Malik's *Sofia Khan is Not Obliged* is a Twenty7 paperback (London, 2016). See also: Judith Butler, *Gender Trouble: Feminism & the Subversion of Identity* (Routledge, London, 2007). Further details on the International Meeting on Co-operation and Development, informally known as the North-South Conference can be found at: http://bit.ly/2f0tfmN

Annie by Aamer Hussein

Qurratulain Hyder translated three of her novels and several of her short stories into English. The titles of two of her novels are literal translations: *Aag ka Darya: River of Fire* (Kali for Women, Delhi, 1998); *Mere Bhi Sanam Khane: My Temples Too* (Women Unlimited, New Delhi, 2004). However, the original title of *Fireflies in the Mist* (New Directions, New York, 2010) *Aakhir-e-shab ke hamsafar*, means 'Travelling Companions at the End of Night'.

Among the stories mentioned here are 'Patjhar ki Avaz', translated by C. M. Naim as 'The Sound of Falling Leaves'; in Urdu, 'patjhar' has the connotation of autumn, as the title implies. 'Jalavatan' was translated by the author as 'The Exiles', though the Urdu title does not specify the plural form of the noun. 'Ek makalma', which means 'a dialogue', was translated by the author as 'Point Counterpoint'.

The title of her memoirs, *Kar e jahan daraaz hai* (2 volumes, Educational Publishing House, Aligarh, 2003) means 'The World's Work is Long'. See also: Rakhshanda Jalil, editor, *Qurratulain Hyder and the River of Fire* (Aakar Books, Delhi, 2011).

Of the untranslated word in the text, 'Khala' means maternal aunt.

Best of All Patrons? by Syed Nomanul Haq

There are at least four primary sources that are essential for reconstructing the biographies of the main scholars that appear in the essay. Abu'l-Fazl Bayhaqi, *Ta'rikh* (History); Zahir al-Din Bayhaqi, *Tatimmat Siwan al-Hikma* (Continuation of 'The Cabinet of Wisdom'); Nizami 'Aruzi, *Chahar Maqala* (Four Discourses); and Ibn abi Usyabi'a, *'Uyun al-Anba' fi Tabaqat al-Atibba'* (Sources of Information Concerning the Classes of Physicians). Full bibliographic details are a bit cumbersome, but can be found in the secondary sources which I have also used for this essay. I have greatly benefitted from the works of Clifford Bosworth, particularly *The Ghaznavids, their Empire in Afghanistan and Eastern Iran, 994:1040* (Librairie du Liban, Beirut, 1973). Sonja Brentjes has been doing remarkable work on patronage, particularly of the mathematical sciences, and her work and private communications have proved uniquely important for my own studies. I have closely consulted her essay 'Patronage of the mathematical sciences in Islamic societies: structures and rhetoric, identities and outcomes' in *The Oxford Handbook of the History of Mathematics*, edited by E. Robson and J. Stedall (Oxford University Press, 2008). For Ibn Tufayl, the anthology of Lawrence Conrad is a work of superb scholarship and his Introduction has been written in a highly readable style; the title of the work is *The World of Ibn Tufayl: Interdisciplinary Perspectives on* Hayy ibn Yaqzān (Brill, Leiden, 1996). For Ibn Sina, there is hardly any scholar who can match Dimitri Gutas in erudition, rigour, and historical stamina. His work is literally indispensable for any researcher on the Grand Shaykh, in particular his *magnum opus, Avicenna and the Aristotelian Tradition* (Brill, Leiden, 2014).

The Zahir al-Din Bayhaqi citation is taken from the entry 'Al-Khāzinī' in the *Dictionary of Scientific Biography*, edited by Charles Gillispie (Scribner, New York, 1970). The E. G. Browne, Abu'l-Fazl Bayhaqi and Nizami Aruzi quotes have been taken from Bosworth. Juzjani's words are quoted from the citations of Gutas and reproduce his translations.

Where I cite myself, it is from my article, 'The Chimes of Hayy ibn Yaqzān: From the Divine Comedy to Robinson Crusoe and Onward ...' that appeared in the newspaper *Dawn* of May 25, 2016

Borders by Piro Rexhepi

Blerta Zeqiri *Stigma* (EULEX, 2014) is available online at: http://www.eulex-kosovo.eu/en/news/000495-a.php; and Astrit Ismaili's 'trashformation' can be seen at: https://vimeo.com/84777939. Reports and manuals on 'normally different' projects are available at: http://normallydifferent.com/ and Ludwig Boltzmann Institute of Human Rights – LBI and Research Association, Annual Report 2014 (quote from p. 17) is available online at: http://bim.lbg.ac.at/sites/files/bim/attachments/annual_report_2014_0.pdf. The report of the EU Office in Kosovo, 'Challenging homophobia – Building support systems for LGBT people in Kosovo,' (2013) is available from: http://www.kosovoprojects.eu/en/content-challenging-homophobia-building-support-systems-lgbt-people-kosovo

Various news reports include: 'Semi' – the brave: Living openly gay in Kosovo's homophobic society' Nadine Kreuzahler, Emilie Sok, Dardan Zhegrova. Available online at: http://www.facethebalkans.com/2012/10/semi-the-brave/ ; Agence France-Presse (2014) 'Hooligans injure three at Sarajevo gay film festival,' Available from http://www.globalpost.com/dispatch/news/afp/140202/hooligans-injure-three-at-sarajevo-gay-film-festival>; and Finland helps Kosovo fight against homophobia and transphobia: https://www.thl.fi/en/web/thlfi-en/-/finland-helps-kosovo-fight-against-homophobia-and-transphobia

See also: Fatima El-Tayeb, *European others: queering ethnicity in postnational Europe*. (University of Minnesota Press, 2011); J Puar, *Terrorist Assemblages: Homonationalism in Queer Times* (Duke University Press, 2007); Svetlana Boy, *Another Freedom: The Alternative History of an Idea* (University of Chicago Press, 2010); Mahmood Mamdani, 'Good Muslim, bad Muslim: A political perspective on culture and terrorism.' *American anthropologist* 104.3 (2002): 766-775; and Piro Rexhepi, 'From Orientalism to Homonationalism: Queer Politics, Islamophobia and Europeanization in Kosovo.' *Southeastern Europe* 40.1 (2016): 32-53.

EU's Others by Annalisa Mormile

The quotes from Jacques Derrida are from *The Other Heading* (Bloomington: Indiana University Press, 1992), p. 15; and Michael Naas, *Derrida from now on* (New York: Fordham University Press, 2008), p. 21. See also, the new edition of Jacques Derrida, *The Gift of Death* (University of Chicago Press, 2008).

Jan Patočka's 1966 essay 'Is Technological Civilization Decadent, and Why?' appears in his *Heretical Essays in the History of Philosophy* (Open Court Publishing, Chicago, 1999) pp. 95-118.

Other quotes from: Rodolphe Gaschè, *Europe, or the Infinite Task. A Study of a Philosophical Concept* (Stanford: Stanford University Press, 2009), p. 10; Talal Asad, *Formations of the Secular* (Stanford, Stanford University Press, 2003), p. 1; Wendy Brown, *Walled States, Waning Sovereignty* (Zone Books, New York, 2010), p. 61; and William Walters, "Imagined Migration World: The EU and the Discourse of Anti-Illegal Immigration", in M. Geiger and A. Pecoud (ed.), *The Politics of Migration Management* (Palgrave, London, 2010), p. 89.

See also: Paul A. Silverstein, 'Immigrant Racialization and the New Savage Slot: Race, Migration and Immigration in the New Europe' in *Annual Review of Anthropology*, Vol. 34 (2005), p. 363-384

The Dublin Convention of 1990 can be read at: http://www.cvce.eu/en/obj/dublin_convention_determining_the_state_responsible_for_examining_applications_for_asylum_lodged_in_one_of_the_member_states_of_the_european_communities_15_june_1990-en-8299847c-3aff-426c-a990-675774627e5a.html

Caetani and East/West Relations by Benedikt Koehler

Lean Caetani's *La fonction de l'Islam dans l'évolution de la civilisation* can be downloaded from the digitised library of scholarship on Islam at the Martin-Luther-University of Halle-Wittenberg, Germany. Sameul

Huntington's 1992 lecture 'Clash of Civilisations?' appeared in *Foreign Affairs*, Summer 1993. The book version, Clash of Civilisations and the Remaking of World Orders was published by Simon and Schuster, New York, in 1996.

Dissolving Difference: A Dialogue by Julian Bond and Fatimah Ashrif

The translations of the Qur'anic verses are from Muhammad Asad's *The Message of the Qur'an* (The Book Foundation, Bristal, 2003). The Rumi quote is from the *Mathnawi* I: 1598- 1601, *The Rumi Daybook,* transalted by Kabir & Camille Helminski (Shambhala Publications, Boulder, Colorado, 2012). The Christian Muslim Forum website is at: www.christianmuslimforum.org

Kith and Kin in Japanese Politics by Mohammed Moussa

A new edition of Ibn Khaldun, *The Muqaddimah: An Introduction to History*, translated by trans. Franz Rosenthal has been published by Princeton University Press, 2005. The quotes from Bryan S. Turner are from *The Religious and the Political: A Comparative Sociology of Religion* (Cambridge University Press, 2013), and Roger Bowen's quote is from *Japan's Dysfunctional Democracy: The Liberal Democratic Party and Structural Corruption* (M E Sharpe, New York, 2003). On Japanese politics and its roots in family networks, see: Ronald J. Hrebenar and Mayumi Itoh, 'Japan's changing party system', in Akira Nakamura and Ronald J. Hrebenar, editors, *Party Politics in Japan: Political Chaos and Stalemate in the 21st Century* (Routledge, London, 2015), pp. 1-21; and Marius B. Jansen, 'Meiji Restoration', in Marius B. Jansen, *The Emergence of Meiji Japan* (Cambridge University Press, 1995), pp. 144-202; and the following articles:
Martin Facklermarch, 'Japan's Political Dynasties Come Under Fire but Prove Resilient', *The New York Times*, 14/03/2009, available at: http://www.nytimes.com/2009/03/15/world/asia/15japan.html?_r=0

Clyde Haberman, 'Nobusuke Kishi, Ex-Tokyo Leader', *The New York Times*, 8/08/1987, available at http://www.nytimes.com/1987/08/08/obituaries/nobusuke-kishi-ex-tokyo-leader.html

Akiko Hashimoto, 'Family matters in Japan's war commemoration', *East Asia Forum*, 6/08/2015, available at http://www.eastasiaforum.org/2015/08/06/family-matters-in-japans-war-commemoration/

Ayako Mie, 'Japanese politics a man's world as few females stand in 2016 Upper House election', *The Japan Times*, 5/7/2016, available at http://www.japantimes.co.jp/news/2016/07/05/national/politics-diplomacy/japanese-politics-mans-world-females-stand-2016-upper-house-election/#.V4edvLh97IU

David Powers, 'Japanese politics: A family affair', *BBC News*, 21/06/2000, available at http://news.bbc.co.uk/2/hi/asia-pacific/800564.stm

Giorgio Shani, 'Understanding Japan's collective trauma', *open Democracy*, 18/08/2015, available at https://www.opendemocracy.net/giorgio-shani/understanding-japan-collective-trauma

Linda Sieg and Mari Saito, 'Japan's Obuchi – Political "princess" could be first female PM', *Reuters*, 3/10/2014, available at http://uk.reuters.com/article/uk-japan-politics-princess-idUKKCN0HR2GF20141003

James Sterngold, 'Shintaro Abe, Japanese Politician And Ex-Cabinet Aide, Dies at 67', *The New York Times*, 16/05/1991, available at http://www.nytimes.com/1991/05/16/obituaries/shintaro-abe-japanese-politician-and-ex-cabinet-aide-dies-at-67.html

'Japanese prime minister's another DNA', *The Dong-A Ilbo*, 28/10/2013, available at http://english.donga.com/List/3/all/26/407222/1

Bruce Wallace, 'Japan's dynasty politics losing favor among the public', *Los Angeles Times*, 22/01/2008, available at http://articles.latimes.com/2008/jan/22/world/fg-pedigree22

Reiji Yoshida, 'Formed in childhood, roots of Abe's conservatism go deep', *The Japan Times*, 26/12/2012, available at http://www.japantimes.co.jp/news/2012/12/26/national/formed-in-childhood-roots-of-abes-conservatism-go-deep/#.V4f3xrh97IV

Homogeneity by Elma Berisha

For statistics on diversity, see: James D. Fearon, 'Ethnic and Cultural Diversity by Country', *Journal of Economic Growth*, Vol. 8, No. 2 (Jun., 2003), pp. 195-222, available at: http://www.jstor.org/stable/40215943

And 'Global Religious Diversity, Numbers, Facts and Trends Shaping the World' Pew Research Center, April 2014.

The Zygmunt Bauman quote is from Ricardo de Querol, 'Interview with Zygmunt Bauman: Social media are a trap', *El Pais*, 2016; available from: http://elpais.com/elpais/2016/01/19/inenglish/1453208692_424660.html

Feminism is for Everyboy by Michael Vicente Perez

The quotation by Asma Barlas is from 'Engaging Islamic Feminism: Provicializing Feminism as a Master Narrative' in Annitta Kynsilehto, editor *Engaging Feminism: Current Perspectives* (Tampere Research Institute, Tampere, 2008), p. 22. Other works mentioned in this essay include: bell hooks, *Feminist Theory from Margin To Center* (South End Press, Boston, 1984) and *Feminism is For Everybody: Passionate Politics* (South End Press, Boston, 2000); Catherine MacKinnon, *Toward a Feminist Theory of the State* (Harvard University Press, Cambridge, 1991); Alain Locke, *A New Negro: An Interpretation* (Martino Fine Books, Eastford, 2015); Edward Said, *Orientalism* (Vintage Books, New York, 1979); and Gayatri Chakravorty Spivak, *A Critique of Postcolonial Reason: Toward a History of the Vanishing Present* (Harvard University Press, Cambridge, 1999).

Reading Aloud by Saulat Pervez

The works mentioned in the article include: *Becoming a Nation of Readers: The Report of the Commission on Reading*, prepared by Richard C. Anderson, Elfrieda H. Hiebert, Judith A. Scott, and Ian A.G. Wilkinson, The National Institute of Education, U.S. Department of Education (1985); Robert Fisher, *Teaching Children to Think* (Nelson Thornes, Cheltenham, 2005); Betty Hart and Todd R. Risley, 'The Early Catastrophe: The 30 Million Word Gap by Age 3', *American Educator*, Spring 2003; and Samina Parvez, 'A Nostalgic Look Back at Radio Pakistan,', *The News on Sunday*, Sept. 7, 2014 (http://tns.thenews.com.pk/nostalgic-look-back-radio-pakistan/#.V_KF9TT3anM).

See also: Irene C. Fountas and Gay Su Pinnell, *Guided Reading: Good First Teaching for All Children* (Heinemann, Portsmouth, NH, 1996).

Two Books and an Auntie by Ziauddin Sardar

This article first appeared in *Asia Literary Review* Spring 129-142 2008. *Bihishti Zewari* is translated by Barbara Daly Metcalf as *Perfecting Women* (University of California Press, reprint edition, 1992). Someone has stolen my copy so I cannot provide the page number for the quotations! *Mirat ul-Arus* is translated by G E Ward as *Brides Mirror: A Tale of Life in Delhi A 100 Years Ago* (Orient Longman, Delhi, 2004).

Holy Ignorance! Hassan Mahamdallie

The HT activist quote on the organisation's attitude towards Stop the War can be found in journalist Ian Sinclair's account of the movement in his book *The March That Shook Blair: An Oral History of 15 February 2003*, published by Peace News Press, 2013, and available at https://ceasefiremagazine.co.uk/nobody-listened-me-ignoring-anti-war-movement-fuelled-violent-extremism/

Adnan Rashid's quote can be found at 'Alternative mosques for all genders and sexualities' by Rahila Bano BBC Asian Network 14 June 2013 http://

www.bbc.co.uk/news/uk-england-22889727 and 'Feminist Islam in the West: Inclusive Mosque Initiative' by Christopher Thomas – June 2, 2016 https://www.moroccoworldnews.com/2016/06/188008/feminist-islam-in-the-west-inclusive-mosque-initiative/

French political scientist Oliver Roy's thesis that globalisation's tendency to the separation of culture and faith – by secular as well as religious actors – has fuelled a 'holy ignorance' which paves the way for fundamentalist claims to authenticity is explored in his book *Holy Ignorance:When Religion and Culture Part Ways*, translated by Ros Schwartz (Hurst, 2010). The growth of the New Muslim Cool is documented by Hishaam Aidi, *Rebel Music: Race, Empire, and the New MuslimYouth Culture* (Pantheon books, New York, 2014).

The Inclusive Mosque Initiative can be found online at http://inclusivemosqueinitiative.org/

Last Word On African Chieftaincy by Henry Brefo

Ben Okri's quote is from his *Guardian* article, which is available at: https://www.theguardian.com/commentisfree/2014/dec/27/mental-tyranny-black-writers

The novels mentioned include: Chika Unigwe, *On Black Sister's Street* (Vintage, London, 2010); Tendai Huchu's, *Hairdresser of Harare* (Freight Books, Glasgow, 2010); Pede Hollist, *So The Path Does Not Die* (Jacaranda Books, London, 2014); No Violet Bulawayo, *We Need New Names* (Vintage, London, 2014); and Teju Cole, *Open City* (Random House, New York, 2011).

See also: E. A. Ritter, *Shaka Zulu: The Rise of the Zulu* Empire (Longmans Green, London, 1955); John Wright, *Reconstituting Shaka Zulu for the Twenty-First Century,* University of KwaZulu-Natal: Southern African Humanities, Vol. 18 (2) 2006; and Tom McCaskie, State and Society in Pre-colonial Asante. (Cambridge University Press, 1995).

CONTRIBUTORS

Fatimah Ashrif works as a consultant advising on philanthropy projects in education, politics and media ● **Elma Berisha** is an expert in consumer research and consultant on public perceptions based in Kuala Lumpur ● **Julian Bond** was director of the Christian Muslim Forum from 2006 to 2015 ● **Henry Brefo**, co-founder of Afrikult., an online forum for people to connect, explore and expand knowledge on African literature and culture, is undertaking PhD research on African Chieftaincy at the University of Birmingham ● **Aysha Garaeva**, who was born in Tatarstan in Russia and is of Azeri origin, is studying International Relations and English Language and Literature at the University of Istanbul ● **Nadiah Ghani** is a PhD student in English Research at King's College London ● **Syed Nomanul Haq** is Professor of the Social Sciences and Liberal Arts and Program Advisor at the Institute of Business Administration (IBA) Karachi ● **Aamer Hussein** is a renowned Pakistani writer who has published five collections of short stories, most recently *Insomnia* ● **Mohja Kahf** is an Arab-American poet, writer and Associate Professor of Comparative Literature, University of Arkansas, Fayetteville ● **Hannah Kershaw** is a PhD student at the University of York, researching British Muslim Literature ● **Benedikt Koehler** is the author of *Early Islam and the Birth of Capitalism* ● **Hassan Mahamdallie** is a playwright and Director of the Muslim Institute ● **Ayisha Malik**, the author of *Sofia Khan is Not Obliged*, is currently working on her second novel ● **Annalisa Mormile**, who recently completed her postgraduate studies at Goldsmiths College, University of London, is researching EU migration and asylum policy ● **Mohammed Moussa** has recently been appointed Assistant Professor in the Political Science and International Relations Department at Istanbul Sabahattin Zaim University ● **Michael Vicente Perez** is Lecturer in Cultural Anthropology at the University of Washington ● **Saulat Pervez**, an educator, is working at the International Institute of Islamic Thought's Research Department in Herndon, VA, USA ● **Samia Rahman** is Deputy Director of the Muslim Institute, London ● **Muddasir Ramzan**, who is a regular blogger for the Muslim Institute and is a writer based in Kashmir, India ● **Safeena Razzaq** is an Edinburgh-based artist who specialises in printmaking and illustration ● **Piro Rexhepi** is a research fellow at the Max Planck Institute for the Study of Religious and Ethnic Diversity ● **Perzada Salman** is a writer and journalist based in Lahore, Pakistan.

www.ingramcontent.com/pod-product-compliance
Lightning Source LLC
LaVergne TN
LVHW040615250326
834688LV00035B/569